THE ORIGINS OF CIVIC UNIVERSITIES
Manchester, Leeds and Liverpool

THE ORIGINS OF
— CIVIC —
UNIVERSITIES
MANCHESTER, LEEDS & LIVERPOOL

DAVID R. JONES

ROUTLEDGE

First published in 1988 by
Routledge
11 New Fetter Lane, London EC4P 4EE

British Library Cataloguing in Publication Data

Jones, David R.
   The origins of civic universities:
   Manchester, Leeds and Liverpool.
   1. Universities and colleges — England,
   Northern — History — 19th century
   I. Title
   378.427   LA636.7

ISBN 0-415-00355-5

Printed and bound in Great Britain by
Biddles Ltd, Guildford and King's Lynn

Contents

Acknowledgements

Acknowledging debts of gratitude is one of the unalloyed pleasures of academic research and writing. A wide-ranging, though I fear incomplete, list of these pleasurable debts includes thanks to the following, none of whom are responsible for the work's errors and inadequacies:

Professors B.R. Clark, R.R. Palmer, L.M. Thompson, F.M. Turner, and R.W. Winks, of Yale; T. Kelly, of Liverpool, G. Moodie, of York, H. Perkin, of Lancaster, and Mr R. Eustace of the SRHE.

All the members of the Higher Education Research Group at Yale. Much of my research was supported by the HERG.

The archivists and librarians of Manchester, Leeds, Liverpool, and Yale, and Dr. M. Hampar and the staff of the Bursar's office at Manchester.

Those who have wrestled with my statistical tables, handwriting, grammar, and syntax: Ms. Pamela Baldwin, Ms. Wendy Cramp, Ms. Lois Hetland, Ms. Mary Hyson, Ms. Evelyn McCann, Ms. Stephanie Marder, Ms. Cindy Strahle, and Ms. Florence Thomas.

Dr. V.L. Meek of UNE, who has turned a manuscript into a book.

My parents, to whom my debts are limitless.

For M.W.J. and R.G.J.
and in memory of W.B.W.

Introduction

This work is primarily a study of the influences which mid-Victorian Britain brought to bear on its embryonic universities and of the position which the universities assumed in Victorian society. The new institutions bore little resemblance to universities as they were then known, or to the large and important places they were to become. They were founded in many English cities, often on shoestring budgets, for assorted reasons and various purposes. Many failed, as had many predecessors since the 18th Century. Some succeeded and became the "redbrick" or "civic" universities of 20th Century Britain. After Manchester (1851), colleges were founded at Leeds (1874), Bristol (1876), Birmingham (1880), Liverpool (1881), Reading (1892), and Sheffield (1897). Manchester, Leeds, and Liverpool, which formed the Victoria University, are examples both diverse and interconnected, as well as in many ways representative and influential, and therefore form the basis of this study.

The influences were often dissimilar to those which have shaped more recent universities. There was no large-scale demand for university places, nor was there a large pool of qualified candidates for admission. The state gave little of either direction or money, and there was no equivalent, in scale, of the contemporaneous American philanthropy. The civic universities remained small until the 20th Century, and the influences studied are those which affected relatively few, but which caused those few to weather the lean years and to build perhaps better than they knew, so that their institutions were found ready to hand and invaluable by the students and public of the new century.

By 1900 the originally tiny civic colleges[1] of Manchester, Leeds, and Liverpool had formed a respected federal institution and were almost ready to dissolve it and stand as independent universities. They had stimulated and met demands for advanced education in the arts, sciences, and certain technologies. They had made local benevolence a sufficient if not munificent source of financial supply. They had evolved a system of academic self-government which became the dominant model for 20th Century Britain and its Empire. Finally, they had made a place for themselves in society and in British higher education.

Universities play an important role in most modern societies, and historians have come to appreciate that fact. But it remains difficult to analyze the university as a societal phenomenon. The materials for institutional studies are often uncatalogued and uncertain. Archives are sometimes disorganized or even uninvestigated, while many university histories are still celebratory or antiquarian in character. In the absence of sophisticated studies, too often the university is used as a mere make-weight in an historical or sociological argument, or considered as an adjunct of a class, industry, or government.

The complexity of the university and its purposes, and of the motives and needs of its supporters, directors, members, and users, is enormous. Recently scholars have tackled many aspects of this complexity, from the professionalization of university teaching to the links between the university and various parts of wider society such as government or industry.[2] Their methods and results should inform and assist future institutional historians.

The dimension of time adds to the university's complexity and increases the chances of errors of perception. The most common is an essentially a-historical view. Institutions in the past are seen as similar, perhaps smaller, versions of their present selves, founded upon similar assumptions and shaped by similar influences. Because a university meets certain needs today it is supposed to have met similar needs in the past. It is commonly supposed that the civic universities of Victorian England were created to meet a demand for technical education; in fact other demands were more imperative and influential, at least at some new colleges.

Another common pitfall is the assumption that human actions result entirely from the rational calculation of potential benefits. In fact there are always discrepancies between apparent rationality and actuality. Traditions, errors, inertia, and many other factors may inhibit or altogether negate rational calculation. A detailed study of the actual influences upon those involved is necessary for any real understanding of universities. The following work is in part a sort of *catalogue raisonné* of the influences which produced and shaped the civic universities of 19th Century England.

By stimulating and responding to demands the colleges made places for themselves in Victorian society. They served the social, intellectual, economic, and professional needs of individuals. They also provided services to the community, offering museums, libraries, and public lectures, working to improve the quality of secondary and other education, and providing the experts demanded by society's growing complexity. In addition the colleges were perceived as both expressions and agencies of a provincial culture striving for self-assertion.

The civic colleges constituted a new form of higher education in England. Their response to demands produced new curricula in which Classics and Mathematics lost their primacy, though they remained important, other Arts subjects including English Literature, History, and Economics became prominent, the physical sciences were assiduously cultivated, and technology made its somewhat tentative entry into higher education. Professional education also assumed a new importance. Faced with little competition in the newer fields, the colleges quickly distinguished themselves as centres of scientific, historical, and social studies.

Once created, the colleges were also shaped by internal influences. The interplay of founders, trustees, and faculty produced a form of government which helped make the civic colleges academically efficient and responsive organizations. The constitutions and the customs which they developed became the norm for British universities in the 20th Century, and for the universities of the British Empire as well. Academic self-government and a relatively cordial attitude of non-interference on the part of the state were products of the formative years of the civic colleges.

Chapter 1 describes the social, political, and educational milieu in which the civic colleges appeared. In addition to providing background it permits an estimate of the extent to which the new colleges evolved from older institutions, reacted against them, made entirely original departures, or simply copied traditional foundations. Chapter 2 discusses the necessary preconditions for the success of any new venture in higher education: sufficient preliminary education, an available economic surplus, and interest in and desire for education. Chapter 3 describes the cities concerned, and includes a brief narrative of the founding and growth of each college.

3

The next two chapters deal with influences best characterized as those of supply and demand. Chapter 4 analyzes and compares the demands for liberal, scientific, technical, and professional education. Chapter 5 deals with the supply of funds. The dichotomy is not complete, however. The demands of students and the colleges' responses were affected by the availability of knowledge and teachers; the direction of benefactions was influenced by the benefactors' perceptions of society's demands.

Chapter 6 describes the evolution of administration and government in the colleges. The process was often one of accommodation rather than conflict, and the reasons for accommodation, and the eventual dominance of the faculty, are analyzed.

Chapter 7 defines the importance of these new institutions, both in the life of the surrounding communities and in the history and development of education. The colleges represent both the essence and the limits of British higher education's response to the problems of the industrial, urban, and democratic society of the late 19th and 20th Centuries.

1
Background

The new civic colleges of Victorian England were part and parcel of an active, dynamic era. The air of stability and even placidity which sometimes seems to us to have pervaded the latter decades of Victoria's reign is largely a figment of hindsight. The Victorians themselves saw their society as in a state of flux; even complete dissolution seemed possible. Growth and change in almost every field from population and territory, through commerce and industry, to knowledge and education brought great uncertainty.

The period began with a growing awareness of massive problems. Industrialism was creating new wealth, new classes, new slums, and new ideas, all of which were unsettling. A half reformed parliament was unlikely to offer effective political solutions, while religion was hardly in a more stable or flourishing state. Chartism, the Oxford Movement, and cholera revealed malaise in the body politic, religious, and physical. Carlyle spoke both to and for the Victorians when he told them that theirs was a critical, revolutionary, age.

By the 50s some of the violence, if not the uncertainty, had gone out of change. Industrialism was a fact of life in the Midlands and North, London and the newer cities were developing the range of institutions suitable to modern metropoli, and political violence appeared to be a thing confined to the Continent. It was this cooling of passions which led Burn to refer to "The Age of Equipoise",[1] and to date its commencement in 1852. And in many senses the era was a calm one. The Great Exhibition had signalled Britain's industrial supremacy to all the world, and its philosophy was the replacement of conflict by peaceful social and commercial intercourse. The Exhibition also symbolized that faith in "progress" which, when acquired by both the middle and working classes, provided what Tholfsen calls "The Intellectual Origins of mid-Victorian Stability".[2] Burn's catalogue of the legal and social disciplines which were applied to mid-Victorian society provides further reminders of a growing stability: the ostensibly laissez-faire state was increasingly willing to coerce its citizens when it came to matters of public health, social betterment, and the abatement of nuisances; the worship of home and the family, the concept of gentility, and the importance of religion were all stabilizing factors. Many of these phenomena are important for the growth of education, perhaps most notably economic strength and the idea of "progress".

The age had not entirely lost its revolutionary, or at least its stressful, character, however. The idea of progress is neither static nor stable. Rising real wages, technological change, and the expansion and changing character of business and industry were signs of a progressive, not simply stable, economy. Political stability was merely relative, apparent only by comparison with the Continent. The years from 1846-67 saw eight administrations and even these frequently lacked a reliable majority in the Commons. The family, that apparently perfect symbol of the calm of the Victorian era, was actually a living embodiment of many of the stresses of society. For the working class family, geographical mobility, industrial employment, and consequent alteration in social norms replaced the certainties of an earlier era[3] with a far more problematic state of social and economic affairs. To rise through education and self-help, or to sink through unemployment or drink both seemed much easier.

The middle class family of fiction and photographs is perhaps the centre-piece of our vision of Victorian stability. Yet it embodies many of the gravest stresses of the Victorian world. Two of these, the role of women and the need to preserve social status, are particularly relevant to education. Education could serve as social, professional and economic preparation for achieving or improving middle class status (see Ch. 4), and this was the class which was expanding most rapidly in number and prestige.[4]

The position of women was unimportant in Owens' first years, but by the 70s it concerned all the colleges. Women's supposed position on a pedestal was, after all, only the ideal of one class, and short-lived in its most exaggerated form. Secure elevation only occurred in the 50s and by the 80s increasing numbers of middle class women were determinedly climbing down, and the largest new class, indeed a potential majority, were beginning to enter the system of higher education.

In catering for the middle classes, the new colleges were affiliating themselves with a group that was not only growing, but also steadily increasing its economic and political power. Most of its upper strata had been enfranchised since 1832, 1867 saw the vote given to the rest, and its representation in parliament, office, and the Civil Service grew commensurately. And, while a great deal of England's wealth remained in the hands of the aristocracy, a growing amount, and a particularly high proportion of new wealth, belonged to the middle classes, ranging from the merchant like Owens who could found a college and the engineer/industrialist like Whitworth who could create a national scholarship scheme, to the ninety or hundred a year clerk who could contemplate paying the admission fees for his children. In the late 19th Century the combination of decreased infant and child mortality, followed by reduction in family size, made greater investment in the individual child both safer and more likely.

The life of the mind was even less settled than that of the family. Science was not new, but its ramifications and applications were both expanding at a great rate, and the expansion interested an unprecedented proportion of the population. While its applications transformed such fields as transport and communication, more theoretical work such as the *Origin of Species* (1859) was equally unsettling, especially when non-scientists also questioned the state of religion. (*Essays and Reviews* followed Darwin's work almost immediately.) The expansion of knowledge also implied the expansion of the agencies for its creation and diffusion. A brief sampling of this sort of activity in the "Age of Equipoise" would include the establishment of free libraries under the Act of 1850, the Working Men's College movement begun in London and Sheffield in the early 50s, and such signs of parliamentary interest as the Military Education Commission (1857), the Museums Committee (1860), the Newcastle Commission (1861), and the Clarendon Commission (1864).

The events catalogued in the previous paragraph all appear in the "Chronological Table" of Young's *Portrait of an Age*,[5] and a further look at the list suggests other mid-century events which, though less immediately connected with education, offer food for thought.

1853 saw the institution of competitive examination in the Indian Civil Service, reform of recruitment to the Home Civil Service, and the establishment of a Charity Commission which would both reform educational trusts and divert other funds to them. In 1855 the growth of big business was legislatively recognized and encouraged by the Limited Liability Act, and while the age of the self-taught businessman was certainly not over, professionalization would soon begin.

The growth and movement of population formed one of the most powerful dynamics of the Victorian era. The population of England as a whole grew quite steadily.[6] The cities and surrounding conurbations which the colleges served also acquired their modern scale during this period. By 1871 South East Lancashire had a population of 1,386,000, West Yorkshire 1,064,000, and Merseyside 690,000. (London at the same date had 3,890,000 inhabitants.) After 1850, more Englishmen lived in urban areas than everywhere else. This growing and shifting population was also increasingly employed in new ways. Booth's analysis of occupations shows substantial expansion in all the middle class occupations between 1851 and 1881 and a growing proportion of the population engaged in literary and scientific professions closely linked to advanced education, and in commerce and trade.[7]

An enlarged electorate and a liberal administration after the Reform Act of 1867 suggested the possibility of further change in Victorian society. The most obvious monuments of the 60s, 70s, and 80s are perhaps those great municipal buildings which seem to embody monumental stability. And yet they reflect the rise of an enlarged power and scope for public action and administration, a new and apparently unpredictable force arising out of great changes and considerable strife.[8]

At a national level organized change was also proceeding and even accelerating. In 1870 it was finally admitted unreservedly that elementary education was a responsibility of the state; competitive examination became the rule in the Home Civil Service in the same year. The corps of Her Majesty's Inspectors enlarged its roles and powers.[9] Centralization was decried in theory and extended in fact.

The economic life of the public and the economic position of the nation underwent changes in the late century as well as in the earlier era of expansion and supremacy. New industries, which would eventually and belatedly replace the old staples, began to appear. The so-called Great Depression created concern, without disrupting the economy so far as to make responses impossible. Internal and psychological life was as increasingly uncertain as the externals of politics and economics. The certainties of religion, society, and the family were disappearing for many members of the middle classes; education, whether as social insurance or intellectual stimulus, was a possible response.

Religion and Education

Religion was undoubtedly a great stabilizing force in Victorian society. But, simultaneously, it was the subject of great controversy, and of controversy with tremendous impact upon all levels of education. Religion and religious tests were two bitterly debated and enduring issues in Victorian Britain, and most people were involved, if only in attacks on the state's support of a church. The duration and intensity of this debate arose out of the conjunction of several factors. The complacency of 18th Century religious opinion was supplanted by new enthusiasms. Religious fervour moved some Anglicans toward Rome, others toward Methodism, and still others toward the revival of enthusiasm within the established Church known as Evangelicalism. At the same time, political theories argued against a religious establishment and various secular philosophies attacked the spiritual and more frequently the worldly position of religion.

The Church of England was accustomed to view education as an Anglican monopoly in theory, with dissent a de facto but not de jure competitor, and purely secular education an abomination. Primary education before 1870 was largely in religious hands, divided, in descending order of importance, among the Church of England, Dissent, and the Church of Rome, and debates among these were to hinder the creation of an efficient school system at least until late in the century, as each wished either to control state support or prevent it from going to the other competitors. Endowed secondary education was predominantly Anglican, though efficient proprietary and private schools were founded by other sects and in general the grammar schools did not restrict admission. The public schools were, of course, largely Anglican. The debate between Establishment and Dissent remained important until it was overwhelmed by the secular wave of the 20th Century. Higher education was equally bedeviled and yet encouraged. Like the question of religious instruction and control in schools, university tests were a national battleground. Under the circumstances there were demands both for the opening of old institutions and for the creation of new ones which would offer new subjects and admit new people.

Education for the ministry of dissenting sects had long been provided in academies of various kinds, but these neither answered the demands for secular education, nor possessed the funds and breadth of vision necessary to offer the new sciences and modern education to larger numbers. Many of the early exponents of new universities had attended one of the great dissenting academies of the Midlands and the North.[10] The religious freedom of foreign institutions provided a more direct and obvious precedent than sectarian academies. Continental and American institutions were cited, and advocates of non-sectarian education like James Yates ranged from Belfast to the Academy of Fine Arts in Mexico for their examples.[11] The founders of London University had the American example conveniently at hand. Brougham, Horner, Birkbeck and others who were to establish London had entertained a representative of Jefferson's non-sectarian University of Virginia in 1824.[12]

Conservative arguments were also bolstered by supposed foreign examples. In an 1834 article advocating the abolition of University tests, the *Edinburgh* found it necessary to refute a Tory argument based on German examples. It had been claimed that the non-sectarian admissions policy of many German universities had led to much aberrant theology, abhorrent to a good Anglican possessed of the true Protestant doctrine. The *Edinburgh* replied with detailed arguments. In general the weight of foreign example was with the reformers while their opponents depended on the tradition of insularity so strong in many Englishmen.

The problem of providing non-sectarian education was complicated by the fact that few reformers were willing to countenance a complete lack of religious instruction. Though the backers of the "godless college" in Gower Street could find no workable compromise on religion except its removal, they consistently argued that this indicated not its insignificance, but its extreme importance, and the impossibility of a makeshift, compromise solution of the problem. They expected the student or his family to find religious instruction and welcomed the establishment of religious teaching of various kinds in the near vicinity of Gower Street.[13] The trustees of Owens College faced similar difficulties. John Owens, who had attended both Church and chapel in his life, expressed the new liberal principles both in free trade where he battled against the Corn Laws and in education where his will declared that in his college members: "... shall not be required to make any declaration as to, or submit to any test whatsoever of, their religious opinions, and that nothing shall be introduced in the matter or mode of education or instruction in reference to any religious or theological subject which shall be reasonably offensive to the conscience of any student ...."[14] The trustees nonetheless considered religion to be a necessary part of education and reconciled their position with the testator's directions by offering voluntary lectures on presumably non-controversial religious questions. The debate did not end there. When the college fell upon hard times, Manchester's more radical critics were quick to seize on the theology lectures as a cause of the decline. However, the compromise was maintained in various forms until late in the century when a cooling of religious passions allowed the formation of a separate theology faculty.

Religious reaction to criticism and innovation produced additional higher education. Thoughtful ecclesiastics realized that criticism of a worldly and wealthy established church was bound at some point to focus upon the immense revenues of the Bishop, Dean, and Chapter of Durham. In the 1830s the ecclesiastical authorities therefore founded a university in the interests both of orthodox education, threatened by such new trends as London, and of establishing a use for their revenues less open to criticism.[15] Perhaps it was a combination of the orthodoxy of the education and the remoteness of the region; at any rate the new University of Durham failed to flourish. Its curriculum remained quite traditional at least until the 80s, with English still excluded, science moribund beyond the needs of medicine, and the failure of an attempt to found an engineering department. Enrolment remained low in the 70s, but undergraduate numbers rose to 205 in 1882. This rise preceded major curricular reform, suggesting that the social and other demands for traditional higher education were rising, not just the oft-mentioned demand for new, scientific, and utilitarian studies.

Newer subjects and an urban location undoubtedly had more appeal, however. The College of Science at Newcastle was affiliated to Durham from 1871 and provided the counterweight which perhaps prevented Durham's decline into a mere theological seminary of the Church of England. Newcastle arose out of the demand for a mining school, and began as a general science school of small scope. After affiliation with Durham, the university vaguely considered an associateship in science for a few years, and then offered a BSc. The college's popularity and reputation grew, and by the 80s its success as a mining school was marked by the endowment of a chair by a group of coal owners. Clerical connections, non-urban location, traditional curriculum: Durham was practically a negative definition of a successful civic university, and it long remained small and parochial, even losing its connection with Newcastle in recent years.

Oxbridge

While Durham stagnated, the Establishment's major universities were criticized and reformed, and eventually flourished. Even before their progressive alteration in the latter half of the century they were the precedents, predecessors, object lessons, and sometimes awful warnings to new institutions. Unsatisfactory as they had become in the 18th Century and in part remained in the 19th, despite a shrunken student body and an antiquated curriculum, for most people and purposes they were higher education. They were the sole degree granting bodies in England before the 1830s as they had been for hundreds of years. The state saw higher education in their terms and often through the eyes of their graduates in public life. Educational precedents at law were those of the ancient universities, an important consideration under a common law system. Briefly, the chief visible characteristics of this sort of higher education were: 1) it was expensive, collegiate, classical and, at Cambridge, mathematical; 2) its institutions were well-endowed, oligarchically self-governed and free to ignore and even defy the state; 3) it was an education for the Anglican gentry (including clergy) and increasingly the upper middle professional (though not business) classes and whatever sprigs of the nobility might wish to roister or indulge scholarly tastes.

Many of the persons who contributed to the establishment of new universities had little firsthand knowledge of the ancient ones. Even at the turn of the 20th Century few businessmen had attended, and almost none of the Northern industrialists would have done so.[16] Their information came from secondary sources of very varied reliability.

Least reliable but quite widespread and popular were the steadily increasing number of novels about university life.[17] Even the most popular of these, *Tom Brown at Oxford*, with the most successful of heroes, is by no means an advertisement for the ancient establishments; Tom Brown succeeds in spite of a system which might easily have made him another of its supposed common product, the upper-class snob, unknowing and uncaring. This was a perfect reinforcement to the natural parental fear of creating a son who would leave and despise his origins and class.

A constant theme of university fiction was debt, high necessary expenses being vastly increased by student extravagance which was encouraged and almost required in an inbred, corporate society where one aped one's betters. In this matter fiction appears to have mirrored truth with surprisingly little exaggeration. Rothblatt is only the most recent of a long line of secondary and primary sources testifying to the large and often unwarranted expenses of Oxbridge. And for the new middle class, debt was the sin of sins; the briefest perusal of Dickens testifies to that. Thus fiction presented a model of universities to be avoided; there must be other institutions and they must be different. Only in the 80s do university novels of the sort with which we are still familiar, detailing the good old days at college, become common, and their influence must post-date the great civic foundations.

Led by Sir William Hamilton's essays in the *Edinburgh*, the great reviews provided a more balanced but equally discouraging picture of the universities. They hoped to reform, not to discard and replace, but they certainly did not encourage emulation of Oxbridge, and in fact supported new institutions as one part of the remedy. Brian Simon has remarked that "By the early 1830s all publications in any way expressive of the middle-class standpoint are in full cry against the state of university learning ...."[18] But this criticism was by no means uniform. While the *Edinburgh Review* called for an improved liberal education, with continued emphasis on the classics, the *Westminster* demanded a complete reorientation of learning. The unsatisfactory state of the colleges and the powerlessness of the university were the major points in this sort of criticism, but the unlikelihood of a young man getting a good education was clearly implicit in the reviews' attitudes.[19]

The most significant criticisms were probably made by those most active arms of Victorian government, investigative committees and Royal Commissions. Beginning in 1850 and continuing to the present, a succession of Commissions have pointed out both the weaknesses and strengths of universities, and proposed various improvements. Commission criticisms were the usual catalogue of expense and corruption, archaisms in teaching and learning, etc. The civic universities would be different. The Commissions' blue books also put forward recommendations, at one time or another canvassing every possible solution to the problems of higher education.

Sheldon Rothblatt has suggested that 19th Century Cambridge, and presumably Oxford as well, possessed another characteristic which would not endear them to a large part of the bourgeoisie, an antipathy towards business.[20] Rothblatt argues convincingly that a decisive number of dons viewed business as grubbing for filthy lucre. The traditional professions were exempt from this fault by reason of their service character, and the notion that their practitioners were suitably rewarded with an honorarium rather than being demeaned by the receipt of a wage or relieved of their finer feelings by the crassness of a stock exchange. While perhaps significant, the importance of this characteristic should not be overrated. Religion, expense, and curriculum were far more effective bars to the admission of students intending a business career. The Oxbridge students and dons who came to staff the new universities successfully stifled any antipathies they may have felt. On the other hand, whatever the reasons, the business classes of the North certainly did not flood Oxbridge with their offspring. Lancashire and Yorkshire provided substantially less than 10% of Oxford's matriculants in 1835 and less than 19% 50 years later.[21]

In some senses then, the civic universities were to be characterized by a reaction to Oxford and Cambridge. This is obvious in terms of curriculum and students, but equally true in such less visible areas as organization and administration. The attack on corporate abuses, and particularly those of charitable foundations, was widespread, and a large part was directed at education. The legally sound but practically untenable position that grammar school foundations were meant to teach only the classical languages was being steadily undermined. The status of collegiate foundations at Oxford and Cambridge, while less visible to the public, was at least equally shocking. Teaching was moribund, as was a high percentage of the co-opted college fellows. The appropriation of funds answered neither the letter nor the spirit of the founders' bequests. Most significant, and most complained of by reformers at the time, the collegiate establishments had overwhelmed their parent and supposed governor, the university. Certainly the civic universities were to be very different organizations. Costs were to be kept low, and residence was not originally considered desirable. A busy professoriate was to replace a class of idle college fellows.

Agitation for university reform and for new institutions was not entirely devoted to the destruction of Oxbridge prestige or the establishment of utterly different institutions. The essence of the battle against the Tests was a demand for admission to the benefits and privileges of a more or less traditional higher education. Men like Owens and Firth and the founders of London University specifically stated that a major purpose of their foundations was to provide the advantages of a higher education much like that at Oxbridge to persons prevented from attending those institutions.

The inadequacy and not infrequent absence of teaching at Oxford and Cambridge led reformers to look abroad for other models. The Scottish tradition of a lecturing professoriate as the main means of tuition was found laudable and generally encouraged in new foundations. Owens College began with a staff consisting entirely of professors and did not appoint a tutor for some years. The Northern tradition of open fellowships and a relatively fair distribution of revenues was applauded from an early date.[22] The age of developing economic liberalism could not help but notice the competitive character of a German professoriate. Freedom of teaching and payment by number of pupils were seen as incitements to a diligence unknown at Oxford and Cambridge. The *Westminster* remarked, "With a host of opponents no man can sleep at his post,"[23] and founders of new universities hoped to ensure proper teaching by paying by results.

London

As the 19th Century advanced, Oxbridge and the Establishment evolved; the North and Midlands, mercantile, industrial, and non-conformist, created a new culture and its institutions. Meanwhile, new groups and old naturally acted in London, the seat of ancient aristocracy, a parliament of gentry mixed with a mercantile and financial elite, and the home of significant industries as well. It had long been the "third university of England," justifying the title both by the informal educational opportunities of a metropolis and a range of more formal educational enterprises including the Inns of Court, scientific societies, medical education, and a variety of endowed and proprietary institutions for education and research. Liberal, non-conformist, middle class action, and Establishment reaction, were now to give it a formally recognized university.

The liberal, secular, and middle class institution came first: an establishment in Gower Street begun as the London University and eventually to be University College. Its tone and intentions may most easily be characterized by listing a few of its supporters: Brougham, Hume, Macaulay, and assorted Benthamites.[24] While all represented some form of liberal and reformist opinion, any institution supported by all of them had to be based upon tolerance of diversity. The pragmatic, if not exactly liberal, wing of the Establishment organized a response to this "irreligious" institution. Wellington, the archbishops , and Peel attended the meeting which resulted in Kings College.[25]

In theory Kings College was to be an Anglican rival of London, but the actual case was different. As early as 1838 an *Edinburgh* reviewer heralded the foundation of Kings but warned that it would wind up following the new trend in education: without tests or sectarian bias.[26] The rising demand for admission, foreseen by 1825,[27] swept tests before it and the amalgamation which formed the University of London ended the practical, if not the theoretical, debate. The charter provided for the affiliation of other colleges whose students might then take London degrees, and though the standards for affiliation were variable if not lax, affiliation was worthwhile for provincial institutions; Owens sought and received it soon after its foundation. In 1858 an alteration of the University charter opened its degree examinations to any student, regardless of his place of education. Previously affiliated colleges protested, and there was much talk of the value of systematic and supervised study, but the provincial colleges in fact lost little, remaining as they did the most suitable places to prepare for the London degree, and for London matriculation, which itself became a widely accepted certification.[28] London thus provided a vital service to new colleges which had not the power to grant degrees, and eventually helped them to achieve this pinnacle of status as well. H.C. Dent has summed up the situation: "It was by preparing students for London University's 'external' degrees that every English university college for close on a century proved its right to full university status."[29]

London was precedent and exemplar as well as certifying agency for the new colleges. It had been founded in a major city by members of the intellectual and professional middle classes; it survived without significant endowment; it offered new types of education and catered to new demands; it was relatively cheap and entirely non-denominational. The curriculum set the standard for the Victorian foundations: matriculation and degrees would both require a wide range of knowledge of classical and modern letters, history, mathematics, and science, while, on the other hand, the colleges would also open their courses to those seeking only some specific skill or knowledge. The needs of business, the professions, and the growing bureaucracy and its examination system were met by professing Oriental and modern languages for the Imperial administrator and the merchant, modern sciences among which chemistry in particular was to be increasingly applicable to industry, and professional studies such as medicine, law, and engineering. The intricate relations with medical schools, which needed science and general education courses as well as degrees, while the colleges needed the steady supply of medical students, became a characteristic feature of institution-building in the provinces, just as in London.

A secular institution was to be governed, in theory, by laymen. A lecturing professoriate, frequently trained on the Continent or in Scotland,[30] would do the teaching of an increasing variety of subjects. A variegated student body largely from within the city, but drawing students from an expanding area with increasing ease as the railways developed, would receive a liberal or professional or technical education, while living at home, in lodgings, or in the "halls", frequently linked with some religious denomination, which grew around the colleges. A plausible model of the modern and middle class alternative to Oxbridge had been created.

Civic Colleges

After London and Durham, Owens College was the next institution to appear and grow toward university status. Before looking in some detail at the cities and colleges of Manchester, Leeds, and Liverpool, a brief survey of other significant institutions of the time will help to provide context. University College, Bristol, was established as a limited liability company in 1876.[31] Its Southwestern location in an ancient trading city separates it obviously from Manchester and Leeds, though less so from Liverpool. There was neither a major founder nor widespread support, as in the cases of Manchester and Liverpool respectively. The powerful initial impetus provided by Oxford colleges under Jowett's influence had no equivalent in Manchester, and was far more practical and potent than the influence of Oxbridge extension courses at Leeds and Liverpool.[32] The college remained quite small until the 90s, when the first major influx of students and money, notably from the Wills tobacco fortunes, began.

Nevertheless the college conformed in many ways to the developing model. It quickly affiliated itself with the local medical teaching. It offered evening and teachers' classes, which represented a majority of enrolments for some time. Much of its early teaching was secondary in character, and a degree-seeking student body, a fairly complete faculty, and a campus were all acquired gradually.

Sheffield's beginnings resemble those of Owens College.[33] Mark Firth, an engineer and industrialist, made a large contribution to establish a college which would teach university subjects to largely local students, without religious restrictions. Mutually advantageous links with the local medical school resulted in eventual amalgamation. The differences from Owens' early days are reminders that thirty years had passed when Firth College opened in 1879. Oxford and Cambridge had begun to extend their activities, and the original concept of what became Firth College was of a permanent home for the Extension Lectures and related activities. The growing interest of the late century and Firth's experience as an industrialist (Owens had been a merchant, a very different thing) caused him to hope that technology might quickly be added to his college's curriculum, and a technical school appeared in 1886.

Mason College, Birmingham, was founded in 1880, and followed what by now was the usual path: it had been preceded by a variety of unsuccessful colleges, it was linked with a medical school, it was secular, etc.[34] Two peculiarities are perhaps noteworthy, both of them connected with the character of the founder. The original trust deed excluded literary and other arts subjects, and these only appeared under the combined pressures of Josiah Mason's advisers and the requirements of London matriculation and degree exams. Perhaps it is the fame of this testamentary stipulation which has led to the peculiar notion that the new civic universities were founded primarily to teach science and technology. London and Manchester were essentially concerned to offer higher education of a more or less traditional sort without religious teaching or discrimination. Firth stipulated the teaching of the then customary university subjects. Liverpool was powerfully oriented towards arts subjects by a local elite long accustomed to a "liberal" and classical education. In fact, the least support was given to those institutions with the heaviest technological bias, like Leeds.

The founding gift was also of unprecedented size. With Mason's £200,000 in hand, the college was able to achieve a size and stature which made it the first independent civic university in only 20 years, admittedly with the able assistance of Joseph Chamberlain. Owens had taken 30 years to become merely a constituent college, though the only one, of the Victoria University.

Other Precedents and Predecessors

The significance of other British predecessors and supposed precedents for civic universities is debatable.[35] The one fairly clear line
of descent is from the Dissenting academies of the 18th Century.
Many leading non-conformists, including early 19th Century advocates of new universities, were educated in these academies. However, there are obvious flaws in any assumption of great influence,
and great dissimilarities between the two types of institutions. The
academies are generally assumed to have shot their bolt by 1800,[36]
leaving a seventy year gap before the great age of new foundations.
They were notably peripatetic institutions, and were generally
short-lived. Their often-mentioned science teaching was undoubtedly innovative in its day, but did not amount to much. The presence of a Priestley does not make a scientific centre of Warrington
Academy, particularly since he taught history and other subjects.
They may, however, have provided an example of institutions setting out to fulfill newly felt and defined needs as opposed to places
resorted to for a pre-defined education.

Two sorts of educational institutions preceded civic universities
in every provincial city: medical schools and mechanics institutions. Medical schools appeared in the 19th Century to supply the
want of medical education outside of London, Scotland, or the
Continent, thus setting an obvious precedent. They came to need
laboratories and teaching facilities for chemistry and other basic
subjects which could best be shared with or provided by a more
general educational institution. In addition, concern over the general and liberal education of members of the profession led to
examinations in general education, and a new college was a convenient place to prepare for these.

The mechanics institutes were the 19th Century's first major attempt to deal with the educational problems of the dawning scientific age. Largely a creation of the middle class in the interest of
their inferiors, they failed as a means of technical education for the
working class.[37] As a source of recreation and mildly educational
entertainment they throve as middle-class establishments until more
functionally differentiated organizations began to usurp their purposes in the latter half of the century. While never offering the education they may have intended, they offered precedent and stimulus. They had been formed by the well-to-do classes who would

have to support successful universities. Better-off artisans and the lower-middle class had sent their older children (14-21) to the institutes' classes, thus suggesting that there was a potential clientele for colleges. Equally important, they had been a genuinely new attempt to solve the problems of a changing society.[38]

Less formal and direct means of education also grew in London and the provincial cities of mid-Victorian England. Most obviously important were libraries. Public interest and state concern were first noticeable in London, where the early years of Victoria's reign saw the British Museum expand enormously in reader numbers and physical size.[39] The state's interest was broadened to include the provinces with the passage of the Public Library Act of 1850, which authorized the levying of a library rate by local authorities. Manchester and Liverpool were among the first to adopt the Act, in 1852.[40] Of the seven cities which had established university colleges by the end of the century, by 1872 five of them were providing the largest free public libraries in Great Britain at the ratepayers' expense, authorized by public vote.[41] The libraries were intended to serve all classes, though at first they were of particular service to workers, as the middle classes continued to patronize the proprietary circulating libraries. In some sense the new libraries, along with technical schools, night schools, etc., represented that functional differentiation which replaced the mechanics institutes with a variety of institutions. At their dissolution local institutes often left their libraries and premises to the new public libraries.[42]

Societies and associations, in which the English tend to embody any mutual interest, were growing in number and frequently devoted to educational and intellectual matters. *Primus inter pares* was that already ancient institution, founded in 1662, the Royal Society. London saw a steady growth of societies, among which the Society of Arts and the Royal Institution, founded respectively in the mid and late 18th Century, were prominent. The trend moved to the provinces, where the Birmingham Lunar Society (1766) was followed by the more permanent Literary and Philosophical societies of Manchester (1781) and other civic centres. These societies and the 19th Century Athenaeums for the discussion of more or less academic subjects both advanced knowledge and made it an object of more general repute and desire. Indeed, with this growing interest in mind, they often discussed proposals for colleges and other more formally educational institutions.[43]

More narrowly defined and clearly differentiated learned societies proliferated in both capital and provinces in the 19th Century.

Geological and other societies gave support and often valuable collections and museums to the new colleges, as well as serving the generally helpful function of encouraging intellectual interests. Some were peculiarly concerned with education, as was the famous Manchester Statistical Society, which devoted much of its time to some of the first statistical analyses of educational provision.[44] At the same time the establishment of the British Association for the Advancement of Science (1831), and later of the Association for the Promotion of Social Science (1857), provided a powerful voice for the general interests of science and the intellect. In fact the British Association deliberately held its general meetings in provincial cities to stimulate nationwide support and interest.

Mid-Victorian society was rearranging its institutions and creating new ones to serve a changing and growing variety of needs and people. Intellectual and cultural services were in increasing demand. The specific circumstances which made civic colleges a logical response are the subject of the next three chapters.

2
Preconditions

A variety of colleges led brief lives in the provincial cities of England before successful, permanent institutions were established. Want of capital or students, inappropriate aims, poor locations or management, trade cycles, and other factors all share the blame. Certain preconditions were necessary to the successful establishment and growth of a college. An educated population had to be available in sufficient numbers, and they must have an interest in education which would produce both support and attendance. The demands of status and the conditions and growth of the economy encouraged such attitudes. Victorian England, and the Northern commercial and manufacturing districts in particular, established these prerequisite conditions in the mid and later 19th Century.

Education

A sufficiently educated population was the most obvious prerequisite. Without institutions of secondary education colleges would either founder for want of students or be reduced to a secondary level. The type and content of available secondary education also defined the interests and achievements of students, with great effect on the curriculum of new colleges. As Principal Scott explained: "But what we should teach, it was thought must depend on what and how the better prepared candidates were qualified by previous attainments to learn ...."[1] To a lesser degree the education of benefactors, their connections with local schools, and their perception of local educational inadequacies might all affect their benefactions.

The education available to the vast majority of the population during the 19th Century neither led toward, nor prepared for, attendance at a civic college. Prior to 1870 the provision of education, and attendance, were voluntary matters. Provision appeared in the forms of ancient endowment, contemporary charity, and commercial institutions both profit and non-profit. To begin at the bottom, this meant that considerable numbers of children received no education whatsoever. Above this level education was divided, as Matthew Arnold saw, into three planes, more or less corresponding to the three obvious divisions of society.

This correspondence was neither coincidental nor merely a result of the class divisions within society. Rather, schools deliberately and quite efficiently set out to both define and perpetuate the divisions. As the 19th Century advanced the idea of education as a necessary social emollient, an antidote to crime and pauperism (the supposed great lower class threat of the latter half of the century), replaced the idea of ignorance as a defense against revolution (the earlier fear of the privileged). A docile population was no longer enough; increasingly a trained, perhaps also indoctrinated one was necessary.

For the majority of the Victorian population, the working classes, there was elementary education, intended to fit the recipient for the most subordinate duties of the social and commercial state, which he would begin to undertake at an early age (perhaps ten at mid-century, and not reaching the mid-teens until the 20th Century). The elementary "system" which was adopted, adapted, and enlarged by the Education Act of 1870 in no way contradicted these principles, but the concept of the education desirable for the proletariat did expand towards the end of the century, rising in both level and variety of subject matter. The pinnacle of elementary education as provided by the school boards (established under the 1870 Act) was the higher-grade school, which appeared in increasing numbers in the great cities from the 80s onwards.[2] Many of these schools offered a sound modern education which would equip their best students, if not for immediate entry to a college, at least with the tools to prepare themselves, independently or via the various informal and formal agencies of adult education, either for direct admission or to compete for a grammar school scholarship (see below). Only a very few of their first students could have entered the colleges during the 80s, but they were the harbingers of a small but socially significant future clientele. In general, however, elementary schooling was and was intended to be terminal for the majority of its recipients.

Formal and informal ways might be found around the cul-de-sac of elementary education, and finding them required an intelligence and persistence, as well as preparation, which could lead to the civic colleges. Autodidacticism was one answer celebrated throughout the vast Victorian literature of self-help. It produced the heroes of Samuel Smiles, and also much of the radical leadership from Francis Place to Keir Hardie and Tom Mann. Such study could be supplemented by any of various more systematic arrangements which increased in number and scope as the century advanced. The wide span in time and degree of organization between the first mutual discussion groups and the WEA and university extramural departments has been well surveyed.[3] Two major organizations of considerable interest for this study are discussed elsewhere: the mechanics institutes in Chapter 1, and the working men's colleges in Chapter 4. Adult education in all its forms was a notable phenomenon of the new, Northern industrial areas. In 1851 Lancashire and the West Riding possessed over a third of the evening schools for adults available in England and Wales,[4] and were soon to open the earliest public libraries. Obviously, study in the evening classes of a civic college was a logical and fairly easy step to take in the process of adult education.

There was also an alternative and more formal route from elementary to higher education. This was the so-called "ladder" by which a bright student might proceed via scholarships to progressively higher grades of secondary schools and eventually to the universities. Traditionally this route had been comprised of charity schools followed by the local free (i.e. endowed charity) grammar school where the exceptional student could prepare to win a university scholarship, or qualify for one of the various forms of geographically or institutionally restricted admission. The decay of the grammar schools and the reform of Oxford and Cambridge had largely eliminated this route by the 1860s and considerable effort from then on was devoted to restoring and broadening the ladder. Full acceptance of this principle, with the concomitant assumption that elementary education was otherwise and in a majority of cases terminal, was embodied in the Education Act of 1902, which provided for a mandated scholarship ladder. This was not a sudden decision. Since 1869, the revision of educational trusts by the

Charity Commissioners had often included the provision of free places and scholarships.[5]

The further step from the secondary schools to the new civic colleges was also increasingly provided for by scholarships. Two examples are particularly relevant. Exhibitions to Owens College from the Manchester Grammar School were solicited by both institutions and grew in number, thus capping the considerable number of exhibitions, free places, and scholarships to the grammar school. By 1884 the Samuelson Commission noted that a full if narrow ladder from elementary to Central School (School Board), to Grammar School, to university, was in place and in use in Manchester.[6] A more wide-ranging example was the famous Whitworth Scholarships and Exhibitions in Mechanical Science, which provided for both high level study and the preliminary preparation necessary to compete for the scholarships.

A somewhat different form of ladder was provided by the growing demand for teachers and the concomitant growth of teacher education. The recruitment and training of lower class teachers expanded steadily after the Minutes of 1846 and especially after 1870. Pupil teachership,[7] formal teacher training, and particularly Queen's Scholarships, could prepare people for admission to the colleges. (For a further discussion see Chapter 4 on Demand.) The number of potential students so prepared is uncertain, but there were over 12,000 certificated teachers in 1870 and their numbers had increased fourfold by 1895.[8] At a minimum, any of them would have been well qualified for evening study in the colleges.

The type as well as the amount of preparation received by potential students affected the new colleges by influencing students' choice of courses and the colleges' notions of what to offer. The education of the proletariat, (and of members of the lower middle class, particularly in the higher grade schools and lesser private schools) already discussed, emphasized literacy and numeracy. Beyond this a great variety of more or less efficient teaching in other subjects was offered in increasing quantities as the century drew to a close. Some amount of maths, sciences, history, geography, English literature, and modern languages might be available, and individual variation between schools might well exceed that between the generality of schools in one class and another. The offerings of various schools in such a non-system represented a continuum of curricula rather than hard and fast lines.

The typical education of much of the middle classes in 1870 was that which had recently been decried by Matthew Arnold: "In England the middle class, as a rule, *is brought up on the second plane*."[9] "What these middle class academies fail to give in social and governing qualities, they do not make up for in intellectual power."[10] At any rate this education consisted of most of the subjects listed above, with perhaps an increased emphasis on modern languages, commercial subjects, and, in later years, science. There was also a certain amount of classics, and it is between the partially classical education of some of the middle class and the almost wholly classical training of the upper middle and the aristocracy that it is least possible to draw a clear line. In general, as schools ascended the social and economic ladder they increasingly emphasized classics at the expense of other subjects, until eventually they reached the first plane, that of the great public schools and their most successful imitators.

These grew in number as newer public schools joined the ancient foundations and as the revived grammar schools increasingly conformed to the public school model, which was well established by the 80s.[11] Academically this model consisted of a classical education with trimmings of English and history and a tincture of science, these latter parts often relegated to despised "modern sides". It had also another aspect, that of the provision of those "social and governing qualities" whose absence in middle class education Arnold deplored. Emphasis on games, leadership, and the manners and deportment of a gentleman, all provided in a consistently regimented setting, replaced the alternation of anarchy and severity and the occasional concentration on the intellect which had characterised older styles of secondary education. This classical and more or less anti-intellectual education was the socially dominant mode, and as it was imitated in the education of all who could afford it, the civic colleges could expect a fairly low standard of classical knowledge to be the preparation of many of their better-off students.

There were of course exceptions, and the industrial and commercial North, with its independent bourgeois culture, undoubtedly resisted the new gentry-cum-middle class education, and continued to provide a sound general education for many students. Testimony to the efficiency of the modern as well as the classical teaching in such schools as the Manchester Grammar School and the Liverpool Collegiate School was widespread. Indeed the youth of the first students of the colleges and the constant complaints of the faculty about the necessity to do relatively elementary teaching suggest that

Northern parents found the new colleges a logical alternative to proprietary schools or the new wave of public school foundations.

The intricacy of class distinctions permeated both the theory and provision of secondary education for the middle classes. For the sons of bankers, merchants, and the upper strata of the learned professions, there was the education of the upper classes. With the decline of private instruction this meant attendance at a great public school,[12] possibly followed by Oxford or Cambridge. Attendance at a civic college would be an anomaly so rare as to make this type of preparation irrelevant to this study.[13] Below, or including, the great public schools, most late Victorian theorists, practitioners, and critics saw secondary education as divided into three parts. The Taunton Commission defined these in 1868 as: a first class education which was classical, given mostly in boarding schools, and continued until at least 18; a second grade which placed more emphasis on modern subjects, was offered largely in day schools, and ended at 16; and a third grade, terminating at 14, which concentrated on basic literacy and numeracy, with perhaps some scientific, commercial, or technical training. In 1895 the Bryce Commission accepted the Taunton divisions as both a sound prescription for and a reasonable description of the provision of secondary education.[14]

All these divisions provided some candidates for education at a civic college, but the second grade and the lower portion of the first were most important. The third grade assumed the necessity of employment at an early age, and did not provide anything like a thorough preparation for admission, at least not to a full-time day course. By and large its recipients were in the same position as that of the proletariat described earlier. At the other extreme of the great schools the late leaving age as well as social considerations militated against admission to a civic college (or, more precisely, a student likely to attend a civic college would not have been sent to such a school). The major public schools were increasingly retaining their pupils until the age of 19, and entrance to the university after that meant a greatly delayed entry into business, which was generally unacceptable to the provincial business community.[15]

Thus it was schools roughly of the second grade or shading into the first, which were most likely to prepare candidates for the civic colleges. They offered modern subjects and a considerable amount of Latin, and their age of graduation was between 16 and 18, probably increasing toward the end of the century, as also was the emphasis on classics (as in the great schools) in some cases, and on science in others. These schools were of three more or less distinct types: public, grammar, and proprietary, and all three types were growing in size and number during the latter half of the 19th Century. The fifty years from 1840 to 1890 were the heyday of public school foundations, with something between thirty and fifty such schools founded, depending on definition.[16] While grammar schools did not greatly expand in number, their reform became a matter of concern, and a growing number of them were raised from a moribund or elementary state by the Charity and Endowed Schools Commissions. The size of these increasingly efficient schools also grew, sometimes enormously.[17]

A city had to have sufficient population in receipt of some form of education if a civic college was to survive. New colleges began with a local catchment area and attracted a tiny proportion of the local populace; the area had to provide sufficient student numbers for viability both as an educational institution and as an object of philanthropic and other support. Manchester was first to achieve this, and first to create a permanently successful college. Birmingham and Liverpool followed suit, while the other university colleges remained smaller and poorer until other factors broadened their scope, income, and appeal in the 20th Century.

How many potential students were available when? Neither half of the question is susceptible to exact statistical analysis, but even a notional answer suggests the increasing likelihood that a new civic foundation might meet with success as the century progressed. How many is an impossible question when dealing with lower class education, particularly since the genuine potential student was not merely one who met the educational prerequisites but one sufficiently stimulated to enroll and who possessed the means to do so. A very small percentage of this category of people met these further criteria. That the potential numbers rose greatly is, however, easily demonstrable. The numbers who received elementary education and thus could at least attempt to go further, rose throughout the century. After 1870 rising elementary enrollment rates were increasingly accompanied by chances to receive further formal education. At the same time, the alternative education of, by, and for the working class shifted its character to provide more distinctly secondary and advanced work as elementary education became a public responsibility.[18] The steady growth of evening enrollments and the appearance of working class students in day courses at the civic colleges demonstrated this.[19]

Proprietary and private schools formed a significant portion of middle class educational provision. The nature of their organization makes any estimate of their number and efficiency less certain than in cases where there was public oversight. Musgrove and Taylor,[20] using the data gathered by the Taunton and Bryce Commissions as well as other sources, talk of 10,000 schools of relatively small average size in both the 60s and the 90s, though witnesses in the 90s spoke of a decline. Numbers in such schools are very uncertain, as is the percentage of these schools capable of or likely to prepare students for the colleges.

In spite of all the variables and lacunae, some estimates of student numbers exist. Musgrove and Taylor think there were about 37,000 in grammar schools, 12,000 in proprietary schools, and 40,000 in private schools in the 1860s.[21] Lowndes, drawing on the Bryce Commission's report, speaks of 75,000 in endowed schools and 34,000 in non-profit proprietary schools in 1895, by which time there were also 24,584 students in higher grade schools, with the heaviest concentration in Lancashire (7,664) and the West Riding (8,263).[22]

There is even some reliable evidence of the proportion of students from these various sources who attended the new colleges (see Table I, p.31).

Obviously, the second category, which contains the preponderance of students, corresponds closely to some of the first and all of the second of the Taunton and Bryce categories; in fact it is the typical middle class education. That its students were the best equipped to meet the criteria of the colleges is demonstrated by the ratio of students to scholarships won in this category. The ratio is only higher in the proletarian category and there reflects the simple impossibility of admission without financial aid for most potential candidates. To extrapolate backward from these proportions to arrive at those of the 60s and 70s seems reasonable, so long as several allowances are made: foreign students are unlikely to have appeared prior to the chartering of the university in 1880; the proportion of students in category 4 was probably considerably lower earlier on, at least among the full-time day students who are the earlier equivalent of undergraduates; it is possible that within category 2 less distinguished schools provided a greater proportion of earlier students, before the attraction of a degree was offered. Increasing cosmopolitanism would also alter the mix of schools across time.

Table I
Previous Place of Education of Undergraduates
of Victoria University 1893-94[23]

	Male		Female	
	Students	Scholarships	Students	Scholarships
(1) Seven Public Schools	18	1		
(2) Other Endowed, Proprietary, and Private Schools of a Secondary Nature	623	142	68	24
(3) Private Tuition or Home Study	71	12	9	2
(4) Training Colleges, Pupil Teacher Centres, Technical Schools & Public Elementary Schools	126	78	16	12
(5) Wales, Scotland, Ireland & Foreign Countries	52	1	5	1

New Attitudes Toward Education

The growing provision of education in Victorian England represented new ideas as well as new practices. Previous systems of primary and secondary education were seen to be defective for the middle and upper classes and non-existent for vast numbers of the labouring poor. The growing complexity of business and the new professions required drastic revision of middle-class education; enfranchisement and employment in industry made education a necessity for the labouring classes. Debates over the character, amount, and control of this education made it a prominent political and social issue. Politicians like Brougham made education part of every program; literati like Macaulay kept the question before their readers. A vast range of experiments, from monitorial schools for the poor through Arnold and Thring's revolution in the "public schools" to new universities, adult education at all levels, and reform of Oxford and Cambridge marked an age of both reform and new departures in education.

All this required a particular attitude which was developing or reappearing in the 19th Century. Education must be viewed as a social necessity or at least a benefit to society if it is to receive the attention of patrons, philanthropists, and reformers. Tudor endowment of secondary and university education had insured the presence of a clerisy, both secular and sacred, for the purposes of the state. In fact it created a genuinely national system of endowed grammar schools, colleges at universities, and scholarships.[24] This system, fallen into varying degrees of decay and desuetude, was still the basis of higher education in the 19th Century, the object of a vast assortment of proposed reforms.

During the 18th Century, however, education was habitually viewed as sufficient in quantity and quality for the purposes of society. Clerics were trained, or at least supported, in the ancient universities, and private tuition, the Inns of Court, and the capitals of Europe trained the great men of affairs. Neither philanthropy, hoping to benefit society, nor the state, aiming at efficiency and security, was particularly interested in education.

This attitude had already begun to change markedly by Victoria's accession. Education as something a man might wish to purchase for himself, the prevailing 18th Century view, began to be replaced by the idea of education as a public interest, even a public necessity; a logical field for philanthropic and even legislative effort. A great variety of social stresses produced the opinion that the lower classes might safely be educated, indeed were safer when educated than when ignorant. Lawson and Silver rightly see the essential problem as the growing concentration of population, and provide a useful list of the groups and theories which produced an educational response by the end of the 18th Century: "the political radicalism of the 1790s, traditions of philanthropy, the utilitarianism associated with Jeremy Bentham and the laissez-faire economists, the evangelical movement in the Church of England, and the educational radicalism connected with the ideas of Rousseau."[25] The Sunday School movement of the 1780s was followed by the monitorial day schools at the turn of the century and the steady growth of the two great non-conformist and Anglican societies, the British and Foreign School Society and the National Society for Promoting the Education of the Poor in the Principles of the Established Church, thereafter. A succession of Reform Acts added fear of an uneducated electorate to the other stimuli towards the provision of elementary education. Whether the central concern of educational policy was social control or merely amelioration, education was an increasingly prescribed remedy for the social ills of Victorian England.

Middle and upper class concern with secondary education produced new proprietary schools, the reorganization of grammar
schools, and the elevation of some to public school status. Large
scale reorganization, the founding of many public schools, and the
reform and creation of universities occurred in the later part of the
century; the sense of education as a national need and an almost
patriotic duty had begun to develop earlier.

The steadily growing need for an educated electorate, literate
labourers, trained technicians, and cultivation for the new middle
class regardless of religion was brought home to the wealthy and
powerful by their own experience and the periodical press. By the
1830s the *Westminster* and *Edinburgh*, in calling for university reform and new curricula, justified their demands on the grounds of
society's need for educated men. In 1838 the *Edinburgh* called for
a "national system of education,"[26] and in a survey of the growth of
working class education emphasized the necessity for the middle
and upper classes to maintain their positions via education: "It is
no longer a matter of choice: they must bestow the requisite care
upon their education. And here we speak of the middle as well as
the upper classes of society ...."[27] An 1854 essay,[28] significantly titled "Government Education Measures for Rich and Poor," reiterated both the need for a national system and the peculiar requirements of the governing classes. The need for better middle
class education was of course the main thrust of Arnold's influential
writings on education, which added the further stimulus of comparison with foreign examples.

The particular importance of higher education was also emphasized quite early. The famous attacks on Oxbridge led by Hamilton
and the *Edinburgh* in the 30s were not merely protests against
"abuses" and "jobs" in the traditional manner. Nor were they simply attacks on the quality of the education available, though both
these strains were obviously present. Basically the *Edinburgh* was
engaged in redefining higher education as a necessary public adjunct of society and the state, a role not fulfilled by Oxbridge.[29]

This change of attitude redirected philanthropy toward a recently
neglected but traditional path. The massive charitable efforts of the
British and National Societies and their subscribers have been
mentioned. Contributions founded the Woodard and other smaller
projects in secondary education. Higher education benefitted as
well. New Oxbridge colleges, London, the provincial colleges, and
a network of scholarships had all been created by 1900,[30] while the

18th Century had offered little support even to its traditional institutions.

Private philanthropy is evidence of some people's concern. The role of the state offers a broader perspective on the changing attitude toward education. Investigation followed by regulation was the course customarily pursued by the state in accepting some degree of responsibility for social problems, national concerns, or public works. The various levels of educational provision followed this pattern and even went beyond it to the far rarer third stage of governmental subvention. The significance of this activity is best understood by remembering the constitutional reluctance of the Victorian state to expand its regulatory role, and the even stronger desire of all politicians and parties to reduce or eliminate the income tax and many forms of government expenditure. The gospel of self help, the doctrine of laissez-faire, was sometimes violated in practice but its theory was worshipped by the state and much of the articulate public. The most that new universities could hope for until the closing years of the 19th Century was tolerance, permission to incorporate, and eventually charters. Money they could not expect: under Robert Lowe as Chancellor, the exchequer had refused funds for such basic studies as astronomical and tidal observations vital to Britain's maritime power;[31] new institutions of doubtful value were obviously beyond the pale.

Nevertheless, the state's attitude towards education shifted in the course of the century. Increasingly, those necessary things which private enterprise could not accomplish became tasks of the state. The general principle of laissez-faire remained, but many a free-trader and classic liberal like Macaulay came to support government regulation of industry, child labor, and education. Once government took some responsibility for society, its role, perhaps inevitably, grew. Where previously society had known only charity and the privy purse as means to its ends, the 19th Century added a far more efficient means, the municipal rate.[32] From mid-century on, the private bequests which founded and supported schools and universities were matched and then exceeded by growing public rates for a variety of educational purposes. The state's assistance sacrificed the principles of self-help as little as possible. Throughout the century the most common form of funding was the authorization of a local rate for primary and later technical education, locally approved, levied, and administered. Schools, libraries, and a variety of municipal works were funded on this basis.

The trend towards state support was not a trend towards a monopoly of education. The right of private and sectarian education was and is presumed in Britain. Education was to be regulated by both the state and the laws of supply and demand. Business joined philanthropy and the state throughout the range of 19th Century education. Many private schools, at all levels of financial scale and educational pretension, were established as business speculations.

Public responsibility was first admitted at the lowest levels of education and in an indirect manner: public funds were offered to religiously-oriented societies providing primary education. The contribution was small but provocative. The provision of better education at the primary level prepared greater numbers of students for further progress. Coupled with an increasingly democratic franchise, government funded improvements in education would eventually lead to the establishment of a complete though not all-inclusive system of publicly supported education. As the century progressed liberals and reformers called for more funds for different purposes and by 1902 a succession of Education Acts had laid the groundwork of a national system of education from primary schools paid for by local rates and inspected by public officials, through universities increasingly dependent on grants from the state.

The growing interest in education as a public service, or at least a public need, is easily seen by summarizing the progression from investigation through regulation and subvention at the various levels. Reports of Parliamentary Committees on the Education of the Lower Orders (1816-18) and on the State of Education (1834) produced a Treasury Minute (1833) allocating a trend-setting £20,000 grant for buildings to the British and National societies. This support expanded and became routinized via the creation of a Committee of Council for Education (1839), the support of a teacher training system, and the development of an inspectorate and an expanding government department. The 60s saw further inquiries and the institution and subsequent criticism of the Revised Code. 1870 marked the full assumption of government responsibility, though greater control was more slowly developed.

Secondary education of the middle and upper classes became a major concern in the 60s, as shown by the Reports of the Clarendon (1864) and Taunton (1868) Commissions. These were investigations of the schools of the upper middle class; concern with broadening the scope and the catchment of secondary education led to a major report on all secondary education by 1895 (Bryce Commission), and finally, in 1902, to the first definition of a truly national system of primary and secondary education.[33]

Universities received their first major scrutiny in the 50s, by the Royal Commissions on Oxford and Cambridge, and a second round of investigation and reform in the 1870s. The last quarter of the century also saw the chartering of the Victoria University and the investigation and reorganization of the University of London. In 1889 the first of a continuing series of grants was made to various university colleges.[34]

A less obvious aspect of law and public policy also demonstrates the 19th Century's changing attitude toward education. Philanthropy in the form of endowment had created many of England's educational institutions and these were governed and regulated by a body of law concerned with charitable trusts.Over the course of time this body of law and custom had acquired enormous moral and traditional as well as legal force,[35] and any alterations for the benefit of education would reveal a very powerful concern with that social responsibility. And in fact several such major alterations were made, against opposition, in the course of the century.

The state had begun the investigation and subvention of technical education on a very small scale as early as 1837, when a school of design was created, and from 1853 the Department of Science and Art and its successors inspected, regulated, and supported an increasing amount of technical education. The scope and intensity of this interest remained very small until the last quarter of the century, however, when the by now standard process of investigation by commission followed by legislation occurred: the Devonshire Reports, 1872-75 (Commission on Scientific Instruction and the Advancement of Science) and the Samuelson Reports 1882-84 (Commission on Technical Instruction) were followed by the Technical Instruction Act, 1889, the Local Taxation Act, 1890, the Schools for Science and Art Act, 1891, etc., which provided funds, organization, and regulation.

Government action, and its timing, demonstrate the growing concern for technology, but also the slow pace and late start of this growth. As industry grew and became more complex it became increasingly necessary to acquire a body of scientifically based information relating to production, research, distribution, etc., and to equip a class of managers and skilled employees with this information. Craft and craftsmen needed to be supplemented by technology and technicians. The old methods of training by apprenticeship, suited to the maintenance of a stable number of persons and an unchanging body of knowledge, were ill-suited to the training of larger numbers, and utterly incapable of developing the new knowledge, technology. Higher education, linked with research, was eventually to provide an answer.

A need must not only exist, but also be felt, before it can be filled, and the British were slow to become aware of the need for technology and its concomitants, polytechnics and universities. Precedents did exist. The Royal Society had offered awards for practical applications of scientific principles since its foundation in 1663. Throughout the succeeding eras some few men of science, business, and industry had been aware of the need for a marriage of science and industry. Faraday and later Kelvin were scientists with industrial and technical connections and James Watts' work with Joseph Black, professor of chemistry at Glasgow University, foreshadowed the modern development of universities as servants of technology.

Foreign stimuli had appeared and were recognized as such. On the Continent, most particularly in France, knowledge was acquired and systematic technical training commenced in the 18th Century. French works on civil engineering were the standard references for those few Britons who thought in modern theoretical terms.[36] The Ecole des Ponts et Chaussées and, after the Revolution, the Polytechnique, provided a technological education at a level unavailable in England. In Glasgow, precursors of the mechanics institutes appeared in the 1760s. These Continental and Scottish examples of technical education were long ignored by the English, but their results eventually forced themselves into notice. Foreign industrial competition, increasing in effectiveness throughout the century, would force Britain to analyze its industrial weaknesses; and the greatest of these seemed to be the lack of modern education at all levels.

The need for sound general education of workers increased along with the complexity of machinery and industry, and this was evident to reformers of every stripe. It appears regularly in the *Edinburgh* and *Westminster* as a major argument for popular education along with the customary political and social arguments. A real and widespread understanding of the connection of higher science and education with industrial demands developed more slowly. The general proposition that various scientific studies were useful for industry, business, and government was stated quite early,[37] but as long as Britain maintained its lead in world industry, complacency defeated all advocates of serious reforms in higher education and the establishment of new institutions.

The great industrial exhibitions which increasingly became an educational and competitive stimulus to European society after the Great Exhibition[38] revealed that Britain's long industrial lead was shortening, and that education seemed to account for many Continental successes. By the late 60s, and especially after the Paris Universal Exposition,[39] British complacency had given place in some quarters to critical comparison and fears of future failure. The names of Borsig, Krupp, Creusot, and other famous Continental firms were heard in England, and comparative tests showed Britain behind even the one-time colonies in agricultural machinery. The relatively poor education of the English work force was pointed out and invidious comparisons between British and Continental popular education received new impetus. Literacy and technical instruction became universal demands of British reformers.

The limited and antiquated character of higher technical education was also assailed. British managers and technicians were unable to acquire that education and information which was evidently necessary to efficiency and progress.[40] Scientists like Tyndall and Playfair and manufacturers like A.J. Mundella publicly expounded Britain's educational deficiencies, especially when compared with her competitors.

One obvious step towards remedial action was to look to foreign examples in education. The public, or at least the critics, were not unaware of Continental developments. The *Edinburgh* had studied the Polytechnique in 1840, when British industrial opinion was still unanimously complacent. In 1868 when concern was mounting, the Taunton Commission on secondary education had sent investigators to France, Germany, Switzerland, Italy, Scotland, the United States, and Canada. The Devonshire Commission of 1872 found English science ill-organized and advocated, among other things, the complete revision of secondary education to take account of technical and scientific needs.[41] Scientists were familiar with German achievements,[42] and indeed had often received their advanced training abroad. However, it was not the German universities or that pinnacle of French education, the Polytechnique, which were to serve as examples of technological education. The high-quality technical institutes which were developing in France, Germany and Belgium were the objects of admiration. The *Edinburgh Review*, stimulated by the Paris Universal Exhibition of

1867, undertook a critique of "Technical and Scientific Education," and concluded that technical education abroad was providing the impetus for the Continent's enormous gains vis-a-vis the British.

Along with technical training, awareness of the commercial significance of pure science increased. The eventual applicability of scientific discoveries was realized and demonstrated by the *Westminster* in 1873.[43] Britain's failure to support research was documented by a statistic on the number of published papers of scientific research in 1866: Germany, 777; France, 245; Great Britain, 127. While no direct mention of British universities appeared, it was pointedly remarked that in German universities young men were encouraged to do research.

At this point many histories of British education sum up in favour of the demand for science and technology as the chief if not sole stimulus behind the developing civic universities, and technicians and scientists as the end products produced. It is assumed that by the time that higher education began its major expansion from the 1870s through the turn of the century, industry's needs were publicly recognized. The new university colleges would offer technical and scientific education. They would promote basic research and go to foreign countries for personnel and ideas.

This conclusion requires a good deal of modification. The economy's need for new men was not so great nor its demands so imperative as they may appear in retrospect. Graduates were to find few jobs which required their new skills until well after the turn of the century.[44] The foreman, engineer, or technical expert trained on the job remained the standard type of "scientific" employee, and Smiles' *Lives of the Great Engineers*, glorifying self-made men, continued to sell well.

This demand shortfall is not surprising. It continued to be a British presumption that technical training, if needed, was a desideratum for the working classes, while their betters required a general education and, perhaps, business training. As Arnold, among others, pointed out, Britain educated its populace on different planes and neither the aristocratic and professional nor the lower-middle class plane were thought to require the inclusion of science.[45] Certainly the "public" and proprietary schools which furnished the education of such a large part of the middle classes and sent some on to Oxbridge had little use for science. Furthermore, this attitude was not entirely the result of a blind failure to recognize a primary need. Habakkuk has argued convincingly[46] that the relative decline of Britain's industrial position in the world was largely a function of such factors as population, resource availability and capital accumulation, and not the failure of scientific knowledge as perceived by men like Playfair and reviews like the *Edinburgh* and *Westminster*. If Schelsky's analysis of the occupational structure of industrial society is correct, then the large scale demand for the university trained scientist or technologist appeared only in the 20th Century.[47]

Social Status and Economic Circumstances

Other aspects of social and economic reality provided less direct but no less vital preconditions for the success of civic universities. The social and economic circumstances of the growing middle classes provided impetus and funds for enrolments and gifts. An economic climate compounded of continued growth, but at slackening rates, and in face of increased competition, could encourage new curricula and new students. The diversification of both professional occupations and intellectual disciplines provided new roles and new niches in an expanding academic world. The material conditions of life made attendance easier as time progressed.

The uncertainties of the growing middle classes were important to the colleges. For some time before the Victorian era the levels of status in society, and its division into groups of differential prestige, had been fairly clear and stable. While the barriers were permeable, a majority of the members of each of the major classes possessed the same clearly perceived status throughout life. They also remained in an area where their class, ancestry, and credentials were personally known to others. With urban expansion, city-ward migration, and rapid and cheap transportation, society achieved both a new scale and a new fluidity. As formal credentials necessarily replaced mutual familiarity as a measure of technical and professional skill, so assertion and performance increasingly replaced ascription as the measure of status. The use of education to provide credentials is discussed in Chapter 4, and the demand for education, particularly "liberal education," as a mark of status is analyzed there. Here the *desire* for status requires discussion.

The creation of the first modern industrial society involved unprecedented growth in the numbers of the middle classes as the tertiary sector of the economy and the number of non-manual employments expanded enormously along with productive capacity.

Three important changes in people's status thus became common and important. One could move from below into the middle classes, forsaking manual labour, exchanging a wage for a salary or the profits of business, hopefully achieving security of employment, dressing daily in the matter if not the manner of all the classes above. Educationally such a change meant the necessity of literacy and numeracy, and perhaps a desire for further education as an assertion of status.

The second possible change was a rise in status within the middle classes. Greater income, the abandonment of retail trade except on a large scale, political activity, professional employments, conspicuous consumption in housing, transport, and servants, might all define and assist this rise. Education could prepare the recipient for his duties, equip him with his manner, manners, and friends, and reveal his family's ability to purchase such a luxury.

At the third level a movement from the middle class to either the gentry or to the long-accepted, traditionally small, but now growing class of the plutocracy was possible. Abandonment of all but the largest scale of business affairs, land holding, new leisure and social pursuits, and unenthusiastic conversion to the Church of England, if that had not accompanied a previous rise, all are probable evidences of this third transmogrification. Educationally this meant the complete de-emphasis of practical studies, the social necessity of attending one of a small number of schools followed, if at all, by Oxford or Cambridge; an education which in fact separated the recipient from the middle classes. Clearly the first two of these social movements are of greatest importance for the growth of such decidedly middle class institutions as civic colleges and the schools which might prepare students for them. The status anxiety caused by this new fluidity could be partially allayed by education.

Education could support both the economic substructure and the social superstructure of status. Thinking, speaking, reading, and writing like a gentleman provided both inner confidence and outward evidence of position. A public school education might well serve as a form of conspicuous consumption. On the other hand education might be a shrewd investment. The preparation for high status occupations, particularly the professions, represents an amalgam of these two principle motivations, representing as it does both financial security and an assertion of social position.

The middle classes, well aware of the uses of education, created and patronized a vast network of schools in the Victorian era. The tremendous growth of both "public" and proprietary and private schools has been discussed. In many cases they represented the entirety of middle class education, but for some the ancient universities followed, and for a growing number the new civic colleges provided another alternative. The economic character of many middle class occupations made the civic college a particularly suitable means of educating children. The professions, small businesses and manufactories, the upper reaches of clerkdom, were all expanding, and in these employments maximum earnings and income are achieved relatively late in life. The civic college offered social and professional education at a level which had been unconsidered or financially unavailable when children were younger. An educationally or socially inferior previous education was not an insuperable or even a very high barrier; the colleges were well accustomed to remedial work and their social standards were the minimum of respectability, not insistance upon gentility or ancestry.

Social position was not only a private and personal affair. Men were concerned with the reputation of their communities as well. The great mercantile and industrial cities of the North had particular reason to be sensitive. While York had been a great medieval city, more recent times had seen the total economic, political, and cultural eclipse of the North by the South of England, and particularly by London and its environs. The 18th Century defined the provinces as boorish, and the North as the home of Catholicism and Dissent. When the area became industrial and the producer of a new class of wealthy men of apparently dubious principles and antecedents, this did nothing to allay suspicions, and added the country gentry and aristocracy of the North itself to the ranks of the cities' critics. But a new civic class developed, created a provincial culture of its own, and insisted upon a recognized position in society and the state.

The creation of a civic college might serve to leaven the lump of the urban middle class populace both intellectually and socially, as well as being a sound economic investment. It could also serve as a monument to municipal pride, as the central piles at Owens and University Colleges, with their close resemblance to other monumental civic architecture, attest. The intellectual interests of the leaders of provincial society were of long standing, and were already being institutionalized in the 18th Century. These groups would naturally be interested in education, its furtherance and publicization. H.R. Charlton has listed nine among the many intellectual societies formed in Manchester between 1780 and 1851 ranging from the Manchester Academy to the Royal Medical College, but the first and most famous of these may serve as an example.[48] Founded in 1781 the Literary and Philosophical Society established a sufficient reputation so as to receive a nickname, the Lit. and Phil. It studied, proposed and indeed inaugurated several educational experiments and undoubtedly contributed greatly to form a general attitude among Mancunians favourable to innovations in education. Manchester's Lit. and Phil., Statistical Society, etc., were copied in many other industrial centres and did their share to improve the educational climate.

Arnold Thackray has shown that this intellectual interest was a means of individual and communal self-assertion as well. "Given their social isolation, political emasculation, and tumultuous surroundings, Manchester's new and increasingly wealthy elite understandably sought cultural means through which to define and express themselves."[49] Science was particularly attractive as a newly defined intellectual field not monopolized by the traditional intellectual aristocracy of Oxbridge and London. As the 19th Century progressed, more of the civic aristocracy entered the traditional elite, and science teaching became more closely linked with the labouring classes and technical education, intellectual interests might well have shifted back toward traditional, literary and "liberal" studies. Indeed both the title and publications of the Lit. and Phils. in so many cities are a reminder of the catholicity of provincial intellectual interests.

Such interests and personal and civic pride might all go hand in hand, as the analysis of benefactions in Chapter 5 shows. John Owens' trustees are a good example. Two mayors and a variety of public officials were on the Board and in fact certain trustees had backed the bills of the newly formed Manchester Corporation when its legal existence was under attack by Tories.[50] The Baines family, long among the first citizens of Leeds, were powerful supporters of the Yorkshire College.

Given the interest and will, the capacity of the new industrial cities to create viable institutions can not be doubted. Phenomenal growth and lack of representation had left them ill-served and supplied by the traditional apparatus and institutions of the state. Anglican clergy were few, and seats in Parliament even sparser. The ancient universities, ostensibly national, failed to educate their elite.[51] This adversity did not discourage these cities. On the contrary, they remain the most obvious physical embodiment of the Victorian belief in progress.[52] They established their own religious organizations; they governed themselves in the absence and even in defiance of parliamentary legislation.

Victorian Britain possessed the money to build civic universities; it was available in previously unheard of quantities as the century advanced. And a growing proportion of this wealth, far more liquid than the traditional form of real property, was to be found in the industrial Midlands and North. Both average income and the number of wealthy persons grew in the latter half of the century, if in changing and debatable ratios. Greater income for the mass of the middle class and for the aristocracy of labour meant the possibility of attendance; wealth meant the possibility of benefactions.

The availability as well as the quantity of wealth increased with the century. Second and third generation mercantile and industrial fortunes were no longer so completely committed to the support and expansion of the business as were the founders' funds. Later generations might also be more concerned with the type of social status to be derived from charitable generosity.[53] If possessed of large families, they were likely to be seeking socially and financially respectable positions for sons outside the family business, and the professional and liberal education of the civic universities, offered without religious tests or the anti-commercial bias of the ancient universities, might well be appealing.[54]

Legal developments also contrived to free mercantile and industrial wealth from its total commitment to "the business". Limited liability and changes in the laws governing partnerships made the family firm less vulnerable, and made expansion without increased family investment easier. The growth of banks and the expansion of their functions made capital available outside the confines of the private fortune. In short, the stockpiling of private wealth was no longer so necessary either as insurance against misfortune or to provide for expansion. Charity became easier and safer to practice.

No consideration of the economic climate of late Victorian Britain can entirely ignore the so called "Great Depression". Yet its effects, and those of trade cycles generally, on the support of civic colleges seem to have been quite limited. No direct relationship between the long term, nationwide cycles of trade and the level of support for civic colleges can be detected. Two specific correlations deserve notice, however.

On a short term basis (a matter of months or a single year) the fortunes of manufacturing and trade within a city were carefully considered when launching a fund-raising campaign, or accounting for its slow progress.[55]

The second correlation is the relationship between unemployment and evening class enrolments. As a general rule hard times were found to reduce working class enrolments in many places. On the other hand, when the cotton industry was operating at peak levels, overtime and the demand for men could also reduce numbers. Particularly hard times might also produce exogenous stimuli to enrolments, as tuition fees were reduced and free lectures offered to keep men usefully occupied. Sir Henry Roscoe's organization of science lectures during the cotton famine of the 60s is a good example.

In fact, funds and enrolments grew steadily in the period from 1873 to 1896, the era of the "Great Depression". Owens College had grown to respectable size and substantial renown in the economically expansive third quarter of the century, but it moved on to university status and acquired brethren and competitors thereafter. The atypical character of the later era, which makes depression a dubious description of that time, may well be loosely connected with this growth. The basic economic features of the era were a fall in prices and the rate of investment (coupled with greater purchasing power for wages), the development of major threats from foreign industry in world and home markets, and a resulting generalized sense that the opportunities for economic success and growth were declining. Businessmen were unsure of continuing profits; professionals and clerks alike feared the overcrowding of their professions. Such attitudes could provide a number of reasons for supporting and/or acquiring higher education. New techniques and better training might be an aid in international competition and equally in the tighter job market at home. Education might provide a broadened horizon of future possibilities. Furthermore, the economy was by no means universally depressed. New fortunes were made in new leading sectors, and old ones stabilized or enlarged in efficient businesses, while banking, insurance, and the tertiary sector of the economy remained strong and internationally dominant. The money and the will to use it were very much there.

A residual category of preconditions includes aspects of that progressive amelioration of the material conditions of like which marked the latter half of the 19th Century. While improvements in street lighting, sewerage, medical care, etc., indirectly made education along with every other aspect of social life more pleasant and efficient, these general improvements are too varied in type and great in number to catalogue. Many improvements had more direct effects on education, however. Some made education easier for all.

Increasingly rapid and cheap transportation brought students to the new public schools in droves by train. The express train and the local commuter train brought the students to the civic colleges as well, and with the further aid of the tram, suburbs and working class districts could send their students to the day and evening classes for a few pence, saving money and allowing for parental supervision. Gas lighting was common in public buildings by mid-century, and appeared in growing numbers of private homes thereafter, as it became progressively cheaper, more efficient, and less noxious. Evening reading became possible for the poor and cheaper and easier for the rich; evening classes also became feasible.[56] While the importance of this factor is overlooked today through familiarity, the civic colleges recognized its importance; we find professors redesigning and testing lamps when new labs and classrooms were planned and erected.[57]

Other improvements offered to the many benefits which the few had long possessed: sufficient leisure and income among the working class would eventually break the upper class monopoly of higher education. Child labour was declining by the 50s, and shorter hours of work became more common. By the 70s most textile workers were on a 10-1/2 hour day and a 60 hour week.

People and things were being reshaped in ways that made higher education both more practicable and more desirable.

3

Colleges and Cities

Manchester and Owens College

Manchester became the second city of England between 1800 and
1850; indeed it was as visible to the world as London. Both ad-
mirers and detractors recognized its importance. For Disraeli
"Manchester is as great a human exploit as Athens" while for En-
gels much of it was a "hell on earth". The shape of the modern
world was appearing in Manchester: urban blight, suburban sprawl;
the proletariat and the new middle classes. The cultural and educational institutions of the new age were also foreshadowed, from the
18th Century Literary and Philosophical Society to the Owens College.

Size alone would have called attention to Manchester. The
population of the area trebled between 1801 and mid-century.
Growth continued thereafter, but by then it was form rather than
scale that marked Manchester. Its central area lost two thirds of its
population between 1851 and 1900[1] while suburbs exfoliated and
even the working class moved out with the tram lines. By 1851
suburban railroads brought some of the haute bourgeoisie in to
work while omnibuses served Ardwick, Rusholme, etc. Victoria
Park, in its walled suburban majesty, sent merchant princes to the
city in their own carriages. The possibility of cosmopolitanism had
already been created by the main railway lines which had connected Manchester with Liverpool since 1830 and with every major
city soon thereafter.

The expansion of the suburbs suggests the importance of Manchester's middle classes. Manchester was built on cotton, and cotton was the greatest industry of mid-Victorian Britain, but Manchester's relation to the industry was peculiar. Had it been only a production centre, a city of factories, a small middle class and massive proletariat would have resulted. In fact it was the entrepot of the finished goods and the middleman in raw material. As a mercantile city it needed a large body of clerks and other lower middle class persons, and its growing wealth was invested in banking, insurance and other business of a middle class character. Perhaps the most salient industrial product of Manchester was machinery, and the great engineering firms required a more skilled work force, and paid more of their workers an almost middle class wage, than did the cotton mills. The middle classes did not merely exist in Manchester; they asserted themselves. Nationally, the triumph of their Anti-Corn Law League marked the first great defeat of rural and gentry interests by a new class. The "Manchester School" went on to teach the nation the doctrines of free trade and laissez-faire. Recognition of the town's significance came with the establishment of an episcopal see in 1847, a Royal visit in 1851, and civic status in 1853. Locally the middle class governed through the Corporation and various commissions, and through school boards and councils as time went on.

They also created the institutions of civic life. By the 30s "Manchester was beginning to hanker after the refinements of civilized life, public parks, public libraries, higher education and the encouragement of the fine arts."[2] The parks and libraries reveal a willingness to spend money on improvements. In the mid-40s a government grant of £3,000 elicited a ten-fold local response, and the first public parks were created. The creation of public libraries demonstrated both private and municipal concern: private subscriptions approached £10,000, while a municipal rate was approved by a vote of approximately 4,000 to 40.[3]

Love's *Manchester As It Is* provides a picture of the intellectual and cultural institutions of middle class Manchester in 1839. The Athenaeum had been "established for the purpose of affording persons of the middle classes in Society, chiefly young men, a suitable resort for reading the public prints, and for attending lectures ...." In 1838 there were approximately a thousand subscribers and fifteen courses, amounting to 73 lectures, were given. Manchester and Salford had their mechanics institutions, there was a school of design, and, moving down the social scale, lyceums in Ancoats,

Chorlton, and Salford. The Lit. and Phil. had been joined by the Royal Institution, the Geological, Statistical, Phrenological, Botanical and Horticultural, Architectural, and Agricultural Societies, and the Manchester Society for the Promotion of Natural History.[4] Of more formally educational institutions, Manchester Grammar School was undoubtedly most important: its curriculum, organization, and premises had been overhauled and student numbers grew steadily. Some other secondary education was available from religious or proprietary schools at mid-century, and by the 80s a variety of local schools had been established, while rapid transport and the explosion of "public" schools made a distant education far more likely.

Middle class interests and numbers sufficient for the creation of a civic college had thus accumulated in Manchester earlier than elsewhere. Will and opportunity were also available. Asa Briggs has described the way in which the size, newness, and industrial base helped to eliminate old restraints and ways of thought. Into the breach thus made the new leaders of Manchester stepped firmly and briskly. "The settling of the greatest radical issue, the Corn Laws, left the way open for a number of other possible radical priorities-- education, financial reform, extension of the suffrage."[5] And education was a field in which many of a more conservative bent could concur in the radicals' enthusiasm. As monuments ranging from Owens College to the Halle Orchestra still remind us, Manchester was the first of the new industrially based cities[6] to create what Edward Shils aptly described as a provincial culture apart from the Oxbridge-London axis.[7]

Manchester, and the provincial cities generally, produced a variety of predecessors to the civic universities. These included many proposals for universities and the creation of a variety of dissenting academies and colleges which led relatively brief but sometimes quite successful lives. While they do not demonstrate great continuity of activity they show that concern for higher education was usually present in at least some Manchester minds. As Manchester minds came together in societies like the Lit. and Phil. proposals appeared which foreshadow the arrangement and goals of Owens College. By 1836 Harry Longueville Jones was publicizing a plan which mentioned the needs of an underserved area of the country, the special desirability of students residing at home, and the importance of a link between general and medical education, as well as suggesting a curriculum remarkably similar to that of Owens in its opening years.[8]

By the 1840s Manchester contained many men like John Owens; wealthy merchants of at least the second generation, with an interest in their city which was likely to include familiarity with schemes for education, and friendships with others equally concerned with such matters. If such substantial men were Nonconformists, or even, like Owens, simply individualists who might migrate in and out of the established church, they were likely to resent religious tests, in university education and elsewhere. In Owens' case a lack of family or other likely heirs, and the unproven but very probable influence of a friend to whom he had intended to leave his wealth, were superadded to the more general circumstances to produce the founder of the first and greatest of the "Redbrick" universities of England.

Owens College opened in March of 1851. Under the will of the founder a distinguished group of trustees had been appointed, representing substantial wealth and position and a wide range of political and religious persuasions. The trustees in turn appointed a committee which considered the best means of establishing a college, soliciting opinions from English, Scottish, and Irish universities, and Eton and Harrow, getting replies only from London, Aberdeen, and Belfast, and taking particular note of the Scottish example as detailed in the Report of the Royal Commission of 1831. They decided to offer classics, maths, mental and moral philosophy, natural philosophy, and English language and literature for a start; regretted the financial impossibility of offering a full course of applied science as at Kings or engineering as at Durham at first, but pointed to their maths and natural philosophy courses and concluded that a separate chemistry professorship would be necessary. Teaching was to be by lectures and examination, fees were to be moderate and within the means of the middle classes, rewards for scholarship should be offered, affiliation with London sought, and the idea of a university for Manchester kept in mind.[9] All these recommendations and implications eventually came to pass: London affiliation almost immediately, rewards for scholarship and the offering of more applied courses gradually, a university for Manchester eventually.

The trustees then hired a small but very competent faculty who were prepared to offer as much as was immediately possible of "such branches of learning and science as are now and may be hereafter taught in the English universities" to males of 14 and over "without respect to place of birth, and without distinction of rank or condition in society" and under the "fundamental and immutable rule and condition that the students, professors, teachers, and other officers and persons connected with the said institution shall not be required to make any declarations as to, or submit to any test whatsoever of their religious opinions and nothing shall be introduced in the matter or mode of education or instruction which shall be reasonably offensive to any student or his relatives."[10]

The professors soon reported[11] to the trustees that the students were willing but their previous preparation was very poor, a complaint which recurred regularly for decades. Nevertheless, they and the trustees decided to maintain high standards in the hope of eventually influencing secondary and other local education, and this policy was followed thereafter through all vicissitudes. There were few regular day students, and the college soon increased its usefulness by beginning classes for schoolmasters in 1853 and evening classes in 1854. In 1858 the faculty and other concerned persons opened a Working Men's College, which in 1861 was amalgamated with the evening classes of Owens. These enterprises were important in that they provided substantial student numbers and offered a perceptibly useful service to the community, thus encouraging a sense of accomplishment within the college, and financial and other forms of appreciation from without.

After the first flush of enthusiasm had dissipated, the college found itself with embarrassingly few students. While 62 had enrolled in 1851-52 and 71 the following year, by 1857-58 a falling off to 34 day students was inadequately compensated for by only 35 evening students and 24 schoolmasters. The average number of courses taken by each student was very low, and few if any seemed to be pursuing a systematic course of study. This latter problem was to remain long after that of sheer numbers had been solved. Faculty and trustees conferred on the reasons for the dreadful slump of 1856-59 and concluded that the poor preparation of students, inadequate local demand for and appreciation of higher education, and the college's lack of an established position and relationship to employments and professions were all contributing factors. The college's first historian added that a traditional fear that higher education unfitted a man for business life was also prevalent. In 1858 the *Manchester Guardian* declared the college a failure, and pointed to its provision of undesired classical studies, the absence of more popular courses, and the loss of the first professor of chemistry.

The college persevered in offering a high standard of education and a relatively traditional range of subjects. The brilliant choice of a new chemistry professor and his concern with both advanced research and the practical side of chemistry improved matters, and the college gave careful attention to the needs of those studying for the growing range of professions and examinations. A market for both chemistry and classics was found and encouraged. By 1860 the worst was over, and numbers began to rise to 113 day and 280 evening students at mid-decade, and to 264 and 527 respectively by 1870-71.

Growth necessitated a move from the converted residence in an undesirable quarter which had housed the college since its inception. In addition to growing student numbers there were plans for the incorporation of a medical school and the collections of the Natural History Society. Discussions within the college led after several years to the public announcement in 1867 of an appeal for funds to extend the college. The trustees and professors worked together on planning and fund raising; Professor Roscoe obtained the assistance of Thomas Ashton, whose repute, wealth, and activities lent great weight to the extension movement, and the executive committee of the trustees suggested that Principal Greenwood and Professor Roscoe should tour Continental universities; they returned with a detailed report on German universities and polytechnics. Public response was satisfactory, and the legal difficulties of expanding the work of the college, particularly to include women, were overcome by creating an Owens Extension College in 1870 and then amalgamating it with the original institution in 1871. After amalgamation with the Royal Manchester School of Medicine in 1872, an action which had long been discussed and had always been implied in the extension movement, the Owens College began to look very like a university.

A campus was created in a suburban location, chosen after a survey of student residences found a majority in that area, with easy access to the centre of the city and to the stations of the important suburban railway lines. The choice of Alfred Waterhouse as architect set a precedent widely adhered to by succeeding colleges, and justified by his close attention to the work and tolerance of an unending stream of advice from faculty and Council. Sufficient property was acquired to permit the continued physical expansion of the college as student numbers and research requirements demanded. By the 80s Owens had a considerable and perhaps even distinguished physical presence, at least by contemporary standards. Its income had grown from approximately £3,500 per annum in the first years to over £7,500 in 1870 and more than £21,000 ten years thereafter.[12]

Its academic performance was also definitely and increasingly distinguished. Students of the college were winning prizes at London, scholarships at Oxbridge, and positions in open competition, and some few were beginning to conduct advanced research, notably in chemistry. Scholarship was encouraged by a steadily growing range of exhibitions, prizes, and scholarships endowed by benefactors. A mere listing of the names of the best known professors in 1875 gives a clear picture of the extraordinary quality of the faculty in a wide range of fields: James Bryce, W.S. Jevons, Osborne Reynolds, H.E. Roscoe, and A.W. Ward.[13] International recognition was testified by gifts to the library and museums from foreign universities, businesses, and governments, as well as by comments like the very flattering view of the college taken by the *Revue Scientifique* in 1875.

The above qualities, and a student body which was to reach 400 day, 750 evening, and over 200 medical students in 1880, suggested that Owens had become a university in all but name and privileges. Under these circumstances anything less than a university charter seemed insufficient, particularly as the continuing necessity to sit the London University examinations for degrees meant that in effect the highest levels of college teaching were controlled not by the faculty, but by London. Internally awarded degrees would also form a major attraction to those potential students who might seek them as a professional or pre-professional qualification, or for reasons of prestige. Professors Greenwood, Roscoe, Ward, and Morgan pointed out the advantages of university status for both the college and the medical school, the Court and Council agreed, and in the summer of 1877 a deputation was sent to the Privy Council. Opposition to the petition for a charter soon arose in several quarters. The proliferation of universities was attacked, and particularly the chartering of any more institutions allowed to grant medical degrees as there was already a confusing multiplicity of bodies with this power. Some, particularly supporters of the London University model (most notably its M.P., Robert Lowe) disapproved of a teaching institution examining and certifying its own students. Other variants on the general theme of a depreciation of the value of degrees were also heard. All these objections were successfully met, though the power to grant medical degrees was delayed for a short time. The ancient universities, no longer the bastions of reaction and privilege they had been a half century before when they resisted the chartering of London, were in fact far more sympathetic than London.

A different sort of objections came from the North of England. The Yorkshire College, and various persons and groups in Liverpool including the medical school, feared that a degree-granting University of Manchester would have attractions beyond their ability to counter, and would thus draw both the best and the majority of potential students, leaving them not only temporarily weakened, but probably unable to develop to a point were they could achieve equal status eventually. The representations of Leeds seem to have been most forceful and important, coming as they did from an institution with at least some pretensions to the character of a university college, and apparently capable of expansion. A compromise was effected whereby Leeds and Liverpool would support a petition for the chartering of a Victoria University, to be organizationally and legally separate from Owens College, though based in Manchester and incorporating Owens as its first, and for a time only, constituent college. Yorkshire, and Liverpool if and when a college was established there, might be admitted to the University upon presentation of proofs of the efficiency and level of their teaching and of their possession of adequate means to maintain themselves. They would then be represented by their faculty and others in the councils of the university in the same manner as Owens. As a sort of harbinger, the original governing body of the University included representatives of Liverpool and Leeds.

Leeds, as a result of slow growth in numbers and funds, a heavy technological and scientific bias which left the arts subjects relatively weak, and a peculiarly unacademic form and manner of government, was not admitted to the University until 1887. Liverpool, starting late, rapidly made up time, opening as a college in 1881 and gaining admission to the University in 1884. The arrangement continued with considerable success into the 20th Century, when Liverpool and Manchester felt themselves capable of standing alone and inconvenienced by the continuation of the federation. Over the objections of Leeds, which feared itself to be too weak to compete independently, the federation was dissolved in 1902, and its members received individual charters, with the name of the old University memorialized in Owens' new designation as the Victoria University of Manchester.

Leeds and The Yorkshire College

Leeds was another of the fast-growing industrial and commercial cities of 19th Century England.[14] Little more than a market town in 1800, by the 1870s it was one of Yorkshire's major cities, far surpassing the old capital of York. Textiles, particularly flax and wool, and the later addition of important engineering works, made Leeds a well-to-do community of the new entrepreneurial and industrial middle classes. The energies of the community were mobilized to create the institutions and services which an older-fashioned England had not provided. The Town Council and a variety of committees and commissions began to provide the necessities and amenities of civic life, including an enormous Town Hall which expressed not only civic pride but also a notably combative determination to compete with both the neighbouring Yorkshire communities and the growing cities of Lancashire.

The intellectual needs of the community were not ignored by its middle class leaders. The Philosophical and Literary Society became a meeting place for many of the Leeds elite. Mechanics institutes sought to educate the working class and at least succeeded in uniting many members of the middle classes in support of education. Another important voluntary association, the Yorkshire Board of Education, concerned itself with various projects. Secondary education was revised and expanded, a task made easier than elsewhere by the substantial charitable endowments of the past. By the 70s the Cambridge Extension movement, with powerful local support, was bringing some higher education to Leeds. Money, potential students, and interest in education were all available in the city by the mid-70s.

Nevertheless, Leeds was not as obviously suitable a location for a university as Manchester, Liverpool, or Birmingham, the homes of the most successful early colleges It was smaller than its rivals in Lancashire and it may have been even less than proportionately wealthy, as the woollen industries mechanized slowly and never experienced an extraordinary boom like that in cotton textiles. It was not the undisputed centre of its region: Bradford could lay equal claims to local and cultural pre-eminence. Leeds certainly lacked the cosmopolitan atmosphere of a great port or the world centre of cotton manufacture and sale. It had no equivalent of the Halle Orchestra or the long cultural tradition of the "Liverpool Renaissance". In these circumstances not only Bradford but even smaller communities like Huddersfield were inclined to support their own voluntary endeavours rather than those of Leeds.

The Yorkshire College of Science,[15] like its parent city, was notably different from what Owens College was or University College, Liverpool, was to be. Its name suggests its intended purpose as a technical science school. The Paris Exhibition of 1867, which is often said to have produced recognition of the need for technical education among the English, at any rate had such an effect in the West Riding. Influential men began to consider the possibility of higher technical education. Woollen manufacturers, engineers, and Lord Frederick Cavendish, working through such local organizations as the Yorkshire Board of Education, had established a College of Science Committee by 1869. The Committee concluded that there was need for a college which would concentrate on those sciences necessary to the West Riding's industries. A public appeal for funds was launched in 1872.

In the absence of a munificent founder like John Owens or Josiah Mason the success of the college was entirely dependent on widespread public support. The first appeals were naturally directed toward those who were likely to benefit from the college's intention "... to supply an urgent and recognized want, viz., instruction in those sciences which are applicable to the Industrial Arts ...."[16] Unfortunately, the urgency does not appear to have been widely felt. The £60,000 the committee sought would have been little enough to meet the likely expenses; in fact the college opened in 1874 with only £20,000. In these circumstances the hired premises' previous use as a bankruptcy court was no doubt disconcerting.

Support for technical subjects remained discouragingly limited. The textile technologies which seem so natural to the locale had to be established and supported by the charitable endowments of the Livery Companies of the City of London. Only engineering received substantial if belated local support in the 80s. Attendance on technical courses was similarly limited; only 17% of class enrolments for 1879-80 were in specifically technical subjects.

Another 45% were in the sciences; the three foundation professors taught chemistry, physics and maths, and geology and mining.[17] Chemistry and geology obviously had industrial uses. A considerable part of the demand for science derived, however, from medical students. As elsewhere, the local medical school was anxious to associate with a college offering chemistry and other sciences. Amalgamation took place in 1884. A greater interest in technology seems to have obtained among the evening students, many from the working class. The college had correctly assumed that they would be interested in technical skills which would lead to better jobs.

The city's limited but significant interest in Arts subjects was soon expressed through the college. The supporters of the Cambridge Extension Lectures, including the Yorkshire Ladies Education Association and the Baines family, proprietors of Leeds' most influential newspaper, transferred their efforts to the establishment of Arts teaching in the college. In spite of objections to any diversion of the college's original purpose and funds, and a fear that middle class Arts students would discourage working class attendance, the support of the original science professors, the requirements for London matriculation and degrees, and growing demand for liberal education ensured a place for Arts courses. This broadening of scope probably added to the general appeal of the college and to its prestige in the eyes of those familiar with more traditional forms of higher education.

The addition of Arts courses did not, however, produce either the unity of purpose or the similarities of operations and intent which marked Owens and University Colleges. The Arts subjects were separately and often problematically funded, and debates over their place and importance in the curriculum divided the Council, though not the faculty. Perhaps such divisions within the Council exacerbated the problems of governance which resulted from poverty, and from a tendency to view the faculty as employees rather than collaborators. For whatever reasons, academic self-government developed more slowly and painfully at Leeds than in Lancashire.

Similarities to Owens were as significant as differences. Middle class support and clientele, non-sectarianism, moderate fees, non-residence, the importance of evening classes and of part-time and non-degree students, and a strong desire to adapt to local needs were basic characteristics shared by all the civic colleges. Equally basic was the idea that a civic college was both a useful local institution and an expression of civic pride and power. The influence of the first successful civic college can also be seen in Leeds' adoption of Owens' formulation of professorial duties, the hiring of Owens-trained faculty, and perhaps even the choice of Waterhouse as architect when the college began to plan its own buildings.

The possibility of joining the Victoria University made the Owens and University College models even more influential at Leeds in the 80s, since the university's curricular, constitutional, and financial requirements were modelled on those of its first college. Faced with the probable loss of its best medical students and any others interested in taking degrees, as well as the embarrassment of University College's almost immediate success in gaining admission, the Yorkshire College knew it must become part of the federal institution it had helped to create.

Admission to Victoria affected the college in many ways. The university demanded a firmer financial base and greater emphasis on a wider range of Arts subjects. The Yorkshire College made this an effective argument in appeals for more funds. The university was governed primarily by its academic members; the position of the professors at Leeds was enhanced by membership. As Leeds remained the weakest of the three federated colleges in finance and prestige, which was generally accorded to success in Arts subjects, it undoubtedly sacrificed some individuality to its more powerful neighbours. The college nevertheless retained something of its original purpose. To this day it has the strongest technological bias, in enrollments and budget, of any civic university.

Liverpool and University College

Nineteenth Century Liverpool possessed great and growing wealth and a significant cultural and intellectual tradition. The West Indies and slave trades built the port and the city's fortunes were maintained by its position as entrepot of Northern England's products. The city was mainly commercial rather than industrial, though shipbuilding and the heavy chemical industry were nearby. The city's cosmopolitan commercial character helps to account for its highly developed intellectual culture in the 19th Century, most notable in the efflorescence of the early century often associated with the name of Roscoe. The cultivated elite produced the usual crop of intellectual societies and a number of more specifically educational institutions. The Royal Institution and the Liverpool Institute joined Liverpool College as distinguished secondary schools and also provided a meeting place and organizational basis for other educational endeavours, including a science school and Queens College, which offered courses preparatory to London degree exams during the 60s. The courses were fairly popular but very few took degrees.[18]

The Liverpool of the 70s and 80s was led by the members of a cultural and economic elite of merchants and shipowners, of whom

the Gladstones, Rathbones, and Holts were perhaps the most famous exemplars, who acted together in a variety of organizations to
advance education. The necessity for non-partisan or bi-partisan
voluntary activity in this area was constantly emphasized by the
bitter religious feuds which divided first the quasi-public, church
controlled provision of elementary education, and then the later efforts of the school boards. The intellectual and social elite thus
found themselves bound together in the interests of all sorts of education; having created middle class education (with its eventual potential for preparing students for a civic college) earlier in the century, struggling with reluctant ratepayers to provide museums and
libraries from mid-century on, acting to improve the sorely divided
and underfinanced elementary education via a voluntary Council of
Education (founded 1874), and then creating University College.[19]

Liverpool was late in establishing its college, considering the
city's age, size, and pretensions. Much of the earlier interest in and
funds for education had gone into the provision of secondary education; Liverpool was peculiarly lacking in endowments, having
neither a great foundation like the Manchester Grammar School nor
a variety of smaller charities which could be effectively reorganized
by the Charity Commissioners.[20] Liverpool College, the Royal Institution School, and the Liverpool Institute had absorbed money
and energy. For Liverpool's middling sort these schools represented a considerably advanced education. As for Liverpool's
elite, this was much older than that of most Northern cities, and its
members had found their way to traditional forms of higher education in substantial numbers. While Oxbridge might not suit the
Nonconformists, the cosmopolitan character of a mercantile elite
made even the adventure of a foreign education seem less unusual
than elsewhere.

The city's apparent size is also deceptive. A large part of its population was poor and transient, particularly great numbers of the
Irish. White suggests that a merchant aristocracy in the absence of
industry implied a particularly large gulf between upper and lower
classes. At any rate the city did not possess those large numbers of
technical employees in engineering works who in Manchester were
an object of concern to their employers. A Whitworth or Beyer,
deeply concerned with the further education of artisans, was not so
likely to appear in Liverpool. An older middle class in a more settled society than that of Manchester in the 50s was apparently in
less of a hurry to complete its local system of middle class education.

Delay in founding a college could make it seem less necessary in some ways. The public schools had developed a socially acceptable form of terminal education; Liverpool's best schools, though small, could match much of the work done in many civic colleges. The Tests were a thing of the past and Oxford and Cambridge were growing in size and breadth of curriculum. London's colleges had well-established reputations, while Owens College had acquired size and prestige. Rapid transportation made all these options readily available.

Some arguments for delay had a reverse side, however. Civic pride found the necessity to resort to other cities distasteful; the local press complained particularly of Liverpudlians resorting to Manchester. Liverpool's formal designation as a city in 1880 must have enhanced the force of this argument. A brain drain, particularly among medical students, was feared. In May, 1878, the *Daily Post* analyzed the need for a local college: the available schools were either terminal or preparatory for Oxbridge, which in turn was preparatory only to the Church, the Bar, and the higher levels of teaching. An alternative was needed for general further study and for degrees, available cheaply and locally. Not all professional persons could send their children away, yet "... almost every professional man is more concerned about the effective education of his sons than about anything else in the world."[21] The very success of Liverpool's relatively new institutions of secondary education created a potential clientele for a university college.

These interests helped to create a Liverpool Association for the Promotion of Higher Education in the 70s, concerned with a variety of things including extension lectures. The real and immediate pressure to establish a college came from the medical profession, however.[22] As in many cities, a medical school was funded and operated by the members of the profession. Finance was on a hand to mouth basis, with no endowment and a minimum of expenditure on plant, apparatus, etc. The growing range and depth of medical education made this method of operation increasingly precarious, and in the mid-70s London University's changed requirements, which involved more chemistry and the introduction of practical lab work in physics, made the pressure on the physicians and their school unbearable. The solution seemed to be a partnership with a college or school of science as was already the method of Manchester, Leeds, etc. At first the establishment of a science school seems to have been contemplated, but after a conference with the Association for the Promotion of Higher Education a proposal for a university college offering liberal, scientific, and technological education emerged.

This more or less private interest was converted into a public concern by the calling of a public meeting in May, 1878. Considerable care was taken to involve the public in all aspects of the new proposal; a series of meetings defined the College's purpose and organization, appealed for funds, and then reinforced the appeal with reports of what had so far been collected. Every precaution was taken to assure the success of the enterprise. Important public figures were associated with it from the first. "The requisition for a [Town Meeting] was signed by the clergymen of all creeds, by the headmasters and principals of the large public schools and the various scientific and literary associations,[23] by the most eminent in the medical and legal professions; and though last, not least, in this commercial town, by the merchants."[24] The Earl of Derby and the Rathbones represented the interests of both old and new aristocracy, and the Reverend Charles Beard testified to the interest of respectable and wealthy Nonconformity. William Rathbone appealed to the memory of a distinguished civic past when the city's intellectual eminence had been second only to that of London and Edinburgh, and suggested that a college might help to recover this position.

The founders wisely defined their purpose in reasonably broad but quite specific terms from the first. The requisition for the first Town Meeting had stated their intention: "To provide such instruction in all branches of a liberal education as would enable residents in the town and neighbourhood to qualify for degrees in arts, science, and other subjects at any of the universities granting degrees to non-resident students, and at the same time to give such technical education as would be of immediate service in professional and commercial life." Level of instruction, range of subjects, intended clientele: all were clearly set forth. There would be none of the debate over purpose and division of counsels which vitiated much of Leeds' effort. The founders and their successors were well aware of the value of such a clear statement and they repeated it at every opportunity in their appeals for funds, their advertisements for students, and their petitions to the government, first for a charter and then for money.

Determined to begin the venture on a sound footing, over £100,000 was raised by a succession of appeals before the college was opened in 1882. The large contributions of a few great merchants and peers were supplemented by a wide range of endowment funds collected from among such specific groups as shipowners, Scottish merchants, literary and professional men, etc. The city itself provided a site worth about £30,000. Lacking a munificent benefactor, the college arose as a genuinely civic enterprise.

University College, Liverpool, opened in the winter of 1881-82 in the middle of the traditional academic year, a reminder that it did not expect to depend solely upon the traditional sort of student or offer a traditional education.[25] (Owens had begun in the same fashion.) Ninety-three students enrolled for the first term, and numbers rose fairly steadily.

Careful planning had provided a small but well chosen faculty, and the roster was designed to allow easy expansion. Lectureships could be elevated into professorships and several chairs could be divided; indeed two cried out for division. While the professors of chemistry, natural history, physics, mathematics, and philosophy and political economy may each have been expected to fulfill their duties for some time no one man could undertake to teach english, literature, and modern history, or be Principal and Professor of classics (both Latin and Greek) for long. Growing student numbers would soon have warranted expansion, but an even more immediate crisis intervened.

Amalgamation with the medical school had brought additional faculty, students, endowment,[26] and physical plant to the college almost immediately. Some autonomy, including ownership of buildings, remained temporarily with the medical school. In 1882 the Victoria University received a supplemental charter enabling it to give medical degrees. Its medical school was thus in a position to attract all the best students from other provincial schools of the North. Both faculties and the governing body of University College recognized the danger immediately and private solicitations followed by the by-now traditional Town Meeting and public appeal produced the funds necessary for the expansion demanded by Victoria University as a condition of membership. The obviously overburdened professorships were divided, and an engineering chair was soon endowed in keeping with the founders' original intention to develop this subject when possible. Further expansion of the faculty then took the form of lectureships until the 90s, allowing some development but no radical departures in curriculum.

By the mid-80s a steadily applied policy of faculty first and buildings later had born such fruit in repute and consequent size that buildings were desperately needed. A further fund drive was launched and continued in one way or another, via such expedients as the Queen's Jubilee Fund, beyond the period under study, and provided the University College with a central pile in the approved Waterhouse Gothic.[27] University College, Liverpool, had definitely "arrived", and surprisingly quickly.

Table II
Student Numbers Owens, Yorkshire, And University Colleges
1854-1885

		54-55	59-60	64-65	69-70	74-75	79-80	84-85
Owens	Day	58	57	127	209	375	392	393
	Evening	69	77	312	434	855	732	565
	Medical					158	232	308
	Women							50
Yorkshire	Day & Medical*					194	339	
	Evening					269	655	
University	Day					112		

*The numbers in the different colleges are not strictly comparable, as the distinctions between regular and occasional, day and evening, and even medical and non-medical, are often unclear. For example, the Yorkshire College day enrolments probably represent fewer courses per student than the roughly equivalent category at Owens.

Owens College opened in 1851 with 25 students and enrolled 62 in its first full year of operation.

Yorkshire College opened in 1874 with 24 students, increasing to 65 day and medical students in its first full year.

University College opened in 1881 with 93 students.

Table III
Funds*
Owens, Yorkshire, And University Colleges

OWENS   Owens opened with approximately £110,000. By the late 70s, when a university charter was sought, this had increased to over £300,000, with another £150,000 to come in the early 80s.

YORKSHIRE   Yorkshire College opened with approximately £20,000. By the time of its admission to the Victoria University in 1887 this had increased to approximately £150,000.

UNIVERSITY   University College opened with approximately £130,000, including the gift of a site from the city, and quickly raised another £20,000 to ensure its admission to the Victoria University.

    *These estimates are based on cash contributions. The value of the amalgamated medical schools, museums, etc. is impossible to determine with accuracy.

4

The Dynamics of Demand and Supply

Growth and change in 19th Century society created demands for both expansion and innovation in education, and civic universities were shaped largely by these pressures. This chapter analyzes the sources of demand for increasing amounts and varieties of education and the new colleges' awareness of and reaction to these demands. Many of the demands for innovative education were just beginning in this period as new employments on the one hand, and new disciplines on the other, were in their infancy. While such demands were at first slight, they were relatively very important to institutions equally new, unfamiliar, and small in numbers. In many cases the institution, its new departments, and the demand were to grow together from insignificant 19th Century to mature 20th Century form. The comparative and total weight of demand cannot be measured precisely. In the pre-degree and pre-university era, statistical certainty about enrolments and uniform biographical data on students are no more to be expected than an immediate awareness of new employments on the part of the census bureau.

Nevertheless, a modest use of historical hindsight, coupled with evidence of what the new colleges thought and hoped they were offering to students, produces a fairly clear picture. It is not the picture of many technical courses and predominantly industrially-based demand which has often been painted. Social and economic demands for Arts subjects were substantial. The demand for pure science came as much from the medical students and those seeking general education as from industry. The colleges prepared more professionals than technologists. The middle classes were the principal consumers of the civic colleges' offerings, and the financial and social rewards of liberal education and white collar and professional employments were their primary goal.

Liberal and General Education

The necessary precondition of a potential supply of educators and subject matter to meet new demands was well fulfilled in Victorian England. Someone was available to teach almost any subject, and even in fields not previously institutionalized, such as technology, there was a substantial information base from which to construct a discipline. Innovation could take place. However, the most substantial and readily available bodies of both information and teachers were in the subjects of the then common curriculum of the universities and upper class schools; that is, the subjects which comprised a "liberal education". New and enlarged demand for the more or less traditional liberal education, and for those variants and additions which might be included within a "general education" were therefore most quickly understood and met. This category of demands included almost all of that for classics, a great deal of that for history and English, and progressively lesser portions of the demand for mathematics, modern languages, and "pure" sciences. The various curricular combinations of these fields can be called general education.

The most widely touted value of general, and especially of liberal, education was its function as social preparation and emollient, along with the less-expressed but often more considered concomitant of conferring social status. Status ascription by type of education was certainly not unique to England, but it was peculiarly widely accepted there, perhaps because of the unusual opportunities to achieve such an education and consequent status. Liberal education was that offered by the universities and public schools, whose social status, steadily recovering during the Victorian era, was transferred to their curriculum; it was the education of the social and governmental elite; hence and with surprisingly little argument it was the mode of preserving or elevating one's status. With the reform of Oxbridge and the growth of public schools came new and reiterated justification for liberal education, and especially the classics. They were supposed to provide the most effective form of mental training or gymnastic. The classics would also provide the discipline and examples to prepare the student for moral and practical leadership.

Given the enormous 19th Century expansion of classes concerned with status, and the increasing extent to which the large and impersonal scale of an urban and mobile society confirmed the proposition that a gentleman was anyone who looked, spoke, and acted like one, concern over social position represented a great potential demand for higher education. This is not to suggest the absence of the disinterested pursuit of literary and scientific culture among the middle classes. Literary and philosophical societies and all the other paraphernalia of provincial intellectual culture provide institutional evidence of this interest.[1]

While the more grossly materialistic aspects of this demand might not be easily discussable by educators, the social value of a liberal education was part of the stock in trade of speeches. At Owens the founder himself had prescribed a liberal curriculum and his trustees, in preparing to carry out his wishes, were particularly concerned that classics and mental and moral philosophy should be provided for their ability to combat the narrowing tendencies they found inherent in the commercial and materialistic world of Lancashire.[2]

Their first Principal lost no time in publicly expressing these values: his inaugural address emphasized the great value of general culture for the recipient and the public, and the intrinsic value rather than the usefulness of scholarly pursuits.[3] The theme of cultivation, and its particular necessity in Lancashire, continued to be heard on every public occasion, and was transported to Liverpool without damage or notable alteration.

The best certification of a liberal education, regardless of the reasons for which it was desired, was a university degree, and the colleges' steady attention to this reveals its importance.[4] The colleges gave constant attention to London degree requirements, became affiliated to London where possible, and unceasingly advertised their students' exam successes and the colleges' efficiency in preparing for them.[5] They even created a grade of Associate which would serve to honour graduates and also to mark the achievements of their best students who for one reason or another did not take a degree. Their eventual demand for university status was based to a large extent on their desire to award their own degrees. As the century progressed, and small employers and selection by patronage were replaced by large firms and necessarily impersonal methods of selection, a degree came to represent what it still most frequently means for employers today: not necessarily a certification of particular or technical training, but a testimony to the diligence and general intellectual competence of the recipient. A London degree also became a route to the more rarefied heights of Oxbridge study for those provincial students whose secondary education had not been such as to qualify them for immediate admission.[6]

Further implications of the status of liberal education enhanced its attractiveness and increased demand. The growing system of examinations, originally developed as a means of stimulating and testing academic achievement, was increasingly used for selecting candidates for employment, and as a certification of the receipt of a general education acceptable for non-academic purposes. Examinations testing minimum capacities were perhaps most common, being the first form used in public employment and continuing to be used for many purposes, but it was the competitive exams which became most famous and influential, as had already become the case in academia. Those for the Indian and home Civil Services, and for admission to the various military schools, were the most important. The relative importance of the various subjects examined reveals what sorts of demand candidates at these examinations might previously have made on the colleges.

Table IV
Percentages of Total Marks Awarded in Examination, for certain subjects[7]

| | Indian Civil Service[8] | | Woolwich | | Direct Commission |
	1858	85[9]	1857	85	1859
Classics	22.0	23.0	14.5	19.0	26.0
Maths	14.5	16.0	29.0	19.0	26.0
English	22.0	15.0	10.5	9.5	8.5
Modern Languages	16.0	23.0	14.5	28.5	8.5
Sciences	7.0	13.0	14.5	9.5	17.0

The most immediately striking aspect of the table is the predominance of classics and mathematics, the core of the curriculum of the ancient English universities. This is hardly surprising given the examiners' purposes. Macaulay and his committee intended to attract to the Indian Civil Service (ICS) the sort of man who had done well at Oxford or Cambridge,[10] and reform in the home Civil Service followed their lead. The military were greatly concerned that the introduction of competitive examination should not mean the end of the concept of the officer as gentleman, and so they tested for the education of a gentleman. This pattern tended to become self-reinforcing, as the universities reacted to the exams and the examiners continued to want university men and also tended to be university men themselves.

The prominence of English is perhaps the most radical characteristic of the examinations, but seems less surprising when it is remembered that Macaulay led the first important committee on the Civil Service. Early Victorian England saw a great upsurge of academic interest in English language, literature, and history, and such a modern study was in keeping with the reforming intent of examinations. The political emphasis in historical studies made them a particularly appropriate part of the public servant's education. The subject did not dig itself in in the ancient universities, however, with the possible exception of its historical aspect, and examiners seem to have sacrificed it to the increasing demands of science for a place in the exams. English studies were, on the other hand, institutionalized in the new colleges, perhaps partly in response to examination demands, and it was there, particularly in Manchester, that the subject flourished.

The demand for modern languages was rapidly met in the new colleges, with Liverpool delaying only because they considered the subject to be well taught already. Clearly the great examinations were not to be the stimulus to any massive expansion of science teaching, when its low examination priority is set against the large expenses and problems of novelty involved in teaching it. Candidates for exams would bring to the colleges a demand for the elements of that mid-to-late Victorian compromise, a middle class general education, consisting of the traditional liberal elements with the addition of English literature and history, modern languages, and a tincture, but little more, of science.

The civic colleges responded immediately and continuously to the demands caused by the growth of competitive examinations for public employment. Throughout the 1850s and 60s the Indian Civil Service was the most important in terms of prestige and numbers of appointments, and was only slowly overtaken by the home Civil Service after the Order in Council of 1870 opened greater numbers of positions to competition[11] and furthered the trend toward competitive placement, not only for general administrative but also for technical positions within the great departments like the Admiralty and War Office. The colleges emphasized their suitability as preparatory establishments by publishing detailed descriptions of the exams (see footnote 7 above) and announcing students' successes.[12]

At Owens College Principal Greenwood gave regular and immediate attention to those questions which arose in connection with Civil Service exams. In 1860 he reminded the trustees for the second time that ICS candidates needed to offer Oriental languages and that a teacher was available.[13] Mr. T. Theodores, a polyhistor and superb teacher, was made Lecturer in that year and Professor of Oriental and Modern Languages and Literature in 1866. The opening of the evening class session of 1870-71 found Greenwood speaking of his fear that the new changes in the Civil Service, with increased emphasis on exams, might lead to rigid, stereotyped teaching in preparation for them. He called for a Service open to merit but remaining a liberal profession both in the education of its members and in their sense of service.[14] Whatever their fears, the Trustees approved a suggestion of the professors that the Civil Service Commissioners be asked to hold exams in Manchester.[15] In the later 70s the Indian Civil Service began to select younger candidates and then require them to spend two years receiving further education in Britain after their selection. The Principal and Council worked to ensure that residence at Owens would be an acceptable form of such training.[16]

The growth of the traditional professions of medicine, law, the Church, and the military, and the regular addition of new professional and semi-professional occupations produced a steadily rising and diversifying demand for higher education. The establishment of a profession involves developing self-esteem among members of an occupational group, the accumulation of a regular body of knowledge considered necessary for all practitioners, and the desire to testify to the competence of the group's members and to exclude the unfit from the profession. Some form of organization is created to espouse these principles and goals. The organizations thus formed in 19th Century England impinged upon the civic colleges at many points, both directly and via the requirements they set for membership. Least directly, the services of the colleges might be used to prepare for the tests of general and professional knowledge which were the increasingly common mode of entry to the professions. The colleges' examinations, though created for other purposes, would often be accepted in lieu of the organization's own tests. More formally, the professional association might collaborate with the colleges to design courses and administer tests. The most intimate association occurred when the profession developed an entire system of education and then transferred it to or amalgamated it with the colleges, as was eventually the case with medicine.

Growing numbers of professional associations increased the size and variety of this demand.[17] Not all of them examined candidates for admission, and many were unable to control entry into a profession, but in the latter half of the century examination became increasingly common, as did a defined course of academic study, and the importance or even necessity of membership increased. The growth of professional associations constituted a new demand for education, not merely a recognition of its previous provision. Geoffrey Millerson has demonstrated that the professional association was rather a reaction to the paucity of professional education than a recognition of its presence.[18]

The new colleges quickly recognized the importance of professional demands, particularly with the precedents before them of Oxbridge and Durham's connections with the Church, and London's close links with medicine and the professional classes generally. At Owens, the Principal's first annual report remarked on the college's deficiency in not having well-defined links to the professions.[19] The college authorities set out to remedy this, both by broadening the curriculum and by emphasizing the availability and value of pre-professional, general education. Within a decade the calendar was describing the exams and general requirements for the Queen's Civil Service, the Indian Civil Service, Woolwich, Sandhurst, direct commissions in the Army, solicitors and attorneys, the Royal College of Surgeons, and the Society of Apothecaries, and demonstrating the college's ability to prepare for them.[20]

By the 70s the principal discerned a major trend toward longer lasting and more thorough education, signalized by the demands of medicine and the law for evidence of both preliminary and professional training, the examinations under the Pharmacy Act, and the establishment of professorships of engineering in Edinburgh, Manchester, and elsewhere. The college was prepared and anxious to adapt to this demand, which would at first involve some relaxation of standards, given the defective previous preparation of potential members of professions.[21]

Leeds paid immediate attention to the demands of new professions and employments. The founders defined[22] the college's primary purpose: "The Yorkshire College of Science is intended to supply an urgent and recognized want, viz., instruction in those sciences which are applicable to the Industrial Arts ...."[23] The specificity of such departments as Textiles, Dyeing, and Coal Mining completes this impression.

Liverpool was equally aware of professional demands. The foundation committee emphasized the needs of medical students, articled solicitor's clerks, architecture and engineering pupils, and nearly 800 pupil teachers for both general and professional education in one of their first public solicitations.[24]

The professions were not solely concerned with specifically professional training. Their concern with general education, particularly of a liberal character, formed a major addition to the demand born of non-professional, non-occupational reasons. Most obviously, a sound general education was the necessary preliminary to the understanding of a course of professional education, and lingual and mathematical skills would be regularly exercised in any professional employment. Many professional persons and organizations were equally concerned with the social standing which went with a liberal education. W. J. Reader has given the best account of both the new and the older professions' desperate concern with the social status of their members and of their callings themselves.[25] Both the general cachet of liberal education and the specific attempts of new occupations to resemble the traditionally accepted liberal professions, with their custom of university education, were involved.

This form of professional demand was progressively institutionalized during the 19th Century so that by the 1930s Carr-Saunders could say "... there are not many exceptions to the rule that two tests are imposed, the first a test of general education and the second a test of professional competence... Where there is a first test, there is always a choice, usually a wide choice, of approved examinations."[26] While any of these general education tests could be prepared for at the new colleges, the colleges' and universities' own exams were perhaps the most obviously and widely accepted. Examples emphasized in the Owens calendars of the 60s included exemption from the preliminary exams of Sandhurst and the College of Surgeons, and from one or two years of solicitors articles.[27]

Medicine

An account of the various professions which made demands upon Victorian higher education may well begin with medicine, in many ways the archetype of 19th Century professional development. Where other professions manifested some of the trends important for education, medicine visibly and powerfully demonstrated all of them. Although an ancient, liberal profession, medicine had a large and socially inferior branch consisting of apothecaries and surgeons, and their concern with status, and hence general and liberal education, was as strong as anyone's in the 19th Century. The latest authority, Peterson, feels that the average Victorian practitioner had not yet achieved the status later accorded to professionals; they pursued it through organization, legislation, and education. Liberal education would enhance the possibilities of a level of social intercourse, and hence status, beyond that accorded to the average medical man.[28]

The Apothecaries Act of 1815 marked the earliest development of what had become by 1858 (Medical Act) a profession thoroughly regulated by examination. The articulation of a body of professional knowledge and a system of education kept pace with this development. New studies and disciplines became important for members, with chemistry teaching the great concern of the first three quarters of the century, physics growing to prominence in the last, and strictly professional studies multiplying, subdividing, and becoming more abstruse. The first half of the century saw the consolidation of the profession from more or less disparate elements; the second half witnessed the hiving off of related professions, notably the pharmacists, whose professional status was marked by the Pharmacy Acts of 1852 and 1868, and dentists (Dentists Act 1878, British Dental Association 1880).

The new colleges reacted strongly to each of these developments. Their eventual response was to establish or amalgamate with medical schools, as the University of London had so successfully done. Indeed, they seem to have envisioned this from the first. In the interim, they tailored a good deal of their teaching to the needs of medical students. The incorporation of medical schools was sometimes a complicated process, but the demands of medical students were being met before amalgamation. General education was provided, leading either to the profession's own exams or to the authorized alternative of London matriculation, which could be taken at the colleges. And the complex scientific subjects which were too expensive for the proprietary medical schools were available at the colleges.[29] Medical schools expected their students to make use of this provision, and formalized the arrangement when possible.[30] The colleges, equally aware of this potential demand, kept in touch with the medical schools and studied the developing regulation of the profession.[31]

The new professions which derived from medicine were also influential, as shown by the case of pharmacy at Owens. In 1867 the Manchester newspapers reported that an Owens student had won all three medals of the Pharmaceutical Society of London, which obviously advertised the effectiveness of college preparation. In 1868 the Pharmaceutical Society asked Owens to offer courses preparatory for the exams mandated by the new Pharmacy Act.[32] By 1869 the evening classes in pharmaceutical chemistry had been so successful that the Manchester Chemists and Druggists Association asked for a further series, which were arranged with careful attention to a schedule suited to apprentices in the profession.[33]

Law

The bipartite division of the law caused the lower branch of attorneys and solicitors to spend much of the 19th Century trying to upgrade both their professional and social status. Lacking the formal organization which barristers had possessed for centuries, the solicitors founded several organizations which eventually consolidated as the Law Society. Raising the standard of general and professional education was a major purpose of the association. General education was needed both to impress liberally educated clients and to deal with the great variety of such men's business which increasingly fell to the attorney.[34] A more liberal education would also bring the social position of the solicitor more in line with that of the envied barristers,[35] who traditionally received a university or other liberal education. In keeping with the trends of the times, association led to Parliamentary inquiry, and inquiry to legislation which mandated tests.[36] The Solicitors Act of 1860, following lines laid down by the Law Society, set up a preliminary exam in such subjects as English, French, Latin, history, geography, mathematics, and book-keeping,[37] an intermediate exam in more specifically legal subjects, and provided for partial remission of articles for university matriculants and for graduates.[38] The general strength of support for legal education is well demonstrated by the extensive discussion and advocacy, throughout the latter half of the century, of proposals for a "legal university". Solicitors were its great supporters, in the interests of both professional competence and status.[39]

Owens College recognized the import of the new regulations. The prospectus for 1860-61 followed the list of the college's London exam successes with the reminder that "Bachelors of Arts and Bachelors of Laws of the University of London may be admitted as Attorneys or Solicitors after Service under Articles for *three* years only" (instead of *five*).[40] By the 70s arrangements were made with the Incorporated Law Society of Manchester to encourage articled clerks' attendance upon the law lectures, and the principal reported a great rise in interest in the Jurisprudence course in 1871.[41] At the same time, more ambitious plans were under consideration. The college, the Manchester Incorporated Law Association, and James Bryce of Lincoln's Inn were discussing the establishment of a more thorough course of legal education which, as Bryce pointed out, would reflect the growing recognition of "The importance of a systematic study of law, its great practical value to the Solicitor as well as the Barrister ..," and would prepare for those exams which were already a feature of the profession and were likely to increase in complexity.[42] The Association would contribute to the costs and encourage attendance.[43]

In 1872 the enlarged law courses, now offered in co-operation with the Manchester and the *Liverpool* Societies, "... constitute, the Council have reason to believe, the beginning of a provincial Law school, such as ... ought to prove an increasingly important branch of the college."[44] The law professor already required and received assistance. A Senate petition to the House of Commons testifies to the college's view of the importance of law students, by calling for the establishment of regular exams for the profession and the recognition of provincial law schools to prepare for these.[45] By 1875 the department had so far advanced that funds were raised to maintain it on a permanent basis, which reveals not only the strength of the demand but the care with which the college had studied, nurtured, and accommodated itself to it.[46]

When University College, Liverpool,[47] was established, regular study and examination had become a normal route into the law, a fact well demonstrated by Liverpool's early arrangements with both the Liverpool Incorporated Law Society and the Law Students Association.[48] Leeds had already agreed on a scheme in connection with the Law Society in 1880.[49] College provision was rising along with the numbers and demands of solicitors.

Church

Of the traditional liberal professions the Church made the smallest demands upon the fledgling civic universities. The Anglican Establishment had the ancient universities and some newer theological colleges, and was in any case not growing as fast as the population. Roman Catholic training was internally established and controlled. There remained, however, Dissent, and dissenting Protestantism in its many forms was in fact the dominant religious mode through much of Mid and Northern England, including Manchester and Leeds, and only challenged by Catholicism in Liverpool. Since the decline of the great dissenting academies of the 18th Century there had been few places for dissenting clergy to receive a first class education, though some theological education was still provided by most sects. This shortage suited the circumstances of the new civic colleges, unwilling in the prevalent social and political circumstances, or even disabled by trust deed, from offering theological instruction, but well equipped to offer general education at a high level. Indeed, relatively serious and mature students of this type might offer a rare opportunity to teach at an advanced level, and a relief from the general run of youthful and ill-prepared students.[50]

This form of demand must have had some effect at all the colleges, a presumption supported by the close involvement of dissenting clergy with the institutions. At Leeds, surely the college least attractive to the clergy, a Clergy School was sending its students for Hebrew during the 80s, and similar forms of participation were solicited.[51] The students of the Lancashire Independent College were sent to Owens from its establishment, forming one-eighth of the regular students in 1853-54, and one-fifth in 1854-55.[52] By the 70s permanent and formal arrangements had been made for them.[53] The Congregationalists were not alone in their support. In 1861 the Education Committee of the United Methodist Free Churches was arranging to send the students at its new clergy college to Owens for their general education.[54] The Baptist College chimed in similarly in 1874.[55] Clearly non-sectarianism had paved the way for the colleges to respond to a significant demand.

Army

The Army, though hardly a liberal, and for long only doubtfully an educated profession, had a history of social acceptability, and concern with education was undoubtedly on the rise after the Crimean debacle. Some awareness of the inadequacy of military education, particularly for technical and staff appointments, was percolating into the military mind, under pressure of civilian criticism and the rise of scientific soldiers like Wolseley. By the end of the century an engineering officer like Kitchener could receive a major command, clearly demonstrating the phenomenal rise of the long despised technical branch. As education became acceptable and even necessary within the Army, as shown by the foundation and growth of the Staff College after 1854, so did the preliminary education of officers come to seem important. This attitude, coupled with the trend towards selection by examined merit in the public service and the professions, led to regulations of substantial import for education.

A Council of Military Education was formed in 1857, its main duties being the establishment of entry exams for the Army, and the reorganization of the system of military education, including Woolwich, Sandhurst, and the Staff College.[56] An examination for direct commissions was created in 1859, and after 1862 Woolwich, the sole portal for admission to the Artillery and Engineers, could be entered only by examination.[57] Sandhurst lagged somewhat behind, establishing only a minimum requirement in 1862, with the passing of a university exam constituting an exemption. It too became fully competitive in 1872. The subjects examined show the possibility of preparing at a civic college, and the appearance of extensive quotes from the abstracts of regulations in the Owens Calendars of the 60s confirms the college's interest in such students.[58] While the crammer was at least as important here as in the Civil Service the variety of subjects and the need for extended study of many of them necessarily implies a substantial education prior to cramming.

The attractions of the Army exams for the middle classes were not confined to the social status accorded to officers, an attraction which was at any rate counterbalanced by the impossibility of earning a living in the more fashionable arms of the service. The technical branches and Indian service offered more practical possibilities, however. An officer in India could not make a fortune, but he had a respectable occupation, could live on his pay, and could

77

hope for promotion. If the middle class family was large and not rich, a relatively cheap preparation at a civic college might launch a younger son into respectability, if not affluence. Woolwich offered further possibilities; before the development of engineering schools on a significant scale, its graduates served not only the Army but the State, railroads, and other industries, and responsible and well remunerated posts were a distinct possibility.[59]

Teaching

Teaching occupied an anomalous position among the employments open to educated persons; it could be anything from a liberal profession to a form of manual labor, with status to match. At the top of the scale, in the better public schools and some grammar schools, status was similar to that of the clergy, who often served as headmasters. Such persons were educated at Oxbridge. At the other end of the scale were those persons providing more or less efficient elementary education for the poor. The expansion of their numbers and professional competence was important to the new colleges. In between were the growing variety of schools frequented by the middle classes and the most fortunate of the poorer, where both expansion and the introduction of new subjects such as science provided a possible profession and a consequent demand for advanced training and education.

The importance of the demands of elementary teachers had been recognized by the colleges long before such recognition was physically embodied in the day training colleges of the 1890s.[60] The growth of this source of potential students accelerated after the Minutes of 1846 gave a boost to the interest in teacher education. 1870 marked both an enormous potential for future expansion and incidentally a temporary appearance of a flooded teaching market soon thereafter[61] which may well have been a stimulus to further education within the profession. The size of the potential demand for further study is revealed by the Education Department's Special Reports for 1896-97: the number of male certified teachers had risen from 6,395 in 1870 to 21,223 in 1895; females rose in number from 6,072 to 31,718 in the same period.[62]

The minimum training of the elementary schoolmaster or mistress was of a lower secondary character, and the colleges were generally reluctant to provide this. Many factors might impel the teacher to seek further education, however. The generally low status of schoolmasters might be, and was, combatted by organization and regulation,[63] as in other professions, but also by obtaining more advanced education. The College of Preceptors exemplified both courses, being both a professional organization and a certifier of educational attainment. Evidence of further education might also be an advantage or necessity in seeking one of an increasing variety of more remunerative and prestigious positions in the field. The most obvious of these were the posts in the developing system of advanced primary and lower secondary education. The increase of science teaching, stimulated by the government via the Science and Art Department from the 1850s and reinforced by various grants leading up to the Technical Instruction Act of 1889,[64] created a demand for teachers educated beyond the resources of most training establishments. The bureaucracy of education was also expanding, offering the possibility of promotion to administrative posts, including Headships of Board Schools and Board Inspectorates, as well as organizing masterships and inspectorships in the voluntary system. These posts were filled by promotion of experienced and successful teachers.[65]

Owens College encountered this demand early, and met it with alacrity and success. They had observed that University College, London, offered schoolmasters' classes,[66] and by 1855 Owens was offering specially tailored courses in Classics and Mathematics and Natural Philosophy, at times and reduced rates appropriate for working teachers.[67] The response was highly satisfactory,[68] and before the classes were absorbed into the general work of the day and evening departments in 1858 they had served notably to fill out the otherwise very small rolls of those lean years, accounting for more than a quarter of the student body in 1852-53, 55-56, and 57-58. The rejection of a proposal for formal affiliation with the government's teacher training program reveals the limits of the college's co-operation and a source of reluctance which remained formidable, however. The faculty found that the proposal would interfere with their right of *lehrfreiheit*.[69]

By the 70s classics and mathematics were no longer necessarily the prime requisites for a schoolmaster, but Owens was eminently well equipped to provide the new desiderata as well. Via an arrangement with the Science and Art Department, limited numbers of teachers were spending three years in the college's science classes preparing for higher teaching positions.[70] Liverpool and Leeds followed similar courses.[71]

Employment in the growing middle class schools below the level of the great public and grammar schools presents a much less clear picture, but certainly few such schools could expect to hire Oxbridge products while an increasing number were capable of offering a reasonable salary and middle class status to their masters. The new colleges provided a suitable preparatory education, and a London or Victoria degree would no doubt constitute a passport to the upper reaches of the system, if system it can be called. Perhaps the colleges provided something more than education in this field; they were intimately concerned with the local development of secondary education, and college representatives sat on a steadily increasing number of boards of governors as the century progressed[72] and the efforts of the Charity Commissioners were reinforced by the provisions of the Endowed Schools Act (1869).

A very small further demand is notable for the quality of the students who might make it. As the new colleges expanded both in size and number and were increasingly paralleled by other institutions of higher education, college teaching began to appear as a plausible profession. While the Oxbridge branch of this nascent profession might be largely inbred,[73] the newer institutions recruited from their own and each others' students.

Business

The phenomenal growth of trade and industry in Britain produced a concomitant growth in the numbers of persons in clerical, commercial, and managerial positions. It also made new educational demands as the expansion of scale and scope involved both increasing specialization and necessarily prolonged training on the one hand, and a class of managers with breadth of vision and information on the other. The civic colleges would provide a good deal of all these various forms of education and training, preparing technicians and technologists, managers and businessmen.

Greatest in number, least in status, and most variable in their educational needs and acquirements were the rank and file of the armies of commerce, the clerks. Their numbers rose tremendously in the years under study: the number of persons in commercial employment and government administration, the vast majority of whom were clerks, was 155,000 in 1851 and 638,000 in 1891.[74] For most of these positions a general secondary education was considered more than adequate, but even this was in short supply and many clerks were employed who possessed merely "the minimum essential qualifications ... of quick and accurate arithmetical calculation, plus a legible hand."[75] If they hoped to advance, they would be likely to seek further education.

> A little instruction in Latin, and probably a very little in Greek, a little in Geography, a little in Science, a little in arithmetic and book-keeping, a little in French, with such a sprinkling of English reading as may enable a lad to distinguish Milton from Shakespeare are considered enough preparation for aught that may turn up in the way of employment.[76]

For the clerk already in a position, one of the few convenient places to get such an education in his spare time was the evening classes of the new colleges, which catered, sometimes quite consciously, for such needs.[77]

From the 60s onward, employment pressures rose steadily. The increasingly common possession of an elementary or lower secondary education, and the increasing employment of women, often at wages which undercut male clerks, lead to competition for places, and greater desire for extra qualifications. The threat of competition from foreign clerks added a special dimension to the problem. While foreigners were accused, like women, of undercutting wages, they were also believed to possess a distinct advantage in being multilingual, obviously a useful skill in the growing field of international commerce,[78] and incidentally in a variety of industries where foreign treatises and production information were important. The equally obvious remedy for the English clerk was study, and the colleges' language courses were available and prepared to adapt to the specific needs of business.[79] Liverpool went so far as to advertise a "French Commercial Course" in local newspapers in 1884.

Above the ranks of the clerks were the businessmen and the developing profession of management. Small businesses increased in number and complexity, thereby increasing the level of education and skill necessary for success. Where Owen Owens had sold a few products to a few countries in the Regency era, his son John found himself trading in a variety of goods and commodities throughout the Western Hemisphere by the 1840s. In the great manufacturing, shipping, insurance, and banking concerns, sheer size as well as growing complexity encouraged the divorce of ownership and management, as did the Companies Act of 1856, which made the establishment of joint-stock companies practicable. While the concept of the manager as the possessor of a fund of peculiarly professional knowledge belongs to the 20th Century,[80] the well educated manager began to appear, partly out of an amalgam of the professions of attorney and accountant, and some members became professionally identifiable as company secretaries by the 90s.[81] The foundation era of the civic colleges was one of substantial growth in the demand for educated managers in the great industrial and commercial centres. Engineering and cotton manufactories had already reached the necessary size. Woollen manufactories followed suit from the 50s,[82] and the Manchester insurance offices[83] and Liverpool shipping houses reached sizes necessitating complex management during the era.

General education for business was not a new concept. It had been a primary purpose of the Dissenting Academies in their heyday.[84] Every college prospectus spoke of serving the classes engaged in business and commerce, and when Owens defined three organized courses of instruction in the mid 50s, one was for candidates for the Civil Service and "for such (persons) as are hereafter to be engaged in Commercial pursuits."[85] However, attempts to offer a course of specifically commercial subjects met problems similar to those which arose in many of the technological fields introduced in the same period. Rather than responding to and further stimulating an available demand, the colleges were attempting to create both new studies and the demands for them.

While some of the traditional subjects might be included, the professional course for a businessman, an engineer, or a textile technologist could not consist solely of a particular arrangement of such courses, as had been the case with teachers and with preparation for the Army and Civil Service exams. A body of knowledge had to be accumulated, codified, and professed. This was within the capabilities of the new colleges, given someone to provide the funds. What they could not do was mandate the acceptance of this form of education and qualification within employments and professions which had a long tradition of training by formal or informal apprenticeship and which assumed the sufficiency and even the desirability of ad hoc planning and problem solving. While reformers may have hoped for a substantial demand, and modern scholars may descry a need for technology and management, it was not then enough to offer instruction and thus tap a latent source of demand. Offers were nonetheless made, with varying success.

Manchester made an early start towards a business program when Christie was appointed Professor of Political Economy and Commercial Science in 1854, with the support of Principal Scott who considered the subjects both academically respectable and useful in the area.[86] No great attention was paid to the commercial side, however, and for all practical purposes no complete course of professional business study was offered before the establishment of a Faculty of Commerce in the 20th Century.[87] Certain courses might prove valuable, however. Instruction in maths, chemistry, and other fields might lead to promotion from the ranks to managerial positions,[88] and the colleges could meet this need, especially in their evening classes. At Leeds, early evening classes in the chemistry of coal and iron and the geology of coal drew 72 and 36 students respectively, most of whom

> were connected with the management of collieries, ironworks and machine-shops in and around Leeds, Bradford and Wakefield. The appeal of the classes lay in the opportunities they afforded those engaged in industry to better themselves. When the spokesman of a class of evening students who had been studying textile design in 1876 thanked the lecturer at the end of the course, he said that 'the fee had been a most profitable investment to himself.'[89]

Liverpool's experience, in the city most exclusively devoted to commerce, was similar. A much advertised business curriculum never really attracted pupils.[90]

Engineering

Engineering was perhaps the most characteristic technology of the Victorian era, and the one whose products are most constantly with us even today. For Carr-Saunders, engineering was the sine qua non of the new professions, necessary to the creation of large scale production and efficient transport, godfather to the concomitant scale of social organization, and hence to the widest range of new professions, from accountants and company secretaries through civil servants to mine managers and merchant marine officers.[91] At any rate, engineers like Stephenson and Brunel were the most widely known of Victorian technologists.

The prestige and success of the engineers was not linked to formal or academic training, however. While chairs of engineering appeared in Dublin and London in the 30s and 40s, the numbers of students were in no way commensurate with the size of the profession, and it is even doubtful how much those who attended were learning prior to the mid-century publication of the first English language texts in the field.[92] Apprenticeship was the customary form of training, self-help and private study the additional keys to success, and Smiles' *Lives of the Engineers* the gospel. The achievements of men trained in this fashion prevented any widespread fear of its inadequacy, and experience remained the qualification for membership in the Institutes of Civil and Mechanical Engineers until the 20th Century. Given the success of British engineering, only major blows to its prestige, coupled with radical changes in the necessary techniques of the profession, would be capable of upsetting this complacency. The blows were continuously administered by the steady relative decline of Britain's technical and manufacturing position from its mid-century supremacy. L.T.C. Rolt sees the developing links between engineering advance and pure science as the major theoretical shift.[93] This happened slowly, and complacency certainly reigned, though not unchallenged, until the 80s.[94]

The demand for university-trained engineers appears to have been as limited as the interest in engineering education generally. Rothblatt's figures on the occupations of Cambridge engineering graduates as late as 1910 suggest a continuing reluctance to employ the university-trained man.[95] The content of the early engineering curricula may not have done much to allay suspicions in this practically oriented field. At Owens in 1863 the physics professor had recommended that a proposed engineering course should have such practical content as would make it a useful and attractive training,[96] but while the department was established five years later, instruction was exclusively by means of lectures until the building of a laboratory in 1885.[97] In fact the expectations of the founders appear to have been limited,[98] and the early reports on the reception of the course were discouraging.[99]

The college made efforts to stimulate demand, which presumably aided the stabilization of enrolments at about 40 per annum in the 1870s, though this fell off in the early 80s. The college achieved recognition as providing a suitable training for admission to the Indian Public Works Department, advertised this recognition in the Calendar, and was concerned that the India Office's new college might become the only venue for such training in the future.[100] The mid-70s found the department adjusting its courses to meet the needs of students and seeking the relaxation of the terms of engineering apprenticeships for Owens students.[101] By the later 80s the early support of engineering firms for the Extension drive had been supplemented by a major bequest from C. F. Beyer, university status had improved the attractions of all courses, and the major expansion of Owens' engineering towards its high 20th Century status had begun. The demand tide had also begun to turn as electrical, chemical, and other scientifically based forms of engineering rose to prominence.

At Leeds there appears to have been equally little demand when classes began in 1876 and in 1878 Professor Armstrong was expressing surprise and regret at the small number of persons taking advantage of the course. He recommended an altered class schedule in the interest of those already employed in an engineering office, and recognition of the college course in the terms of apprenticeships.[102] Numbers began to increase and in 1881 the course further accommodated itself to the profession by offering an early example of the "sandwich course".[103] A steady rise in enrolments ensued, reaching 69 day and 84 evening by 1886-87. By 1884 the college had defined its course as catering for three classes of students:

1. Those who come to the College before they enter upon practice in works or offices.
2. Persons engaged in works or offices, who are able to give part of their time to attendance at the College.
3. Evening students.[104]

In fact, the modern range, if not the modern proportions of students had been achieved.

Liverpool, perhaps forewarned by the indifferent success of engineering theory courses elsewhere, gave considerable attention to the craft aspects of the profession. A five year guarantee for an engineering chair was obtained in 1884-85 and the following year saw the Principal pointing to the need for permanent funds and a laboratory, as the course was proving popular and must not fall behind the needs of the district and the activity of other civic colleges.[105] Both the attention to craft and the interest in all potential students is revealed by the success of woodworking classes especially for "... School Teachers, Trade Apprentices, and for Amateurs ...."[106] Here and elsewhere it was the 90s which first saw large enrolments and widespread interest.[107]

Technology

When the attitude of the leading branch of Victorian technology is considered, the more general disinterest in any form of technological research and education is unsurprising. Indifference predominated. The slow growth of awareness of and demand for technological education has already been discussed in Chapter 2. Technical training at every level was far less available in England than on the Continent, and was least available and least desired at the higher levels of potential interest to a university college.

Those who sought technical instruction in this period often received a peculiar product. The careful job-oriented training of the admired Continental technical school was not imitated for various theoretical, pedagogical, and practical reasons.[108] What was offered was the elements of the pure sciences.[109] This interpretation of technical education was propounded by the Science and Art Department and its successors, and, thus financially supported, it dominated the field throughout the later 19th Century. Hence a double bar to the prosecution of technological studies in the colleges was erected; the level of instruction in favour was not that which colleges desired to offer, and the subjects taught precluded any really large demand for university trained teachers of technology. As for the much-publicized but still little realized need for scientifically trained managers, the Samuelson Commission of the mid-80s still spoke of their education as something desirable but unaccomplished.

Sanderson's study of the links between universities and British industry confirmed that the greatest disjunction was industry's failure to provide a demand for graduates.[110] The action of industry may not even have been as irrational as it now seems. Habakkuk has argued convincingly[111] that the relative decline of Britain's industrial position in the world was largely a function of such factors as population, resource availability and capital accumulation, and not the failure of scientific knowledge as perceived by men like Playfair and reviews like the *Edinburgh* and *Westminster*. If Schelsky's analysis[112] of the occupational structure of industrial society is correct, then the large scale demand for the university trained scientist or technologist appears only in the 20th Century.[113]

The late arrival of technology, at least as a major part of the civic colleges, is clearly shown by course offerings and enrolments.[114] Manchester and Liverpool did not offer significant technological courses other than engineering until the 90s, and even engineering was by no means uniformly strong. Leeds was clearly far more technological, but also less well supported.[115] The effective establishment of a technological course required the suitable conjunction of time and place, and such specialities as metallurgy at Sheffield and brewing at Birmingham were turn of the century phenomena, as well as catering to local needs. Yorkshire College would wait for the 20th Century to grow in size and power, while Owens and University Colleges served the growing demands of predominantly commercial rather than industrial centres, and required no such conjunction.

The Yorkshire College's successes, while small in scale, were nonetheless instructive. Each required some special stimulus to overcome more general disinterest.

Mining

Mining engineers and mine managers were technicians, but a partial exception to the ruling disinterest in formal professional training. Economic incentives to technological advance were undoubtedly present,[116] but that was true of other industries.

What set this field apart from others in which similar conditions obtained was the growth of government regulation. The Coal Mines Regulation Acts of the 70s established boards to examine and issue certificates to managers,[117] and the Act of 1887 required that mines with 30 or more miners be managed by a certificate holder.

The Colleges' reactions to the demands of mining differed, presumably based on the proximity and strength of the demand. Liverpool, founded when the principal mining schools were already established (at Leeds, Newcastle, and, earliest of all, the Royal School of Mines, which had begun in 1851 as the Government School of Mines and Science applied to the Arts) and not proximate to a major field, ignored mining. Manchester was founded before the major increase in demand; geology and mineralogy were offered but attempts to found a complete department got no further.[118]

The Yorkshire College had opened with a chair of Geology and Mining, and the Coal-mining Department was added in 1877 and amalgamated with the Mining portion of the earlier chair in 1897-98. The course was always practical, including visits to various local mines and "practical lessons" as well as lectures. The two year course attracted an average attendance of 20 students for its first 15 years, and a considerable increase thereafter, due in part to the development of extension lectures in the 90s, which attracted large audiences and familiarized potential students with the work of the department.[119] The significance of the certificate under the Coal Mines Regulation Acts was appreciated. In a detailed letter to the Board of Examination for the local mining district written in 1881, the College pointed out the availability and value of its coal mining and engineering classes for candidates for Certificates and asked that two years attendance on the classes might be considered in lieu of two of the five years practical experience required of candidates. The precedent of the similar arrangements between other Boards and the College of Physical Science at Newcastle was cited. The Board accepted the proposal.[120] By the 90s Lupton could cite the success of former students in obtaining "... some of the most responsible positions as Mining Engineers, Colliery Managers, and others ...."[121]

Textiles

Two other notable technical departments appeared at Leeds: Textiles and Dyeing. These would appear to be logical responses to the demands of the most important of local industries, and to some extent this was no doubt the case. Woollen technology was well behind that of the Lancashire cotton industry, and the problem was compounded by the peculiar difficulties involved in mechanizing the production of woollens.[122] Foreign skills in dyeing and designing also appeared to threaten the native industry.[123]

In the light of these facts the need for technological advances, and the desirability of employing technicians and researchers seems obvious. Nonetheless, local demand proved inadequate to establish a department of textiles. However apparently there was a sufficient interest to absorb the students of the departments once they had been established with aid of the London livery companies.[124] Numbers enrolled rose fairly steadily from the inception of each department, averaging 40 day and 70 evening enrolments in textiles and 40 and 30 respectively in dyeing by the mid 80s. The practical nature and the potential desirability of the course can be inferred from the Annual Reports where reference was regularly made to the numbers of new patterns woven and designs produced, to the acquisition of equipment and to the situations gained by past students.[125] By 1882-83 Textiles and Dyeing were attracting students from centres of the industry outside Leeds.[126] The constant and international developments in the field of dyeing meant that demands would be made upon other departments of the college in the process of offering a thorough course. The three year program described in 1884 involved a year and a half of study of pure sciences and modern languages, and an equal time on dyeing itself.[127]

Science

Though little interested in technology before the end of the century, industry did show some interest in the applicability of the more traditional pure sciences. While not a large scale demand, it added to that produced by the requirements for London degrees, the needs of the medical and pharmaceutical professions, etc. This demand centred upon one field. Physics was not perceived as notably applicable to industry until the 20th Century,[128] and the opportunities to engage in research as a profession remained few until the expansion of government research and electrical industries, the enormous growth of university laboratories, and such new departures as the aircraft industry in the World War I era. The biological sciences were still almost exclusively linked with the medical profession, and their places as a part of the educational curriculum and a fully accepted field of independent scholarly endeavour[129] were found in the 20th Century.

Chemistry was the growth science of the 19th Century. It had the greatest applicability to 19th Century industry. Gas production, begun early in the century, grew steadily. In the 50s, the new steel and artificial dye industries marked the replacement of more or less casual empirical methods with those of science in two of Britain's great industries. The heavy chemical industry both reached an early peak and was forced to change its methods in the 70s and 80s, which also saw the scientific rationalization of very old industries like brewing and leather, and the beginning of very modern ones like photographic products and commercial use of various gasses.[130] With the increasing need for chemistry came a concern for the qualifications of chemists, and consequent pressure on education facilities. In 1877 the newly founded Institute of Chemistry of Great Britain and Ireland[131] defined the qualifications for membership as including" ... three years training to the satisfaction of the Council in theoretical and analytical chemistry and physics ..." and three years experience "... either as assistant to a chemist of repute or as a professor or demonstrator of practical chemistry ..." or as an industrial chemist, or in the conduct of some published research.[132]

The demand was by no means unlimited, nor were the attractions of the profession unduly enticing. In addition to the general disinterest in technology discussed above, there is the evidence of salaries in the profession; they remained far below those in other professions at least into the 90s, though the small but growing number of highly respected consulting chemists might do vastly better than the average.[133]

Educational provision, particularly the building of laboratories, had begun by the 40s but made its greatest strides in the latter half of the century, as chemistry as an independent discipline and profession came out from under the wing of the medical profession, whose teaching members had carried it into the Scottish universities and the civic colleges.[134] Manchester was aware of the new demands, as well as those of medicine, from the first.[135] The prospectus for 1854-55 advertised three chemistry courses: general; "Technological Chemistry; or the applications of Chemistry to the arts and manufactures"; Analytical and Practical Chemistry, which taught manipulation and analysis for the purposes of arts, manufactures, and agriculture. Enrolments and the variety of courses rose steadily, aided after 1857 by Professor Roscoe's constant attention to the demands of the growing chemical and allied industries. On the one hand he encouraged industrial recognition of scientific chemistry in many ways, perhaps most notably as a founder of the Society of Chemical Industry[136] and on the other he shared or at least publicly supported the common industrial opinion that much of the applied aspect of chemistry should and indeed must be learned on the job.[137] Roscoe stated that the first 25 years of chemistry teaching at Owens had effected a great change in the demand for chemical education from "... give my boy the chemistry he needs for the family business in 6 months ..." to the later attitude "... formerly, it was difficult to keep our students for more than one session, we now find our Senior Laboratory well stocked with men in their third, fourth, and even fifth years, working at advanced subjects and becoming 'chemists' in the highest and best sense of the word." He also noted that by 1885 Owens had the best institutional record in the City and Guilds' Technical Chemistry exams, and that its students were widely and well placed in industry.[138]

At Leeds attention was naturally directed to the technical aspects of chemistry via the general technical orientation of the founders, the concern of the textile industry, and the appointment of a pupil of Roscoe's as professor. By 1883-84 the first general chemistry course had expanded to include a course in Chemical Technology, with special attention to the distillation of coal, a course on Chemical Physics including Practical Photography, collaboration with the dyeing department, and a full syllabus for those preparing to become professional chemists.[139]

Liverpool did not offer much for the technically oriented chemist in its first years, in spite of the local importance of chemical industries and the presence of eminent chemists and manufacturers among the founders. The first professor, a leader in the efforts to establish the college, was himself an analyst, and particularly concerned with the applications of chemistry to medicine. The great local chemical industries were being eclipsed by newer areas and methods, and in any case heavy chemicals do not involve a demand for large numbers of professional chemists and a great deal of research, unlike the more varied production of the pharmaceutical and other branches of the industry. While a major research laboratory might be desirable, the expense would be enormous, and in any case the growing facilities of Owens were readily available. The attitude is summed up by the order in which a committee considered the various demands for chemistry in 1885: "... the necessity of preparing students for Victoria as well as London degrees, in addition to the training of Medical Students, and those training for scientific Chemistry ... "[140]

Another branch of the chemical profession also rose to prominence in the Victorian era. Legislation and scientific developments combined to make analytical chemistry a well-defined and expanding profession. The Adulteration Acts of 1860 and 1872 respectively made the appointment of Public Analysts possible and likely, and 1875 saw both the enactment of the Sale of Food and Drugs Act, which created the modern investigative and legal role of the Public Analyst, and the establishment of a professional organization, The Society of Public Analysts.[141] While some of the basic analytical tests had been developed early in the century, organic analysis, and indeed most sophisticated forms of analysis, developed in the last quarter of the century.[142] By the 1890s high technical qualifications were becoming the rule rather than the exception both among Public Analysts and in the government laboratories at Somerset House.[143]

The new colleges were well equipped to train the analytical chemist, and the faculties were well aware of the demand, as academic chemists were the first reliable chemists called on to do analyses before the establishment of the profession. Owens became particularly suitable after the appointment of the first Professor of Organic Chemistry in England in 1874. At Leeds, toxicology was being offered in the 80s.[144]

Table V
Class Enrolments

	1852-53[a]	1859-60	1869-70	1879-80	1889-90[e]
Manchester					
Arts	61%	61%	50%	41%	33%
Maths	15%	14%	10%	8%	8%
Science[b]	24%	26%	33%	39%	47%
Tech[c]			4%	4%	6%
Other[d]			3%	8%	6%
Leeds					
Arts				30.5%a	24%
Maths				.5%	6%
Science				4.5%	42%
Tech				7.0%	25%
Other				.5%	3%
Liverpool				(1882-83)[a]	
Arts				68%	40%
Maths				6%	10%
Science				6%	37%
Tech					13%

a. At Manchester 1852-53 was the first complete academic year. At Leeds before the 80s there was nothing like a full range of properly supported Arts courses to choose from. 1882-83 was Liverpool's first full year.
b. Chemistry was the most popular science at all three colleges.
c. Engineering was the only technical subject offered at Manchester and Liverpool. Leeds offered textile sciences and coal mining as well.
d. Jurisprudence and law represented the bulk of Other enrolment at Manchester, equaling engineering in 1879-80 and 1889-90.
e. Women's enrolments are not included in Manchester statistics for 1889-90. They were still few in total number, but 88% were in arts. Arts also represented over 50% of Owens' evening enrolments until the late 70s, declining slowly thereafter.

There was a further, though rather indirect, link between science at the college level and industry. As shown above (Chapter 2), technical education in Victorian England meant, by and large, teaching the principles of science at the elementary and secondary level to superior working men. While the new colleges did not train these students, they were the most logical places to train the instructors, and students arrived both on their own initiative and via arrangements with the Science and Art Department and other official and quasi-official agencies.

An analysis of class enrolments provides a useful measure of the relative strength of demands. It is also at least suggestive of students' intentions. Arts subjects may reflect interest in the civil service, the professions, or other jobs where both the subject matter and the evidence of cultivation might prove useful. Some science enrolments represent similar motives, notably among those seeking London degrees. Chemistry offered the only likely route to industry, but other fields, especially medicine, interested many students. Science teaching, the growing academic profession, and the first research posts in government and universities were attractive to some. Technical courses obviously imply technical jobs, but even here the links are by no means all with industry. Many of the best engineering positions were in government or Indian service, and in civil engineering generally.

The demands of a status conscious and increasingly professionalized society were met by the new colleges. They prepared members of the provincial middle classes to maintain or improve their social and economic prospects; they provided a narrow ladder for members of the working class as well. Liberal, professional, scientific, and finally technical education were all wanted. The colleges' accessibility, low costs, acceptance of the middle class ethos, and willingness to adapt to local requirements made them popular and stimulated further demands To measure the relative or absolute strength of each demand is impossible. What is certain is that the growth of the middle classes and of employments requiring advanced education meant that *all* forms of demand were growing in the latter half of the 19th Century.

5

Founders and Benefactors

The civic universities were built upon charity. The London University sold shares, but if any supporters viewed them as an investment they were speedily disillusioned. From 1851 on each new foundation could look to its predecessors and perceive the absolute necessity of benefactions for foundation, endowment, and usually current expenses. Fees accounted for 50% of Owens' regular income during only four years of the college's existence[1] and never reached that point at Leeds,[2] while total income was generally insufficient to meet operating expenses. Expansion and capital projects were funded entirely from benefactions.[3] The Yorkshire College recognized this immediately. The Annual Report for 1875-76 remarked: "It is satisfactory to find that the fees paid by students amount to a material sum. The contribution of some part of the general expenses of higher education is as much as can be looked for, there being no instance of public education of such a character being entirely self-supporting."

Thus the motives of donors, and the colleges' means of stimulating charity, are principal parts of any explanation of the creation of civic universities. The very fact of substantial contributions is extraordinary; in a world-wide context extensive private benevolence is as rare as self-support. While the amounts contributed to higher education in Victorian Britain may seem small by American standards they are immense in any other comparative context. The sums given must be viewed in the light both of uninflated money and the absence of modern tax incentives. While charities themselves received certain tax benefits, the individual contributor did not. Inflated reputations for benevolence could not be purchased for small real costs.

Every source of charitable support was needed, since the costs of establishing a viable-sized institution were high, and even the great donors did not give on the scale of 19th and 20th Century American philanthropists. State aid followed rather than created permanence at Manchester, Leeds, and Liverpool; indeed evidence of success and stability were generally prerequisites for government support. City government was of significant official assistance only at Liverpool during this period,[4] though civic authorities were of great unofficial assistance everywhere. Foreign charity was hardly likely to flow to the world's richest state; Carnegie was a rule-proving exception. Great benefactors and large subscription lists were the primary supports of the colleges, being about equally important at Owens, while subscriptions and relatively small gifts and benefactions built Leeds and Liverpool. These sources are peculiarly unsusceptible to analysis.

Considerable research has left John Owens pretty much as it found him: an enigma. Subscription lists lack the personal information provided by wills, and even those benefactions made by will seem often to lack that personal, introspective character which provided much of the information for Jordan's classic analysis of Tudor-Stuart charity.[5] The new colleges had clearly stated purposes; testators need not define the purpose of their benefactions,[6] and evidently saw less need than their predecessors to explain their motivation.

Other studies of charity add to the necessarily limited analysis of gifts to the colleges. While extrapolations across time and space have their limitations, informative parallels can be drawn, though not insisted upon. Curti and Nash's analysis of *Philanthropy in the Shaping of American Higher Education* and Jordan's monumental study of *Philanthropy in England* have already been cited. David Owen's *English Philanthropy: 1660-1960* returns the question from more or less distant times and places. All three works consider the motives of benefactors of education, and these and other stimuli, while hardly timeless or universal, certainly affect philanthropy in capitalist, Protestant, and expansive societies.

The London of Jordan's analysis (1489-1660) shared many characteristics with the new metropoli of Victorian England. It was growing enormously, and a new class of mercantile magnates, and their smaller confreres, were rising to economic importance and attempting to acquire political and social power. This mercantile class clearly possessed traits which reappeared among 19th Century urban elites.

It is also most evident that even at the close of the Middle Ages the tradition, the habit, of leadership, and the ability to translate aspirations into institutions were already well-established traits of the merchant aristocracy: that the dominant role assumed by members of the group during the Tudor and Stuart eras represents but an enlargement, a fulfilment, of capacities for leadership already well matured. This class, too, was doubly empowered because its wealth was so largely liquid, so easily and completely disposable, and because it had been gained by men who throughout their trading careers had been obliged habitually to take heavy risks for possibly enormous gains. These men, or at least the greatest of them, were in point of fact speculators to their very core, and surely the disposition to found and endow institutions which reflect one's aspirations for the future of a society is in itself the most speculative of all human undertakings. It is likewise true, and this is important in explaining the great generosity of the class, that these were rising men whose status within their own society was still ill defined, or at the very best in no sense commensurate with the power and wealth which they disposed. They were evidently seeking to lay the foundations of a new England and of a new kind of society, a society animated by values which were all but unknown to medieval men and which were neither wholly accepted nor understood by men of their own age. They were, in fact, fashioning the foundations of the liberal society of which they were in so many significant senses the first exemplars.[7]

Such circumstances caused the London merchants to be unprecedentedly charitable, especially toward education.[8] They endowed both London and England at large with a system of grammar schools which provided an advanced education, intellectually, socially, and economically acceptable to new classes and individuals. Often it was an attempt to provide an opportunity they themselves had lacked. The parallels with the newer cities of Victorian England and the creation of civic colleges are too many, too close, and too suggestive to be merely coincidental.[9] One of the greatest of Tudor merchant/financiers even established a prototypical civic college. Gresham College had professors of both traditional and new subjects and was intended for the further general as well as professional education of those engaged in some professional activity.[10]

Motives

A frequent stimulus to charity is the belief that wealth implies responsibilities. This had been enjoined upon all good Tudor and Stuart Anglicans. Judging from the scale of their contributions the injunction was obeyed, and descended to their Victorian successors more or less mixed with the equally ancient though more secular sense of responsibility felt by gentry and aristocracy for their inferiors. The well-to-do of the 19th Century were exhorted to charity from the pulpit, [11] and pressured as well by considerations of prestige: "Some recognition at least of the obligation to subscribe to charity, from whatever motives, was so widespread among the upper and upper-middle classes that philanthropy became a social imperative ...."[12] As aspirations, theories, and moral principles all filter downwards in a socially aspiring society, the sense of responsibility, altruistic, self serving, or both, influenced small subscribers and great benefactors.

The acquisition of great wealth often stimulated serious thought along these lines, and the philosophy articulated by Carnegie no doubt described many men's convictions. Wealth should be used for the common benefit, and used by its possessors with greater skill and forethought than the commonalty could supply for itself. The philanthropist should provide the means for the elevation of the populace, and the first means mentioned by Carnegie was universities. These, and education generally, were particularly suitable objects, as they obviated what most Victorians saw as the greatest danger of philanthropy, the possibility of contributing to "pauperization".[13]

Josiah Mason's philanthropies embodied the Carnegie philosophy long before it was articulated. Mason's life and actions were in many ways characteristic of Victorian philanthropy. He was knighted in connection with the opening of his first great charitable establishment, an orphanage. As a childless man he was concerned perhaps with perpetuating his memory, certainly about the needs of children and the education of young people. Other great benefactors who shared this attribute and some amalgam of its motives included John Owens, who had no close family ties, Sir Joseph Whitworth, whose two wives bore no children, and Thomas Holloway, of patent medicine fame, whose college for women cost him between £700,000 and £800,000.[14] No doubt other less wealthy or less munificent childless donors found it easy to be generous to charity, and desired to concentrate their benefactions upon the young.

Mason's speech at the cornerstone laying of his college summarized another set of motives likely to affect the philanthropic industrialist, particularly as the propaganda for scientific and technical education mounted after the Paris Exhibition of 1867.

> My wish is, in short, to give all classes in Birmingham, in Kidderminster, and in the district generally, the means of carrying on in the capital of the Midland district their scientific studies as completely and thoroughly as they can be prosecuted in the great science schools of this country and the Continent; for I am persuaded that in this way alone - by the acquirement of sound, extensive, and practical scientific knowledge - can England hope to maintain her position as the chief manufacturing centre of the world.[15]

He also made it clear that his college was intended to smooth the path for those of equal determination who would succeed him.

The provision of opportunity rather than some immediate material benefit was appealing to the charitably inclined for several reasons. Like a variety of public and private measures ranging from the New Poor Law (1834) to the Charity Organization Society (1869) it avoided the demoralization of the recipient supposedly implicit in free gifts. It supported the Smilesian ethic of self-help; it prepared potential winners of the evolutionary battles of social-Darwinist philosophy. Providing opportunity might appeal particularly to those who felt they had risen to wealth by grasping slender opportunities, and were compassionate enough to want to broaden them for their successors, to the eventual benefit both of individuals and society. Curti and Nash found most American educational philanthropists to have been moved by this model, and particularly concerned to provide the practical education which they had acquired the hard way. This emphasis on a new curriculum is sometimes present in England; Mason's original intention of providing a strictly technical and scientific college at Birmingham is a famous case. It was not nearly as universal an emphasis in England, however, as the supply of traditional higher education was much smaller while its potential usefulness was growing with the civil service, new professions, and the growth of education itself. The more or less traditional studies could also be a path to success.

Opportunities might be provided for specific groups as well as for the general public. Notable were those who had been barred from higher education by religious discrimination. The Tests kept dissenters from Oxbridge until the mid-50s, and lingering traces of statute and prejudice remained thereafter. Religion had long been a hindrance to most other forms of educational provision as well. John Owens made religious toleration and the avoidance of controversial theology a fundamental condition of his trust and all other civic colleges followed suit, with Liverpool even statutorily barred from teaching theology. This position appealed to supporters and the public, and was jealously guarded through newspaper commentary and other criticism of any deviation.

By the 70s women represented a growing force in the movement for expanded higher education. Their support of extension lectures established an interest in higher teaching which influenced the curriculum of the Yorkshire College and the very foundation of Liverpool U.C. In Yorkshire influence was wielded notably via the Yorkshire Ladies Education Association led by such notables as Lady Frederick Cavendish, Lady Edward Baines, and Mrs. James Kitson. The Association pressed for more schools, supported the Cambridge Local Exams, and arranged for Cambridge Extension Lectures which grew into the Arts departments of the Yorkshire College. After the foundation of the College the association continued to arrange lectures outside the College's geographical and curricular fields, promoting extension at Leeds and at Sheffield.[16] Given this evident and powerful interest it is perhaps not surprising that the Yorkshire College was always open to women. This liberal attitude brought a specific monetary reward, as well as more scholars and a civilized atmosphere. Edward Baines, as a representative of the college, received the following letter in 1882:

> The Yorkshire College has from the first thrown open its classrooms and laboratories to both sexes alike.
> At the date of its foundation, such ready facilities for acquiring the higher education were but rarely afforded to women; and the fact that a similar course has since been

followed elsewhere is no doubt, in some measure due to the success which has hitherto attended it in Leeds.

It has occurred to a number of Yorkshire ladies that such special service in the cause of women's education deserved special recognition ....[17]

They presented the College with a thousand guineas.

The middle classes' concern with the education of their own children has already been analyzed in Chapter 4. They also frequently felt a paternal and practical concern for their own employees and the working class in general. Scholarships for students of working class schools or employees in particular industries and companies were fairly common (see Chapter 7).

Pride accounted for many benefactions. A major gift could be a blatant advertisement of material success and a bid for public honours. In men like the Rathbones of Liverpool, on the other hand, pride, duty, and cultural interests produced a much more attractive mixture.

Group and professional pride was behind certain specific gifts and subscriptions. The engineering fund at Owens would benefit the trade, but would also testify to the public spirit and success of the members of the profession. Liverpool was particularly successful in tapping this source of charity. Successful appeals were made to manufacturers and traders, corn and provision merchants, Scottish merchants, shipowners, and the Liverpool legal profession. Of special interest was the Literary, Scientific, and Professional List which had been opened early in the campaign for funds with the intention of demonstrating the importance which men of high intellectual attainments though relatively small fortunes attributed to the new college.[18] Over £3,500 was provided by 66 contributors including 14 doctors who gave almost £1,600 and 20 clergymen whose far smaller monetary contribution surely demonstrated the relative financial position of the two professions rather than their degree of ardour for the cause. The clergy included on the one hand such influential figures of the Establishment as three Canons, one the Rector of Liverpool, and on the other a ten shilling contribution from a cleric in Calcutta! DScs,C.E.s, Fellows of learned societies, and the Philomathic and Literary societies help complete the picture of Liverpool's intellectual elite supporting the new college.[19]

Regional pride could be an important stimulus, particularly in the case of the traditional rivalry between Lancashire and Yorkshire.

The Yorkshire College made regular reference to the wants, duties, and capacities of Yorkshiremen, and pointed to the great achievements of Lancashire at Owens and later Liverpool as both worthy of emulation and an embarrassing comment on Yorkshire's position.[20] After years of rather plaintive appeals the College risked a congratulatory note in 1887, when the Queen's Jubilee Fund brought £4,000 to the College: "This is, however, only one of many certain indications that the college is growing steadily in the appreciation of the people of Yorkshire."[21] Even national pride could be appealed to, particularly after men like Playfair, Huxley, and Arnold began to compare English education unfavourably with that of other countries.

Foreign competition stimulated other motives besides pride. Contributions might be viewed as an investment in job-related training for business or industry. All the colleges pointed to this aspect of their work, especially when appealing for funds. The engineers of Manchester and the shipbuilders of Liverpool were investing in their future by supporting engineering education. However, the idea of investment was not so common nor so crudely direct as is sometimes supposed. A perceived need for technology and demand for technologists grew very slowly. The return upon such investment, even to those who desired highly educated manpower, was not necessarily large or rapid. While large numbers of educated middle level employees might be desirable, the very few scientists or managers needed were often already available, trained abroad, in Scotland, or at the earliest of the civic colleges. While an industry at large and in the long run might benefit, a specific firm would gain little quickly. The low level of contributions by companies attests to their realization of this. The frequency of bequests belies the idea of any crude sort of investment orientation. The purpose of testamentary benefactions was charitable, and they partook of the whole range of motives for charity.

The idea of an investment incentive to charity is usually linked with the creation of specific technological studies at university level. However, this connection was not only slow to arise, it was also made more tenuous by the developing English definition of technological education. The scientists and the industrialists agreed that at almost all levels formal technical education should consist of scientific principles, and that more specifically applicable aspects of technique could best be left to on-the-job training. [22] Thus chemistry, and later physics, were more likely to flourish than many entirely technical subjects.

Owens College had opened when there was practically no demand for technology. Manchester's primary industry, cotton textiles, reached a state of technical stasis quite early, and was perhaps exceptionally uninterested in technical education. By the time interest in technology became significant, in the 70s and 80s, the college had established itself, and new subjects were added without overwhelming or even competing with the arts and science subjects with their well established clientele.

Even at Leeds money for technology was quite limited. Only coal mining was supported by local industry, and even there a London Livery Company proved important. The textile departments depended almost exclusively on the support of the Clothworkers Company who were neither local, nor, for that matter, engaged in the textile industry.

Liverpool arose when the concern for technology was becoming wide-spread. Yet the support of merchants with a long cultural tradition, and/or professional men, helped to produce a university college with a strong bent toward arts and pure science. Even great industrialists contributed to this leaning. Sanderson, in *The Universities and British Industry*, expresses surprise that a great chemical manufacturer like Muspratt should not have pressed for industrial chemistry at Liverpool.[23] No doubt the interests of the first professor and the fact that Muspratt, Bruner, Lever, et al had developed research within their firms made this need seem less imperative. Another, and perhaps equally significant explanation may have been their sense of what a university should be. One of the Muspratts had studied extensively in Germany as a pupil of Liebig, and the other chemical magnates were often German or familiar with German education. Wissenschaft rather than the details of soap making was likely to be their idea of a university.

Indeed the idea of a university must have concerned many donors. The prestige of new colleges was significantly dependent on their resemblance to the traditional universities. While the intellectually and socially acceptable curriculum was broadening in the later 19th Century, it was dangerous to forge too far ahead. The desire for a high status institution was more or less incompatible with insistence on new emphases. Familiarity with current ideas of what the university was was not confined to a few German trained chemists. The clergy were influential as donors and supporters of most civic colleges, and were often university trained. In contrast to the self-made men of Mason's stamp were families like the Heywoods[24] of Manchester, with their long and intimate familiarity with higher education. The Oxbridge ideal as modified in the course of the century was to have as much influence on donors as foreign polytechnics or calculations of return upon educational investments.

Publicity

"... Victorian charities in their organization were a fairly faithful mirror of the social hierarchy, and one of the conditions of success was sponsorship by royalty or by representatives of the higher branches of the peerage ...."[25] The colleges were no exception to this rule, and they solicited noble supporters and announced their successes.[26] Governing bodies were headed by peers whenever possible. The Cavendish family served at Manchester and Leeds; Dukes of Devonshire as Presidents of Owens and Chancellors of the Victoria University, Lord Frederick Charles Cavendish as first President of the Yorkshire College. Leeds' second President was the Marquis of Ripon; Liverpool called on the Earl of Derby.[27] The post was not necessarily merely honorific, nor were the services confined to creating cachet. The Cavendishes in particular served the colleges as mediators and intercessors with government.

The seventh Duke of Devonshire, scholar, industrialist, great peer, Chancellor of Cambridge and with relatives distinguished for their scholarship, was well equipped to understand the new institution, explain it to government, assuage the fears of the ancient universities, and provide social tone and respected chairmanship at important meetings. As President he chaired a surprising number of meetings concerning extension in the early seventies and university status at the end of the decade; he spoke at many public meetings. He headed the deputations to Whitehall which finally won a charter for the Victoria University. At a crucial stage in the fight for a charter a meeting at Devonshire House hammered out a compromise between Manchester's pretensions and Leeds' objections; with the duke and his son as presidents of the two institutions accommodation was natural.[28]

Distinguished commoners were also useful. As members of council or trustees, men of wealth, power, and known probity added to the social tone and guaranteed the proper use of other men's contributions. They made effective solicitors of funds as well as contributors. Curti and Nash noted the importance of the example and solicitations of friends and trustees. They also noted that charitable actions by men of one's own class produced class pride[29] and a desire to emulate such actions. As the products of a most self conscious middle class, the English civic colleges surely benefitted from similar attitudes.

Publicity was a vital part of philanthropy. Emulation was necessarily based on an awareness of previous donations; status seekers needed to know that their contributions would become public knowledge. And in the early years potential philanthropists needed to hear of the mere existence of this new sort of institution. Local papers were the greatest potential source of publicity, and they generally obliged with monumentally vast reports of every significant college event. Prize days were staged as public spectacles complete with distinguished guests, long speeches, newspaper coverage, etc. Skillful principals worked assiduously to give their colleges a good public image. Greenwood at Owens was a master of this art. In 1861 he established soirees at the college, one of the stated purposes being: "(1) the creation of a more general interest in the prosperity of the college."[30] He answered public criticisms of the college, often with the assistance of other professors, and engaged in battles in the correspondence columns of the press when necessary.[31] Owens' relationship with the *Manchester Guardian*, though strained in the 50s when the paper described the college as a "mortifying failure", improved steadily thereafter. By the mid-60s the *Guardian* was even broaching the subject of new college premises long before the first extension appeal was launched.[32]

Owens and the *Guardian* under C. P. Scott each reached new heights in the 70s, and their relationship grew closer. The Oxford-educated Scott soon learned to respect the new college's scholarship and culture, and professors, including A. W. Ward and James Bryce, became his close friends.[33] By 1874 the *Guardian* was evidently seeking opportunities to support the college: a review of the Fifth Report of the Devonshire Commission closed with a call for support for the college in light of the good work already done (the Report contained extensive evidence on Owens).[34] The thoughtful and considered enthusiasm of this influential paper was most important in the campaign for university status.

A special relationship was also evident at Leeds. The Baines family's support for the college was expressed through its influential newspaper, the *Leeds Mercury*. Edward Baines' long experience of educational causes and debates equipped him to defend, support, and solicit for the college. Leeds also publicized itself by means of lecture series in neighbouring towns.

Solicitation

Appeals and solicitation reinforced the effects of publicity. Trustees, governors, and supporters of colleges made successful appeals both in public and private. Owens College's first supplement to the founder's gift was solicited by trustees. The £9,550 Auxiliary Fund of 1852 was acquired "... principally on the quiet application of Mr. Faulkner and himself (Samuel Fletcher), who, in every case, had met with great kindness and the most prompt and liberal response to their application."[35] Applications by trustees and councillors continued, no doubt with much greater frequency than the occasional mentions of them can prove. Faculty also engaged in solicitation and suggestion, often with great success.

Applications were not confined to individuals. All the colleges hoped for government aid and solicited it regularly. All the advantages and services of the civic college were rehearsed and every conceivably logical precedent for government funding was mentioned; Glasgow and Dublin were frequently cited. While no general subvention was received during the period under consideration, negotiations led to support from South Kensington and the Education authorities for certain aspects of scientific, technological and teacher training, and this permitted the diversion of college funds to other, unsupported, purposes.

Appeals to the general public were more immediately successful. The elements of a well-designed appeal are best seen at Liverpool, which depended on subscriptions in the absence of a single great benefactor.

Those who requisitioned the first public meeting were themselves generous and wealthy, the meeting was attended by a rich and representative audience, and, as was remarked at the time, the tradition that Town Meetings were only called for very important purposes added to the dignity of the occasion.[36] The broad yet clear statement of intention and the careful emphasis on future planning presented at the first meeting were undoubtedly impressive, as was the decision to appoint an influential and effective planning committee. A pamphlet distributed in 1879 summarized the looked-for benefits from the proposed college.

The raising of the whole standard of literary and scientific training among the vast population, of which Liverpool is the centre: the filling up of an acknowledged gap in our educational arrangements: the offer of opportunities of culture to the thousands of young men, who are sent here to begin a commercial career: the bringing of the best instruction to the home of the poor student: the improvement and extension of the education of women: the more complete and thorough training of the teachers of our primary schools, - these - together with the general elevation and refinement of the common life which must inevitably result - are objects which cannot be presented in vain to a liberality, which often tested, has never yet been found wanting.[37]

The founding committee, determined not to start the project with insufficient resources, postponed their first major appeal until after a trade depression and the appeal for funds for a new bishopric were over. They then set out to raise a minimum of £75,000 (shortly raised to £100,000) with which to begin. The goal was quickly reached.

Commemoration

Publicity, example, and solicitation helped to produce one of the most important encouragements to philanthropy, habit. Jordan found that a major gift would produce further gifts to support the same institution, serve other needs in the same place, or create a similar institution elsewhere.[38] The publicity the Owens College gave to benefactions made them a particularly suitable way to memorialize a public figure, and this was quickly recognized. In 1853 a committee formed to commemorate the life and work of John Dalton endowed prize scholarships in chemistry and mathematics.[39] Further instances followed,[40] and by 1881 when Sir William Fairbairn and the Bishop of Manchester were both so honoured,[41] this method had become habitual. The sheer growth in the number of gifts indicates the development of custom; the Trustees were resolving thanks at every meeting by the mid-60s. In 1865 a proposal was made for a standard deed of endowment to be referred to in the future, which suggests not only the growing frequency of contributions but also the influence which the many lawyers interested in the college may have had on clients considering testamentary or other charitable contributions.[42]

Memorials to both the intellectually and the locally prominent thus produced substantial funds. At Owens by 1886 over £50,000 had been received in gifts specifically honouring some person or bearing the family name of the donors.[43] Leeds and Liverpool benefitted in proportion. Some donors wished to encourage a specific field of study. Gifts included collections ranging from Oriental books to biological specimens. Prize endowments rewarded students of every subject from chemistry to Hebrew. Owens College provides a fascinating example of this sort of interest. Political economy, and the commemoration of its heroes and devotees, was naturally of great interest in Manchester. 1865 saw the £1,250 endowment by Mrs. Shuttleworth, in memory of her husband, of a scholarship in political economy "... both as being a study in which her lamented husband took himself a warm interest, and because, while it is expedient for the welfare of Manchester that Political Economy should be much and profoundly studied here, it is a study which, from its very nature, needs more than many others to be fostered by artificial encouragements."[44] A greater name soon followed Shuttleworth's. On 1st March, 1866, the Cobden Memorial Committee resolved: "That a sum of not less than £1,250 to an endowment of the Chair of Political Economy in Owens College on condition that the Professor deliver each session a course of weekly Evening Lectures to which any of the public primary school teachers or pupil teachers engaged within the Boroughs of Manchester or Salford shall have free admission."[45] A decade later John Bright, S. P. Robinson, and Henry Rawson continued this habit when winding up the affairs of the Anti-Corn Law League by giving £2,000 of its remaining funds to the endowment of the Chair of Political Economy.[48]

The Civic Milieu

A wide variety of associations linked the elite of a Victorian city. Active supporters of colleges might easily influence others in this context. In intellectual and cultural societies they might even produce a corporate response of support for a college. That doyen of provincial societies, the Manchester Lit. and Phil., assembled a large percentage of the Manchester elite and presented them with proposals for higher education from an early date. A "plan of liberal education" was considered and advocated in 1783,[47] and the Society continued to discuss education in general, and, occasionally, higher education, through the years. More specifically educational associations were common in Manchester, and trustees of, or prominent contributors to, the Owens College were also members of the Manchester Society for Promoting National Education (1837), the local branch of the British and Foreign School Society (1840), the Lancashire Public Schools Association (1848), the Manchester and Salford Education Bill Committee (1851), the Trustees of the Manchester Free Grammar School (1867), and the National Education League (1869).[48] Owens was also a concern of the local members of Britain's most prominent club. Of the nine Manchester MPs between 1847 and 1874, seven were connected with the College and five made substantial contributions.[49]

The Manchester Statistical Society's links with Owens College were especially close. Its early leaders included names that would be prominent at Owens: Ashton, Darbishire, Heywood, Turner. The Society concentrated upon educational questions, gaining national fame in the field and practically inventing the statistical study of educational provision.[50] In 1836 the Society was the first forum for Mr. H.L. Jones' proposal for a university in Manchester. The resemblance to the Owens College as later established was substantial. James Heywood then brought the scheme and its proponent to another gathering place of the Manchester elite, the Athenaeum. The idea of a college was in the air, and a man of John Owens' civic position probably heard something of it. At any rate, the committee formed to implement the proposal (it was unsuccessful) included at least seven men who were to be trustees of Owens' will. Of the nine trustees originally named by Owens who actually served, four or five had been committee members [51] The new College maintained various links with the Lit. and Phil. Its faculty became members, and presented papers. The officers of the two institutions formed an interlocking directorate which was also linked to the Athenaeum, the Grammar School, the Mechanics Institute, intellectual societies, etc.

The College thus had both spokesmen and platforms among Manchester's elite and middle class. In addition to the obviously intellectual and educational societies other types also contained numerous supporters of the college. At least 30 members of the Cobden Club were contributors, including three trustees of the College and such important men as Ashton, Bright, Heywood, Mackie, Rathbone, and Whitworth.

The cultural and intellectual elite of Leeds had long entertained proposals for colleges and universities, often via the Philosophical and Literary Society.[52] In the expansive but increasingly uncertain era after the Paris Exhibition of 1867 the Yorkshire College developed from the activities of intellectual, educational, and social associations. A proposal for a central college for the West Riding had appeared in a report to the Union of Mechanics Institutes. It was then submitted to the Yorkshire Board of Education, which in spite of its seemingly official title was a private association which had arisen from the Leeds Conversation Club.[53] The Board appointed a committee under Lord Frederick Cavendish to investigate the question, and thus the Yorkshire College was launched. Given the relatively small size of the Leeds elite, the variety of associations involved suggests the support of the same men in different guises rather than independent actions. This is born out by the connection of the college with the most important of the Leeds societies, the Phil. and Lit.

The Philosophical and Literary Society recorded its support of the new college from the first, resolving in 1872-73 their sense of its "great public importance and utility, in which they hope to co-operate by such means as may be within their power."[54] The Society's good offices were to include meeting space, use of the Society's museum for college teaching, and support of the Yorkshire College memorial in favour of a federal rather than a Manchester university. The connection of Society and College was not merely one of premises. Prospective donors were assembled there in greater numbers than anywhere else, making the Society's formal support a practical reality. The Society had between 600 and over 700 members in the 70s and 80s.[55]

One could hardly have avoided hearing about the College at the Phil. and Lit. The Chairman of Council and the Honorary Secretary of the College were officers of the Society. Of the 225 men who had become Life Governors[56] and/or Councillors of the College by 1890, 45% were affiliated with the Society. The College faculty immediately found congenial company there. Sir T.E. Thorpe later described the arrival of himself and Professors Green and Rucker (then constituting the entire faculty), and their role in the Society.

> It was natural and inevitable that we professors should at the very outset of our connection with Leeds find ourselves associated with its Philosophical Society It was the chief centre of the intellectual activity of the town and those who

directed its affairs were among the most influential supporters of the young and struggling Institution to which we
were attached. It was, perhaps, equally inevitable that we
should be called upon to make our debut before a Leeds
audience in the first session of our membership and each of
us figured on the lecture programme of 1874-75....[57]

College faculty became members, officers, and curator of the Society's museum,[58] while half the Society's Council were also on the
Council of the College.

Family ties were a particularly noticeable link among the supporters of the Yorkshire College. Among those who became Governors by virtue of gifts of £250 or more were five Bainses, five
Marshalls, and six each of Nusseys, Luptons, and Barrans. These
families controlled several of the largest textile and clothing firms
of the West Riding, and the Baines family published the area's most
influential newspaper. Other family members were presumably
encouraged to contribute by one or more relatives who were particularly close to the institution: each family except the Barrans included two members of the College Council (the Barrans had one).
Of the 28 contributors among the five families, 24 were members of
the Literary and Philosophical Society. Clearly this is a picture of a
business aristocracy, led by its great Liberal journal, concerned
with social, intellectual, scientific, and technical questions, and
prepared to support an institution addressing such questions.

The associations found at Manchester and Leeds were also
important at Liverpool. The intellectual and cultural societies were
particularly closely linked with education, having created most of
Liverpool's secondary schools. Great families like the Rathbones,
Holts, and Muspratts provided multiple contributions, presumably
encouraged by the members of each family most closely connected
with the College.

The associations of capitalism and Protestantism were by no
means absent. Some Owens supporters had clearly been linked by
business associations. Bankers, decisive in the founding of the
Statistical Society,[59] became generous contributors to the college,
including the Heywoods, William Langton, Lord Overstone, and
Lewis Lloyd.[60] Engineers also offered support. At Liverpool appeals were made specifically to certain professions and types of
businessmen, and the success of the ploy suggests fairly close
bonds among these men, which would have simplified solicitation.

Religious affiliations had a great influence upon possible supporters everywhere. It was particularly important that no major religious group should disapprove of a college. London had had the resources to support both a non-sectarian college and its Anglican analogue; the smaller provincial cities could only support a single institution if men of all religious persuasions contributed. All the civic colleges were non-sectarian, a stance characteristic of nonconformity faced with an established church. An unfavorable Anglican attitude was thus the greatest danger. Fortunately the example of past successes at London (and Owens as seen by the later foundations), and the character of the individual Anglican leaders involved prevented any serious problems at Manchester, Liverpool, and Leeds. Anglican clergy appeared on the platforms at the colleges' public meetings. Successive Bishops of Manchester were good friends of Owens College, both in public statements and in personal benevolence. The Vicar of Leeds was among the first supporters of the Yorkshire College. At Liverpool Canon Lightfoot's oft-quoted speech was of great value.

Non-conformist congregations were regular meeting places of many college supporters, particularly the members of the independent and Unitarian chapels which enrolled so many of the elite of the Northern cities. The Renshaw Street Unitarian Chapel at Liverpool may stand as an example for such others as Cross Street and Grosvenor Street at Manchester. Charles Beard took charge of the Chapel in 1867. His growing reputation made his support of a civic college in Liverpool most valuable. His status was recognized by other supporters, and he became chairman of both the general and several sub-committees involved with the planning and establishment of University College. His congregation included a good percentage of the economic and cultural elite of Liverpool, led by the Rathbones and Holts.[61]

Liverpool, with its tightly knit mercantile and commercial elite, associated via churches, societies, clubs, and employments, provides perhaps the most perfect example of a phenomenon of basic importance to the foundation and support of every college. The stratum of society in a provincial city which was concerned with cultural and intellectual affairs and the repute of their city in these matters formed a close-knit group which could be mobilized to support such a prestigious and useful endeavour as a college. Their interest was summarized by an appeal "To The Citizens of Liverpool":

The foundation of local University Colleges is acknowledged to be a distinguishing feature of English education during Her Majesty's reign. Among the younger of these institutions, the University College of Liverpool can fairly claim to have achieved the most striking success. You laid the foundation of that success, because as individuals you gave to the provision for education secure financial basis, and not less, because by its gift of an ample site for buildings, your Town Council stamped the College with a municipal character. It rests with you now to make the success so far attained, the beginning of a great future. In that conviction we appeal to your civic spirit and liberty, trusting that you will give to this institution and to the cause of education of which it is its highest ambition to be a worthy representative, the stimulating encouragement of your generosity and sympathy.[62]

This appeal, including as it did a tactical reference to the Queen in a Jubilee year, had the desired effect.

To identify the most common motive or precisely define the most effective appeal is impossible, if only because each benefactor must have been moved by a unique amalgam of many influences. The one fairly common denominator seems to have been concern with the local environment, the city. The provincial civic elites of the Victorian era created all the elements of a full-fledged independent culture. The merchants, manufacturers, and professional men of Manchester, Liverpool, or Leeds were united by financial, religious, and other interests. They worked together to create institutions of local government and civic improvement. They also created an intellectual and artistic culture of which the civic colleges were an important, perhaps a culminating, part.

The cultural institutions of the past were concentrated in older cities and other regions, and were designed to provide an older elite of London and the gentry with a culture based on classical education, the Established Church, and the ethos of gentility and leisure. The new men of the new cities created a different culture based on new studies, religious tolerance, and a business-oriented life. Divorced from the older culture by practical differences and mutual suspicion, they asserted their independence and cultivation by creating the institutions and ethos of a new civic culture: intellectual societies, museums, orchestras, and art galleries as well as more obvious manifestations like the Anti-Corn Law League and

113

Liberal politics. The civic colleges were institutional assertions of independence and means of instilling new values. Their supporters expected them to make the industrial and commercial cities of England something more and different from the Philistine temples of Mammon their detractors claimed to see.

Manchester

Exclusive of the founder's £100,000, Owens College had received about £400,000 from corporate and individual benefactors by 1886. These donations have been categorized according to size and the contributors' occupations.[63] 10% came from businesses and other organizations and 90% from individuals, many of whom gave repeatedly. Corporate and private donors of amounts under £100 produced a tiny proportion of the total.

Among business contributors, those who gave £100 to £499 produced £11,000, while large donors gave £28,000. Of the £11,000, over half came from merchants and 25% from manufacturers, plus smaller amounts from engineering and law firms. The £28,000 represented less mercantile wealth and an almost equal proportion of manufacturing money, while over a third came from engineering.

Medium and large scale individual donors gave £29,000 and £104,500 respectively. Half of each group were merchants, 20% were manufacturers, and engineers formed the next largest group at 10%. The proportions of money and donors were roughly commensurate, though merchants were slightly less and engineers somewhat more than proportionately generous. There were also 13 great donors (in addition to the founder) who each gave over £5,000, and whose gifts totalled £221,000. They were too few in number and too varied in their occupations to be analyzed collectively. C. F. Beyer was an engineer, but it was the success of Beyer, Peacock as manufacturers which allowed him to give the college £105,000. George Faulkner, like the founder, was a merchant who also engaged in manufacturing. Two great donors were ladies of independent means. Charles Clifton was an expatriate speculator who left the college a fortune in American stocks and shares.

Engineers were especially noticeable among Owens supporters, and the variety of their employments also entitled them to a category separate from manufacturers or professional people. They were naturally interested in their field, but made substantial contributions to the general funds as well. The two greatest contributing engineers, Whitworth and Beyer, gave enormous amounts in the 80s to an already flourishing institution, creating a distinguished department.

No particular group was wholly or even primarily responsible for supporting Owens, unless it was the middle class, broadly defined. Even there, the analysis of occupation has concealed the support of substantial numbers of peers, and of a certain number of country gentlemen of scholarly and philanthropic interests who do not appear in city directories. All sorts of citizens possessed of sufficient means contributed in proportion to their wealth and/or their interest in their reputations, children, businesses, or the repute and culture of their city.

The Owens College Extension Movement was both highly successful and also a useful epitome of the means and motives of charity. The very fact that it was a prolonged and planned campaign marks the development both of Owens and of new techniques of charitable solicitation. The scale of operations already achieved made dependence on random, unpredictable support extremely hazardous, and also eliminated that class of munificent donors concerned to found a great original monument to themselves or their beliefs. On the other hand an organized institution could call on the resources of society via large scale solicitation and collection of subscriptions, a method which funded an increasing proportion of Victorian charities. Even the massive gifts of a later era were often connected with the subscriptions. Beyer and Whitworth, who gave approximately £100,000 and £150,000 respectively, were intimately involved in the Extension Movement.[64]

By the mid-60s the college felt the pressure of success, with classrooms overcrowded and labs and scientific apparatus demanding more and purpose-built space. The Natural History and Geological Societies were both in decline and desirous of disposing of their collections to some institution which could house them, and amalgamation with the medical school had long been discussed. The college was conducting London University and other public exams without a large hall. The location of the College was in any case undesirable; it was proximate to every threat to Victorian middle class morality from pawnshops to pubs to brothels.

In 1865 the Trustees formed a New Buildings Committee and the opinions of the faculty were requested. In December, 1866, the committee recommended that the college call in distinguished outside friends such as mayors, M.P.s and local politicians and magnates to discuss the expansion.[65] It was decided to hold a public meeting in early 1867, and to solicit a fund of £100,000, later raised to £150,000. Such a meeting had become a customary way of beginning any voluntary civic enterprise, and its calling by the mayor or other officials, and attendance by the distinguished and wealthy of the community, was a measure of the support for the new enterprise. In this case engineers, cotton magnates, merchants, and trustees and professors of the college addressed the meeting, and the resolution to establish the Extension Fund was made by the Dean of Manchester and seconded by Oliver Heywood, of the great banking family. These were good auspices, including the full variety of wealth and opinions in Manchester.

The college had thus prepared its ground well. Professor Roscoe made a special effort to ensure strong leadership in the new movement by recruiting the services of Thomas Ashton whose position in a family of liberal cotton magnates, and personal experience of university education at Heidelberg made him a peculiarly suitable leader of the movement. His services on committees, as a contributor of nearly £8,000, and as a solicitor of other contributions, and his suitability as a figurehead guaranteeing the respectability and efficiency of the Extension Fund earned him the title of refounder of the college which all commentators give him.[66] Other members of the committee were equally well chosen. Edmund Potter[67] and Thomas Wrigley each gave £4,000 to the general Extension Fund and made further contributions to specific subsidiary funds.

The appeal was based on several premises, repeated throughout the speeches, pamphlets and other publicity which accompanied the campaign.[68] Manchester needed an institution providing a liberal education and the opportunity to study the sciences which are the basis of the local arts and industries. Particular attention was paid to the need for an efficient school of chemistry as well as an engineering department; these emphases followed, however, a rather traditional but also practical proviso: "... due provision being made for the pursuit of classics and mathematics."[69] Owens had already proved its efficiency, as well as its ability to attract students and support. It was providing, and hoped to provide on a larger scale:

... University education to youths of the upper and middle ranks in life, together with the practical advantages arising from daily contact with active commercial habits. The

116

Evening Classes of the College afford to clerks, warehousemen, and artisans, whilst earning their own livings, the
means of higher culture which, in cases of eminent fitness,
will enable them to study either for a learned profession or
with a view to scientific distinction.[70]

Owens' current successes in teaching science and its location at
the heart of a great industrial district were said to suggest its suitability to become a great school of science. The arguments for Extension apparently found public favour, particularly with the
press.[71] The major Manchester newspapers, the *Guardian*, the
Courier, and the *Examiner and Times* gave long, detailed, and
favourable reports of all Extension activities. The Chamber of
Commerce immediately lent its support,[72] and from further afield
the *Preston Guardian* and the *Sheffield and Rotherham
Independent* cheered the movement. No doubt this reaction was
encouraged by the emphasis which was placed on the possibility of
Owens becoming in fact, and even in name, the University for
Lancashire. The Dean's motion at the first meeting had used such
terms, as had Sir Elkanah Armitage (who had also mentioned
French and German educational successes) from his position as
both High Sheriff and Chairman of the Manchester Grammar
School. Kay-Shuttleworth had also spoken of Owens becoming a
university for the middle classes which would not draw them away
from their origins.[73]

A series of published reports[74] kept the public posted on the
progress of the Extension Fund, and on its actual use as building
began. While the primary pressure to begin building was that of
growing student numbers, physical progress was also cited to further the appeal, considerable emphasis being placed upon the fact
that the building had gone beyond the funds in hand, and that the
Manchester public's honour was mortgaged in support of Extension.
The public responded.[75]

The General Fund eventually totalled over £105,000, including
more than £2,000 each from committees in Bolton and Oldham.
Several other special funds were collected, including £52,450 in
endowments, mostly for specific chairs or scholarships, and smaller
but substantial sums for the Medical School, the Chemical
Laboratory, Jurisprudence and Law, etc. With the addition of the
Natural History and Geology Societies' contributions the Extension
Fund totalled £211,150 in cash plus valuable collections.[76]

The attempts to raise special funds sometimes overreached themselves. A Geology and Mining Fund stopped short at £3,800 in spite of appeals stressing Owens' teaching assets and convenient location, the necessity of such instruction in light of the practical and legal requirements of the industry, and contrasts with the munificence of other trades and professions.[77] Funding for the teaching of the "Fine Arts" remained unavailable despite a dual stress on their cultural value and usefulness in practical design.[78] The subjects thus negatived ranged as widely as those supported by the public.

With the closing of the Extension Fund and the temporary cessation of building on the new campus (it was designed to accommodate additions, the first of which were soon made) the College achieved an appearance of permanence. Benefactions had amounted to over £330,000. Student numbers were steadily increasing. The College's scholarship was internationally recognized. University status was soon to come.

Gifts continued to flow in steadily throughout the 80s and beyond. The habit of contributing was now fixed. Rising prestige and varied studies brought more varied contributions from greater distances, ranging from Antipodean geological surveys to crucibles and furnaces from the Patent Plumbago Crucible Company, Battersea Works, London. Alumni gifts were significant, notably the contributions of the day and the evening students to the Extension Fund (£614 and £355 respectively) though this source was never cultivated and developed as it was to be in the United States. Books arrived in an increasing flow as the years passed, with thanks to donors being resolved at every trustees or council meeting from 1868 on. The Principal's report for 1890 included a two page list of contributors to the library, including universities, professional associations, government departments, etc., throughout Britain, and from Australia, Canada, India, Norway, Spain, Uruguay, and the United States.

The circumstances surrounding these gifts had greatly changed, however. No longer did a gift constitute an act of creation or of faith in the future of a fledgling institution. Owens was successful and relatively prosperous; no benefaction of a conceivable size would alter its essential character. The early 80s saw the raising of almost £28,000 for a new buildings fund. This helped to provide for necessary extensions of teaching facilities and space for museums, but also for the gateway tower and other fripperies. An amount which might have altered the character of the college of the

50s could only alter its external appearance in the 80s. New gifts became simply a significant part of income rather than the basis of all expansion or even maintenance. And even old gifts, the endowment, began to shrink in relative importance as the government entered a scene which it would come to dominate over the next 75 years.

Leeds

Lacking a munificent founder, and begun with a small subscription for limited purposes, the Yorkshire College's finances remained haphazard and precarious during its first 20 years. Additional funds did not stabilize the institution even temporarily, but rather precipitated or even followed upon expansions of scope which left the college as underfinanced as before. No clear and broad statement of purpose attracted the attention of donors, as was to be the case at Liverpool. Appeals for specific purposes, in the absence of agreed aims, produced fragmentation rather than generally increased public interest. Small subscription lists inadequately supported individual professors temporarily, and no significant endowment was acquired until the mid-80s. In the absence of institutional prestige and purpose the college's appeal to civic pride and cultural interests was very limited, and student fees and the contributions of those interested in some particular study could not take up the slack.

The very small scale of the undertaking perhaps hindered its finances rather than helping. The college seemed neither prosperous nor impressive, and while wealth may flow somewhat reluctantly to an apparently wealthy institution it flows far more slowly to an apparently poor and shaky one. Physical presence did little to ease the problem. From its first temporary quarters in the ominous precincts of a disused bankruptcy court the college moved to a peripheral location, and apart from the Clothworkers' departments spent much of the 80s trying to complete a reasonable range of buildings while generally and dangerously anticipating subscriptions to its building fund.[79] The scale of operations may best be characterized by the rather pitiful note under the heading "Library" in the Calendar for 1875-76:

> The necessity for a Library is evident. A small grant has
> been made, to purchase books of reference as a nucleus, and

several gentlemen have kindly made donations of books. Any contributions will be very acceptable.

Desperately inadequate endowment continued to be a major problem, alleviated though not solved by annual subscriptions to supplement the endowed and other income of particular chairs and departments. Classics, literature, history, and modern and Oriental languages, as well as other activities, were wholly or partly funded through annual subscriptions guaranteed for a few years. The possible non-renewal of such guarantees was a constant threat. Even with their aid the college annually found it necessary to draw upon capital.[80]

The history of the Literature Fund, which supported the chairs of ancient and modern literature and history, is instructive. Encouragement from the science professors, concern over possible university status,[81] the needs of students studying for London degrees, and the financial support of the Cambridge University Extension Committee[82] combined to establish chairs in 1877.[83] Further financing came from annual subscriptions of amounts ranging from one to one hundred pounds.[84] These sums were always inadequate, and indeed diminished year by year; while the College supplied the deficit it refused (apparently led by a group of Council members committed solely to technical education) to absorb the chairs into the general financial arrangements of the College until 1886, when membership in the Victoria University forced the issue.

As the 80s advanced some evidences of stability and permanence appeared. Buildings were eventually erected, the originally very impermanent faculty began to settle down, and the textile and mining departments showed rising enrolments and a developing reputation. The college nevertheless continued to present a somewhat distracted image, torn between its original technical bent and the combined interests of those who wanted more arts courses and those concerned with recognition as a college of the new Victoria University. In spite of its difficulties, the College did tap many of the same sources of benevolence as Manchester, and by similar means.

The most successful appeal was made to a different and distant source, however. The ancient Livery Companies of London possessed large endowments for charitable purposes, and in the later 19th Century their growing income was matched by public suspicion of the amount and efficiency of their charity. The Clothworkers Company, stimulated in part by members engaged in the Yorkshire textile trade, found a suitable outlet in the support of technical education in Leeds. They created and generously funded the Yorkshire College's textile departments, providing a million pounds over the course of a century.

While London was the only distant place to provide such massive funds, the appeal to Yorkshire beyond Leeds undoubtedly brought important results. The support of the Salt family, especially Sir Titus,[85] the £5,800 in gifts and bequests from Henry Brown of Rawdon, and the contributions of Bradford, Halifax and other towns did much to see the College through its early years.

The 1885 subscription list allows some statistical analysis. While not entirely comparable to the more complete statistics for Manchester, it does represent contributions to an institution which had finally come to offer discernibly higher education in a reasonable variety of fields. Indeed, these contributions were intended to help make Leeds what Manchester already was, a University College of the Victoria University.

The fund amounted to £30,691. Donors of sums under £100 produced 7.5% of this total. Large donors (£500 or more) and medium donors (£100 to £499) provided almost equal sums, 45.5% and 47% respectively. The absence of massive donations and the relatively far greater importance of medium donors at Leeds is of course consistent with the smaller scale of both the college and the community. The greater significance of business donations fits the college's predominantly technical aims while the small total size of contributions to the Yorkshire College shows that this was still a new interest of a minority of businesses. Business and personal gifts were about equal in numbers and total amount among large donors, while businesses represented 25% of middle size donors and donations. The list reveals the importance of multiple gifts. A substantial majority of the donors had made previous contributions, and of the six largest donors of £1,000 or more, all had made equally large gifts in the past.

Liverpool

Powerful leaders, efficient publicity, and widespread support characterized the origins of University College. Public meetings and mercantile backers were soon reinforced by an inspiring speech to the Council of Education by the Rev. Canon Lightfoot in January 1879. As a Liverpool man, a distinguished scholar, and soon to be a bishop, his words, enshrined in the college's mythology as "The Bishop's Dream", were most influential. He defined the nature of a college's services to the city and the way in which these might be supported by the benevolence of the various parts of the economic and social community. He was particularly aware of the importance of habitual, customary benefactions, speaking of an institution which

> ... they regard as the great glory of the place. Accordingly, when a wealthy merchant, or shipowner, or banker, has had an exceptionally prosperous year, almost his first thought is how he may increase the efficiency of this institution.

Recalling the speech and its upshot years later, William Rathbone described in simplified form the process by which a large portion of the necessary funds was raised. He described his own actions but also noted those of such other able solicitors as Dr. Campbell Brown, Rev. Beard, George Holt, other Rathbones. etc. He appealed to his brothers and they founded a professorship among them; calls upon A: H. Brown and the Crossfields with the suggestion that they endow a "Gladstone" chair were politically timely; the Scottish merchants of Liverpool were induced to found a professorship of those notably Scottish subjects, philosophy, logic, and political economy; the corn and provision trades were also tapped; Liberals were asked to follow where Conservative mayors of Liverpool had led so as not to be outdone; the Earl of Derby was asked to follow his father's example by endowing a chair of natural history (his father had given a museum).[86]

Rathbone thus summarized a great many of the factors of importance in creating support for the new college. Solicitation is the most obvious theme; the position of supporters like Rathbone, distinguished member of a powerful family and sometime M.P. , Charles Beard, influential clergyman, and various Mayors of Liverpool made their appeals for funds more effective. The College Council was aware of the importance of continued solicitation; in 1883 and 1884 they were preparing lists of important local persons who had not yet contributed for the guidance of Councillors seeking funds, and asking Governors of the College representing neighbouring areas to solicit there.[87]

Memorials were as important here as elsewhere. One was unique and of special interest, its object being long dead and the memorial symptomatic of an important motive in Liverpool's support of civic culture. The Roscoe Art Chair commemorated the most famous of Liverpool's cultural heroes, William Roscoe, whose historical writings, art connoisseurship, and contribution to such endeavours as the Royal Institution made him the leader of the "Liverpool Renaissance" at the beginning of the 19th Century. The glories of this period, the subsequent falling-off, and the need to re-establish a high cultural position for Liverpool were the burden of many speeches supporting the new college. The great of Liverpool were moved by these considerations. A Holt led the subscription list for the Chair with £1,369, followed by another Holt, three Rathbones, six Tates, and five Roscoes.

To achieve widespread support University College had necessarily to represent a reconciliation of several sets of opposed or tangential groups and interests. Rathbone said that he approached certain political Conservatives with the argument that an institution started by two Conservative Mayors now seemed to be supported mostly by "Radicals and Infidels" like himself, a state of affairs that the Conservatives should not permit; evidently the argument was a success. No doubt this was the easiest reconciliation to make, as politics did not rouse quite the passions produced by religion, nor the personal and social anxieties of the relation between liberal education and business success. In any case the cultural and financial elite had long been integrated across political lines by its business and socio-cultural activities.

The breadth of the new college's appeal and rapid growth of support put the founders in a position to request official civic aid. A strong committee of the College Council, containing ex-mayors and other distinguished persons, was appointed to approach the City Council.[88] The official letter of appeal went to the Mayor in August 1881, summarizing past activity, present needs, and future expectations. Special emphasis was placed on the breadth of public support and potential services to the community.[89]

The first success did not remain sufficient for long. A general desire to offer degrees and possess university status was coupled with the specific threat of the growing attractiveness of Owens College as the sole constituent of the Victoria University, a threat felt most heavily by the medical school. A Town Meeting in January of 1884 placed the matter before the public, complete with an account of the College's development and its future intentions. The device of a conditional gift was coupled with the warning that the continued success of the medical school was dependent upon admission to the Victoria University.[90] The money was found, the teaching power of the institution increased, and admission to the University secured.

By 1884 the College was reasonably well established on its new site. £112,000 had been contributed in the form of five great donations (four of £10,000 and one of £5,000), sixty large donations (£500 to £4,999) amounting to over £48,000, and almost 400 smaller donations making up the remaining £20,000. The Literary, Scientific and Professional List (and the Liverpool Legal Profession Fund) consisted mostly of small donors, but the founders felt that the readiness of these men of relatively small means to contribute, at a time when others were still reluctant, set an excellent and influential example.[91]

This success marked more than the ability to grant degrees and remain solvent. The extra prestige and publicity involved helped to fix the College solidly and permanently in the public mind as a part of the civic environment requiring and deserving support. From 1885 on small gifts from individuals and organizations were the order of the day, including in 1884-85 scholarships and prizes from members of the Council of Education, the Ladies Education Association, a Bushnell Memorial Fund, and Mrs. Muspratt.[92] Major benefactors made new or enlarged contributions.[93]

Perhaps 1889 is the best choice of date for the end of the beginning at Liverpool. Private benevolence was continuing. But in 1889 the first Treasury grant was allocated to the College; the government rewarded success.

6
Governance

The new colleges quickly evolved efficient academic self-government. The successively evolved constitutions of Owens College
and the Victoria University were widely influential, but the developing practice of academic governance was perhaps more significant. British academics were learning to use their constitutions and
diverge from the apparent letter of statutes in ways which have
been widely admired in the 20th Century.

The original governments of civic colleges were composed almost exclusively of laymen.[1] They solicited and supervised the
endowments, defined the purposes of the institutions, selected sites,
and hired faculties. Yet within surprisingly few years the colleges
had developed a very different form of government, dominated by
the academic staff, which was to remain customary at least until
very recently. De jure supremacy resided in large courts composed
of representatives of local and national wealth, power, and status.
In fact these exercised only ceremonial and confirmatory functions,
and delegated their real powers to smaller, similarly composed,
councils which shared real power in the universities with the senates. The theoretical powers of councils were quite absolute, but in
practice were severely circumscribed by conventions which dictated that they should have little say in academic matters: none in
matters of *lern und lehr freiheit*, little in matters of appointment.
They exercised oversight, though not day to day control, over financial matters.

The power of academics was exercised by a senate which made the vast majority of decisions concerning curriculum, examination, admissions, and appointments, and whose expertise was consulted by council in other matters as well. Vice Chancellors (originally Principals) were the chief administrative and academic officers of the universities, though their powers depended upon suasion, not statutes. As academics, they tended to represent academic positions to laymen rather than the reverse.[2]

Lord Ashby has explained how academic self-government is practiced via an apparently oligarchic, lay-dominated constitution.[3] In British universities vital business is initiated at the "bottom" and flows "upward". Originating in the subdivisions of the academic staff, it flows through Senate, Council, and theoretically at least, Court, with the likelihood of additions, alterations, or rejection decreasing at each new level. The system works best with matters where academic expertise is undoubted and vitally necessary, such as curriculum. Appointments may occasion some difficulty, as the Council are notionally the employers of the faculty, and are often accustomed to being employers in other contexts.

Budgetary affairs are the most delicate. Endowments are necessarily managed by the Council in their role as trustees. Finance would appear to be a matter about which many laymen are at least as skillful and well informed as academics. Furthermore, the distribution of that part of the budget not committed in advance is a subject on which faculty unanimity disintegrates; therefore the statutory powers of Councils are in this case reinforced by the need for arbitration and decision making, which can easily lead on to the initiation or alteration of policy. That it seldom does so is a testimonial to the strength of the tradition whose origins are the subject of this chapter.

Rowland Eustace has provided a convenient scale for measuring the relative powers of academics and councils.[4] Its first five stages represent consultation, ranging from a Senate right to report to Council, through Council obligations to receive reports or recommendations, to an obligation on Council's part to solicit Senate's opinion. The next stages consist of Senate powers of veto, followed by a stage in which Council possesses only a veto power, and finally by a ninth stage of independent faculty powers, usually found in purely academic matters. In the very beginning some college faculties lacked even the statutory right to report or comment, though in fact they made suggestions and were consulted. By the mid-80s all possessed practical powers which ranged, over various areas, from level five to complete independence. Statutory recognition lagged, and still lags, behind reality, but the constitutions of the maturing institutions began to recognize the faculties' prominence, if not their predominance.[5]

At first the distribution of real power in the colleges resembled the formal allocation of today; indeed, Council's powers extended to affairs now statutorily reserved to the faculty. The vesting of supreme power in a predominantly or entirely lay body has seemed peculiar to commentators who note its drastic deviance from the Oxbridge model. In fact, quite apart from any natural reluctance to copy universities whose organization was then revealing serious inadequacies,[6] the civic colleges were choosing an historically warranted, legally sound, and contemporarily customary form of government. Oxford and Cambridge were the anomalies.

Charitable foundations had long been governed by trustees. Owens, in its early years as a private charitable trust, was in fact being governed in the only legal manner; what faculty power there was represented a departure from the normally complete powers of trustees. The newer forms of charitable organization, based on continuing public subscriptions and contributions, were similarly governed, and this was the form which the governments of Leeds and Liverpool adopted. Their Councils and Courts were also permanent reflections of their first temporary organizations; the magnates who called, chaired, and made motions at public meetings became the Councils, and the smaller but still substantial contributors and interested parties became the Courts. This was the more or less characteristic arrangement for the provision of many public services in the provincial cities of Victorian England. Improvement commissions, police commissions, etc., were all founded by and composed of prominent citizens.

The grammar schools, long the most important providers of advanced education in the provinces, were charitable trusts which offered clear precedents for the government of colleges. Many college governors had experience as school trustees. Those colleges founded as joint stock companies[7] are obvious reminders of the precedents of all such companies[8] ever since the great Tudor trading monopolies.

Nonconformity offered further examples familiar to many potential governors of civic colleges; Congregational, Presbyterian, Unitarian, and some Methodist churches were governed to varying extents by their prominent lay members. Foreign models provided additional precedents. The trustees, corporations, overseers, and governors of Harvard, Yale, and other colonial establishments were examples of how other, similarly independent, communities had chosen to govern similar institutions.

Thus the position of the trustees or council was well established in the eyes of the law and custom. Nothing so simple as mere assertion was likely to gain power for the faculty, and conflicts would find them in a poor position, as several instances at Leeds demonstrate (see below). Some descriptions of the relations of Senates and Councils suggest an adversarial or antagonistic relationship, but in fact the faculties' means of gaining and maintaining power centred on other factors, notably the willingness of laymen to defer to the faculty's expertise and capacity for full time labour, and the slow, cumulative way in which this transferred power. Statutory alterations, which tend to make changes more visible, were eased by the facts that they frequently represented *faits accompli* and that constitutions were drawn up or altered at moments of expansion and change, when *in situ* powers were likely to be inattentive and otherwise occupied.

Courts, Councils, Trustees

Before describing the steady growth of faculty power in detail, the composition and status of the predominantly lay groups needs clarification. The character of the Courts of Governors, under whatever names, was very similar everywhere, as were the processes by which they were quickly limited to largely ceremonial functions. Membership of the Court was used to reward contributors, to attach persons of consequence to the interests of the college, to create a body of prestigious and weighty appearance, and to provide channels for the representation of local government, industry, and education.[9]

At Owens important contributors, public officials, faculty, and representatives of the alumni were the original major groupings. Leeds added many representatives of local educational institutions, particularly grammar and technical schools and literary and philosophical societies, and made the connection with financial contributions more explicit.[10] Liverpool expanded the scope and number of a similar set of categories. Links among colleges and universities were encouraged by the increasingly frequent nomination of professors as Governors elsewhere.[11]

The sheer size of Courts made meetings infrequent, attendance poor, and regular attention to college business impossible. The Council's theoretical position as a committee acting in Court's name helped to define the Court's role as that of a passive recipient of reports *post facto*. At Owens, where Governors were only created upon the reorganization of the College in 1870 (Extension Act), the likelihood of passivity was increased by the institution's already possessing established means of administration and communication; the new Council also looked very much like the old Trustees, who had possessed *de jure* sovereignty as well as great power. The Courts of the newer colleges quickly reached a similar position. At Leeds the Governor's meetings appear almost farcical: in the absence of large attendance the Council members met in their capacity as Governors to authorize themselves as Councillors. Within seven years of the foundation, the minutes of Liverpool's Court came to consist of a few standardized phrases and a printed copy of the annual accounts.

In the absence of activity, if not abdication of responsibility, by Courts, Councils wielded some formal and considerable actual powers. The precedent of the Owens trustees was of course formidable, as they had been answerable only to Parliament and the law of the land. These powers were based on the Councils' more or less absolute control over finances, with all the forms of persuasion, decision, or veto which this implies. Only disinterest or more or less willing cession by the Councils could give substantial power to any other group.

The Councils' powers were generally wielded by a small inner circle, and frequently via committees. The inner groups were self-selected in several senses. Among original trustees and council members those with a close interest in the working of the colleges were easily distinguished from those whose appointments were honorific or intended to shed reflected luster on the institution. The analysis of attendances undertaken below clearly demonstrates the distinction. Professor Huxley and Sir J. P. Kay-Shuttleworth's perfect records of non-attendance certainly did not worry or disappoint the leaders of Owens College. (Such a record need not imply disinterest or failure to serve the colleges in some other, non-managerial capacity: the services of the Duke of Devonshire and his son to Owens and Leeds, already discussed above, belie the superficial appearance of their non-attendance at regular Council meetings.) Every Council contained members whose academic or community interests, often inherited in a family, made them devoted and active members. Such members produced treasurers, chairmen, and the active portion of important committees such as finance, buildings, and general purposes, where, often with the aid of faculty members who became increasingly common and important members, most regular business was conducted. Councils' power to co-opt members has generally produced a steady supply of such persons, whose selection by elective bodies like Courts is much less certain.[12]

Three examples from Manchester help to define the qualities of effective and active leaders. Members of the Heywood family of Manchester bankers served variously as Trustees, members of Council, and important contributors. This was in keeping both with a general civic-mindedness and with a particular interest in education which included the reform of the ancient universities and the support of all local educational and intellectual endeavours.[13]

Mr. William Nield's public distinction as an industrial magnate and early mayor of Manchester gave his devotion to Owens College particular importance. Intellectual interests were unsurprising in a man who had regularly entertained John Dalton, and these interests were passed on to his son Alfred.[14] Upon the father's death the Trustees not only mourned a valued leader, but offered the son his father's old position as Chairman. Family influence survived the reorganization of the 70s as well; Alfred became the first Chairman of the Council which replaced the Trustees.

Joseph Thompson, Council member, Treasurer, and historian of Owens, came from a family long connected with non-conformist education in Lancashire, but his undeviating devotion to Owens was stimulated by personal experience as well. He was one of the College's first students, enthralled by some of the first professors,[15] and a notable contributor to the library while still a student. His rise to the Council was certainly a landmark on the College's path to maturity.

Leaders of this calibre were clearly strong men, not easily overwhelmed or undermined. And, indeed, the faculty had no need to attempt either the one or the other, since it is equally clear that such men were not the unintellectual Philistines sometimes caricatured in discussions of academic self-government. Dinners with Dalton, study under the professors, or a don in the family were hardly likely to produce a low opinion of academics. The relation of Council and faculty were generally characterized by mutual respect and a pragmatic division of labor and responsibility.

Faculty

In terms of permanence, prestige, power, and the public mind, the professors were the faculty of the new colleges. In the first years of each institution the professors were in fact the vast majority of the full-time staff. With expansion the professors required what was usually described as "assistance", and that is what they got: the new demonstrators, etc., were often the personal assistants of professors, hired and sometimes even paid by them (out of the increased fee income of larger classes). As in many of the world's universities, representation and a share of power followed (at some distance) the development of permanent positions and reasonable prospects for sub-professorial staff, and these were 20th Century phenomena.

In a highly class-conscious society, social equality among laymen and academics was a useful, perhaps even a vital, desideratum of co-operation. Fortunately, there were few problems in this regard. The social standing of a majority of the faculty was that of liberally educated men: high and secure in their own eyes and those of much of the public. (See Ch. 4 for the status conveyed by liberal education.) While traditionally linked to Arts subjects, this status was beginning to be conveyed, more or less intact, to the possessors of the new degrees in Science. The problems and complaints of technical faculty, who frequently suffered from a lack of the customary education and certification, exacerbated by the lesser prestige of their subjects, reveal the importance of this consideration. At Leeds, despite the apparent centrality of technology, its teachers were accustomed, though not reconciled, to sometimes inferior status. The organizers of the college explained, in a letter to their new benefactors the Clothworkers in 1875, that their search for a teacher for textile industries had produced candidates wanting in either theoretical or practical qualifications; that they had chosen a practically qualified man, but with the understanding that the arrangement might be temporary and that he be called "Instructor", not "Professor".[16] In 1885 the titles of the heads of the Coal Mining, Textile Industries, and Dyeing Departments were again under consideration. The Instructor of Dyeing asserted that the importance of the subjects and the activity of the incumbent staff surely justified the title of professor, but he thought it necessary to answer potential questions about the liberal education of the prospective professors as well as the substance of their subjects.[17]

The professors' activities soon brought status in the local community. At the prestigious Literary and Philosophical Societies faculty and council met as equals; indeed many professors became officers of such associations and all naturally ranked high in institutions based on intellectual interests. Some, like Roscoe, even helped to found organizations, like the Society of Chemical Industry, which enrolled important laymen. Heroic or newsworthy activity, like Leeds' Professor Lupton's rescue of two men from a burning mineshaft, no doubt favoured social acceptance.[18] More subtle personal relations were important; many professors were relatively young men in their first highly remunerative and secure position, and thus socially and maritally eligible. At Owens, for example, both Greenwood and Roscoe married into locally prominent families with an interest in the college.[19] At Liverpool, the professors evidently moved comfortably in good society, aided especially by the cordiality of William Rathbone.[20]

Public and national repute, while usually based on professional expertise, had its social component. Roscoe's knighthood in 1884 is perhaps the most important instance, but nominations to Royal Commissions and distinctions like fellowship of the Royal Society had their weight, and were recorded by Councils and reported by the press.[21] The appearance of professors on public platforms, advocating sanitation, charity, and other characteristic Victorian virtues, and their presence on prestigious boards of trustees, as grammar schools and other charities were reorganized, finally confirmed their social position.

Professional standing reinforced social status. The professional competence of the professors of the new colleges was undoubted, and in any case the Councils, which had helped to select them on the basis of their expertise, were in no position to deny this. And faculty qualifications did not stop at mere competence. By the 70s Owens' roster included such famous names as H. E. Roscoe in Chemistry, Osborne Reynolds in Engineering, W. S. Jevons in Philosophy and Political Economy, A. W. Ward in History, and James Bryce in Law; a most impressive faculty for a new and still small institution. Leeds[22] and Liverpool were almost equally fortunate in proportion. The increasing reputation and general acceptance of the colleges and their curricula further enhanced the position of the professoriate.[23]

The status conveyed by professional competence and esteem could also be reinforced by a professor's exceptional success as pedagogue or department head. In 1868 the Owens' Trustees

"...having in view the great success which has attended the Chemistry Department" sought funds to raise Roscoe's salary, which was originally lower than that of the other professors. A circular sent to friends of the college pointed out the risk of his leaving to take a prestigious position, and remarked that: "... during his tenure of the Chair [he] has added to the weekly number of lectures, and by his zealous and successful direction of the Laboratory has so promoted the prosperity of the Chemical Department, that it is second in importance to none in the College ...." They appealed successfully for funds, since "If Dr. Roscoe were to leave Manchester now, not only the College but, still more, the Extension Scheme might suffer serious disparagement."[24] Such feelings on the part of the Trustees were incompatible with much condescension or interference.

Professorial remuneration was a further testimonial to middle class and professional status. The salaries of full-time professors ranged from £300 to £400, plus a share of students' class fees. With the addition of other emoluments such as lecture fees, royalties, or the rewards of private practice, a professor could count on an income of approximately £500, while Principals received higher salaries and such a popular professor as Roscoe, with his large classes and special lectures, might make £1,000. This was commensurate with the salaries of many doctors, lawyers, and businessmen, and permitted the possession of such marks of status as appropriate housing and servants.[25]

The education and academic experiences of the professoriate encouraged them to assert themselves. Many were Oxbridge educated and some had held fellowships; they were thus accustomed to a considerable degree of self-government. Scottish educated faculty were also accustomed to a substantial status for the professoriate, as well as to negotiations with laymen, particularly civic magnates. While London trained men were familiar with a far less representative system, it seems possible that this merely encouraged them to self-assertion: certainly Greenwood ran Owens well, and Campbell Brown was an energetic founder of Liverpool.

Most chemistry professors were German-trained, at least in part, and had presumably imbibed a sense of the importance of their subject to society, and of the professor's high place in the university, from men like Bunsen and von Liebig. In later years new men often had had experience under Roscoe at Manchester, with similar results.[26] The general popularity and success of their subject further enhanced their status.

Powers

Laymen founded the colleges, and therefore possessed the absolute but temporary power inherent in creators. While such powers lasted laymen set the tone of the new institutions in many ways and for long periods to come. The closely linked decisions about curriculum and clientele had perhaps the most far-reaching effects. When Owens' trustees decided to begin by offering classics, mathematics, philosophy, science and English, forming a " ... Regular Course for the general cultivation and discipline of the mind, and to prepare the student for advantageously applying to and effectually mastering any particular department of knowledge ...", decided that they could not immediately afford a course of applied science, and that they would charge such fees as could "... be paid without inconvenience by the friends of students, whose intended pursuits in life may render an education of the kind proposed desirable ...",[27] they had defined the direction, purpose, and priorities of the college for at least 30 years. Equally, the organizers of Leeds laid the strong foundations of a very different style and substance when they defined their college as intended to supply "... instruction in those sciences which are applicable to the Industrial Arts, especially those which may be classed under Engineering, Manufactures, Agriculture, Mining, and Metallurgy", and to serve persons "... who will afterwards be engaged in those trades as foremen, managers, or employers ...."[28]

Laymen inevitably made the first academic appointments as well. The nature of these demonstrates the short-lived character of absolute discretion. Decisions about site, physical plant, and curriculum had already committed a large portion of resources, and faculty contracts increased this percentage. Equally important, the first professional appointees in turn influenced all future decisions, both indirectly and deliberately. Owens' trustees, in accordance with the academic advice they had sought from other institutions, quickly found a principal and vested him with "... general superintendance over all the educational details of the institution."[29] Having appointed a man whose intellect and accomplishments they respected, they naturally consulted him on further appointments, and by 1853 he was reporting in detail on the candidates for a new chair.[30] At Liverpool the Principal, who was again the first professor chosen, participated in the selection of all other faculty members and served on the building committee as well as giving strictly academic and curricular advice.[31]

Curriculum

Once the first creative acts were completed curriculum fell most quickly and completely into faculty hands. Detailed control of a particular subject had necessarily to be conceded to its professor. The collective expertise of the faculty was almost as important in making more general curricular decisions; they were obviously best equipped to define logical courses of study for students. This implied not only the definition and inter-relation of their own subjects but also recommendations as to the enlargement of curricula and faculty as new subjects were demanded by the expansion of the institution, the growing variety and complexity of professional training, and the expansion of knowledge.[32] At Owens by the mid-60s all curricular and indeed other entirely academic decisions which did not involve extraordinary financial arrangements were in faculty hands.

The faculty's control over curricula was also furthered by their powers of examination, which they took very seriously. At Owens the need to define curricula through internally controlled examinations was one of the major arguments for university status and an end to the influence of London University.[33] Academic control over the conditions of scholarships and prizes also helped to define and refine courses and subjects of study.[34]

Of course no one within the academy had an entirely free hand with the curriculum. Real or at least potential demand was a necessary desideratum for a successful course in a new institution, though as the colleges gained prestige the force of this check lessened, as institutional prestige would bolster any new course offering. Other extrinsic factors included the growing range of practical and statutory professional requirements to which the colleges were most sensitive, as well as the enormous growth and subdivision of certain subjects, most notably medicine.[35]

A gift might also produce an addition to the curriculum, and only slowly, after the accumulation of wealth and prestige, could a college begin to refuse gifts for peculiar purposes. On the other hand, both academics and lay members of the colleges could and did attempt to steer donors toward certain subjects.

135

Appointments

The reality behind the apparent mechanics of appointments is perhaps the most nebulous aspect of academic governance. Concern for confidentiality has left the record sparse. Statutes and regulations in this area are generally couched in the language of advice and consultation, which leaves the location of effective power uncertain. It is clear, however, that the faculties of civic colleges acquired considerable powers, and that their "advice" or "reports" were generally decisive. At Owens the Extension Act of 1870 defined faculty powers in this area. The Senate was to appoint and dismiss occasional lecturers, tutors, etc., at its sole discretion. It was to be consulted by the Council in all professorial and lectorial appointments. Liverpool's Charter followed Owens' lead here as elsewhere, and further clarified the Senate's powers of advice.[36]

These statutory powers recognized what had already become customary. Professorial expertise and familiarity with candidates or their referees made faculty advice obviously desirable. In the appointment of assistants within a professor's field this argument was evidently completely convincing. Owens' Trustees had left such appointments in faculty hands from the beginning,[37] and even at Leeds the less acquiescent Council generally followed this principle.[38]

After 1870 the provision that Senate be consulted in professorial appointments at Owens was taken most seriously as was the resulting advice. By 1873 the Senate had established regulations for consideration of applications, in 1875 it was "short listing" candidates for the Council's consideration, and in 1876 new regulations made this practice statutory.[39] The Council thus chose from among the few candidates the faculty considered most suitable, and even more specific advice from the Senate seems to have been generally accepted. Thus the reality of faculty power over appointments exceeded any minimal interpretation of the statutes;[40] Liverpool and Leeds appear to have followed suit.[41]

The final word on dismissal, as on appointment, lay with the Councils. Yet the faculty's power even here is revealed by statutes. The Owens College Extension Act made dismissal of a professor the only act of Council requiring a larger than usual quorum and majority. Liverpool's statutes went on to define an elaborate system of safeguards and due process to protect the professors. In this area the lack of evidence concerning interpretation only serves to further confirm the faculty's position once appointed. No professor was dismissed from Owens or Liverpool during the period studied, and the Arts and Science professors at Leeds were equally safe in fact. While in theory professors served at the pleasure of Trustees or Councils, in fact the formal tenure of the 20th Century reflected the practical fact of the 19th.[42]

Finance

Finance was less completely amenable to faculty control. The statutory duties of Councils, and especially of trustees and treasurers, centred on this area, as perhaps did their inclination to exert some power. Yet even here the faculty acquired powerful influence, an acquisition which deserves study, since all students of university affairs recognize the ultimate nature of the power and sanction of the purse.[43] The controllers of finance are the court of last resort. Well before the 20th Century, and long before British governments came to provide the majority of funds, university and college faculties had acquired sufficient influence over budgets to ensure their practical control of the universities at least until the 1960s.

The faculty held several strong cards in the financial game. The first was their considerable influence over that fundamental determinant of expenditure, income. Professors' regular and successful fund-raising efforts have already been described (see Ch. 5). They were also consulted about the fees to be charged. At Owens, revisions in 1858 and 1859 were based on faculty recommendations, and reports from the Senate and Registrar formed the basis of another revision in 1871.[44] The faculties' control of curriculum and influence over its expansion constituted considerable power over immediate and long-term expenditure. As early as 1860 Owens' trustees accepted a faculty recommendation to establish a chair of physics,[45] and by the mid-70s the Senate was leading a willing Council down the path of curricular expansion toward university status.[46]

The importance of chemistry and the rise of physics, engineering and technical subjects meant large expenditures on equipment and supplies which could only be selected and evaluated by faculty professionals. University College, Liverpool was following a well-worn path[47] when it directed its first physics professor to select £500 worth of equipment (the grant was soon enlarged) and a demonstrator at a salary of £100.[48] Professors of chemistry and other subjects soon received similar powers.[49] Libraries represented another growing, professionally defined, expenditure. By 1870 Owens had an annual library budget fully controlled by the faculty.[50]

At all the colleges the faculties' control of the conditions and award of scholarships and prizes involved increasing sums. As well as helping to define the curriculum, control of this money allowed faculties to "buy" the students they wanted. By the 80s Owens also boasted research fellowships under faculty control,[51] giving the faculty an essentially financial power over the direction and repute of the college.

Faculty expertise and constant efforts on behalf of their institutions thus gave them wide powers of control or customarily accepted advice. These are easily summarized from the records of Liverpool for 1884. That spring the Senate's recommendations and choices for salaries, raises, guest lecturers, and two new professors were all approved by the Council, apparently with little or no discussion.[52]

The faculty contributed heavily to the evolution of college budgets. Annual budgets as we know them were not a feature of the colleges' earliest years; expenditure at Owens in the 50s and 60s, Leeds in the 70s, and Liverpool in the 80s was based mostly on *ad hoc* grants. Budgets seem to have arisen from Council's growing habit of requesting estimates of expenditure from faculties.[53] This habit was increasingly formalized, and annual grants to professors and departments resulted.[54] Acceptance of the faculties' estimates also became customary. At Liverpool in 1888 a "Special Finance Committee" summarized the advantages of fixed annual sums for maintenance and an end to private salary arrangements: these would permit easier calculation *by the professors*, stabilize the finances, and eliminate much consideration by the Council.[55] The full-time experts had, naturally enough, captured the budget making process.

Principals

The Colleges' Principals were immensely important, by virtue of both their formal office and their individual personalities. They possessed the same professional and expert status as other professors, plus additional powers peculiar to their positions. As chief academic officer the Principal could unify the faculty and then represent them to the council, and vice versa. When he became an *ex officio* member of the Council and head of the Senate he was the only person constantly informed of both the public and confidential business of each. The apparent anomaly of being simultaneously an agent of both faculty and council evidently led to no practical difficulties. In part this no doubt resulted from the customary mutual tolerance of the groups; it could be further insured through the Principal's executive powers and administrative skills.

The Owens Trustees, following the advice they had solicited,[56] appointed a Principal immediately. They then consulted him about a wide variety of matters, and by 1858, when the efficient Greenwood had replaced the aging Scott, the Principal was regularly attending the Trustees' meetings.[57] Statutory recognition of this logical[58] arrangement came in 1870 when the Owens College Extension Act made the Principal an *ex officio* member of the new Council.

The executive duties of a Principal grew with his institution, as Trustees and Council members had limited time, while the positions of registrar and bursar only grew slowly to their present dimensions. At Owens from 1859 on the day-to-day business of the College progressively disappeared from the Trustees' minutes, while the Principal began to set fees, arrange new classes, deal with unsatisfactory faculty, etc.[59] At Liverpool the first Principal soon found himself conducting business ranging from the appointment of demonstrators to the repair and maintenance of buildings.[60]

The successful completion of much of this work depended on the personality, skills, repute, and activity of the man in the job. On the whole the colleges were exceptionally well served. At Owens, Scott possessed an academic and intellectual reputation and commanded the respect of all as both scholar and gentleman. Though his bad health and apparent lack of administrative skills made his tenure less than completely satisfactory, he certainly enhanced the fledgling institution's prestige. He was recognized by the public as a distinguished figure, and by the Trustees as a man to be treated as a social equal and an expert professional, not as a subordinate or mere employee.[61]

His successor, Greenwood, also possessed an academic reputation both at London and Owens, and was personally respected. In addition to these qualities, which Scott had possessed, he added formidable administrative skills and tremendous energy for the work of committees, meetings, etc.[62] His relationship with the faculty was excellent, and he and Professor Roscoe formed an alliance which cut across disciplinary boundaries and assured a comfortable relationship between the older arts and the newer sciences at Owens.[63] It also represented the alliance of two dynamic and formidable characters, and the efficiency of the partnership and the growth of college business were both being recognized when Roscoe was elected Vice-Principal in 1873 and began to receive responsible administrative tasks from the Council in 1874.[64]

By the late 60s Greenwood's skills were also recognized by a broader public. In 1868 the Manchester *Free Lance* found him an effective teacher and inspiring leader, and was particularly impressed with his business acumen.[65] Cultivating the images of both individual and college was undoubtedly a major duty which Greenwood attended to constantly; he was particularly careful to answer all reasonable questions about the college which arose in the public press, and to redress any widespread grievances among students.[66]

At Liverpool the position of the first Principal derived from a constitution modelled on Owens', and included such statutory powers as membership of the Council, presidency of the Senate, and control over admissions.[67] To these were soon added all those practical accretions which professional skill and diligence made inevitable.

The constant attention of the Principals, and of the faculty in general, to College business gave them exceptional influence in Councils and committees.[68] Between 1881 and 1890 the Liverpool University College Council generally had four or five members who attended most Council meetings and sat on several committees. Principal Rendall was always one, accompanied first by Professor Campbell-Brown and Professor Hele-Shaw. Thus the faculty always formed a substantial minority of the inner circle of the Council, and the Principal was supported by his unparalleled continuity of office and attendance rate as well as by his expertise. In addition, the laymen of the inner circle were men apparently congenial to the faculty as well as committed to the College.

An analysis of attendance at Owens' Council and committee meetings from 1870-1884 is equally revealing. The primacy of the Principal is unquestionable: Greenwood attended more Council and committee meetings than anyone else in all but one of those years. Alfred Nield, the Treasurer, coupled equal continuity with the second highest attendance rate. In the early years certain laymen on the Council had nearly equal attendance records but the sheer numerical predominance of the Principal and Treasurer increased steadily after 1875 as fewer and fewer members attended fewer and fewer meetings. The relative statistical weight of the professoriate also increased. Among the seven or eight men who appeared most often at Council and committee meetings in each year, Greenwood was joined by one other professor in the early 70s, by at least two colleagues thereafter, and by three, forming a majority of the "inner council", in 80-81 and 83-84.

Special circumstances might also enhance a faculty's position. The most obvious case was the Owens' evening classes. These developed through the amalgamation of some evening courses held at the discretion of the professors with a Working Men's College, modelled on F. D. Maurice's foundation in London, in which Owens' faculty had been intimately involved.[69] It appears that the Owens Trustees therefore viewed the large and important evening classes as peculiarly the professors' province. In 1864, for example, the professors thoroughly rearranged the schedules, fees, etc., of the evening classes and then received *post facto* approval from the Trustees with little debate.[70]

Given the faculty's expertise and diligence, it was natural that they be consulted whenever exceptional measures were considered. At Owens faculty recommendations had been accepted during the crisis of the mid-50s and the college had subsequently prospered.[71] In addition to this encouraging precedent the mere quantities of planning and activity required by the Extension movement dictated heavy reliance on full-time personnel, expertise aside. As early as 1865 the faculty were reporting on proposed buildings to the Trustees, and in 1866 they provided equally detailed reports on extension of the curriculum.[72] From then on faculty advice fills the minutes of the Extension Committee, and it seems to have been both solicited and accepted. Professors drafted plans for everything from the physical plant to amalgamation with the medical school. The public meetings which advertised and solicited funds for Extension were customarily addressed by faculty members, the general Extension Committee included all the professors, and they were represented on all executive committees.[73] The faculty had already earned and established the powerful place which was granted to it in the new constitution (Owens College Extension Act, 1870).

The necessity for faculty participation in extraordinary planning and decision-making was summarized by the Yorkshire College professors in 1877.[74] Concerned with their inadequate representation on a Plans Committee for new buildings, they pointed out the need for their expertise, the impossibility of delegating or simplifying the necessary activity, and the fact that their professional reputations were bound up with the suitability of the decisions taken. Somewhat grudging notice was taken of their arguments, and a "Consulting Committee" comprised of all the professors was formed.[75]

The Case of Leeds

In their representations to the Honorary Secretary of the Yorkshire College the professors also complained of the inadequate notice given to the faculty of the creation of this vital committee, a reminder that faculty/lay relations at the College were not nearly so harmonious as they were elsewhere. The importance of many of the factors discussed above (notably a strong Principal, enough professors of high social standing, and respect for faculty competence in developing academic self-government) is revealed by their absence or weakness at Leeds, and the problems which resulted. For more than a decade a determined if not always united body of laymen retained general and detailed control of the College, successfully resisting faculty pressures at the expense of frequent if usually mild conflict. Only the desire for admission to the Victoria University, with its faculty-based government, seems to have moved the Yorkshire College Council to give the faculty some of what Owens and Liverpool men had easily achieved and often taken for granted.[76]

The minutes of both the Council and the "Academic Board" or proto-Senate reveal the Council's constant insistence on detailed oversight and interference. Perhaps minor slights rankled as much as major problems: the Academic Board objected to such matters as laymen's proposal of scholarship candidates without faculty advice, Council's insistence that it should arrange "Local Lectures" by faculty members, and its assertion of control over such matters as the choice of prize books and all expenditures in excess of £2.[77]

Laymen at Leeds clung tenaciously to power and were far more inclined to treat their professors as employees than were Councils and Trustees elsewhere. The faculty's struggle for the right to *advise* (see above) makes it easy to imagine the lay reaction to faculty *control*! The tone was set from the first: where Owens had immediately delegated "academic control" to the Principal, advised by the faculty, Leeds chose to give similar authority to a committee containing the professors and four Council members, chaired by the Chairman of the Council, and with all other Council members allowed to take part.[78]

The absence of a principal no doubt exacerbated difficulties of communication and status in the early years at Leeds. The growing amount and complexity of business made an executive officer increasingly necessary as time went on, but both finances and differences of opinion postponed an appointment. The Council's first proposals in 1877 were confined to the temporary appointment of an acting Principal, with a nominal addition to his professorial salary, and without the right of attendance at Council meetings. The faculty's reaction was evidently both negative and pronounced, leading to some concessions and a rotating, honorary Principalship until 1882, when the College appointed an able and respected Principal, Nathan Bodington, who slowly began to tread the same path as his colleagues at Liverpool and Manchester.[79]

The Yorkshire College's weak financial position may have been an even larger source of friction. Leeds was less well supported than Manchester and Liverpool, and it may well have been this as much as lack of respect for the professors which kept such detailed oversight of expenditure in the Council's hands. On the other hand, the Council's constant refusal to admit professors to the finance committee argues strongly for a less flattering interpretation of their motives.[80] In spite of the presence of Sir Edward Baines perhaps this was simply a less liberal, cosmopolitan, and educationally experienced governing body than those at Owens and University Colleges, which contained so many men like the Thompsons, Heywoods, Rathbones, and Musgraves.

The peculiar and inadequate financing of the arts subjects at Leeds is evidence of other problems. The Yorkshire College of Science had been founded with an obvious technical bias, and the foundation professors were scientists. Arts and their professors were added sporadically, and financed from a "Literature Fund" whose maintenance was even more tenuous than the general finances. Arts faculty thus possessed little demonstrable prestige or security of tenure in the eyes of the Council. (Within the faculty they were always treated as equals,[81] while the scientists worked steadily to further Arts teaching.) In fact the scientists also apparently possessed little status in the eyes of some laymen, which must have galled the three foundation professors, who came from the different atmospheres of Oxford, Cambridge, and Glasgow. As for technical subjects, they might be emphasized, but the treatment of their teachers was predictable. Their general status is discussed above, and in addition this was an area in which many wealthy citizens of Leeds might feel themselves, and actually be, as expert as their academic "employees".

Efficient government and smooth development were also hindered by divisions outside the academic camp. A faction strongly in favour of the Arts was led by Sir Edward Baines. These were the supporters of the "Literature Fund", and also of its eventual amalgamation with the general finances of the college. The opposing faction, among whom Sir Andrew Fairbairn was perhaps most prominent, demanded a continued emphasis on science and technology and feared the financial burden as well as the shifting emphasis that would come with equal status for the Arts departments. Even the lure of admission to the Victoria University did not entirely ease these fears: as late as 1886 the Board of Governors recommended seeking admission to Victoria "... provided that no engagement be entered into to increase the Staff of the Arts Department, or if, after conference with the Victoria University, an extension of teaching should be deemed desirable, that it shall be in the subject of modern languages ..." and that such steps should be taken only when capital funds were increased to cover them.[82] Only in May of 1888 was the "Literature Fund" finally amalgamated with the rest of the College's finances,[83] and by that time Victoria University rather than local influences may have been responsible.

In general, all the influences which quickly produced faculty government elsewhere were weaker at Leeds. The later and less complete acceptance of faculty expertise, advice, and control is perhaps best seen in the Minutes of the Academic Board. In addition to the frictions discussed above, there appears to have been a constant undercurrent of misunderstanding and potential mistrust between faculty and laymen, largely as a result of the inevitable failures of communication resulting from the lack of faculty representation on the governing body.[84] Presumably what prevented greater and potentially disastrous friction was mutual concern for the College: in December of 1880 the Council was thanking the professors for their £500 gift to the Building Fund.[85] By 1882 the Academic Board appears to have settled down to dealing with the regular business of the College, but with nothing like the freedom possessed by the Senate at Owens College.[86]

Governance at Leeds looked different. Many benefactors and governors wanted a technical institute, not a university college.

The faculty was handicapped by the lack of a Principal and of a full complement of professors of prestigious subjects. A shoestring budget exacerbated every difficulty. Professional expertise and steady application were slowly winning the faculty a substantial place in the college, but apparently a smaller one than elsewhere. In fact, however, the model first evolved at Owens College, and embodied in the Victoria University, was already too strong and prestigious to be resisted. If Leeds wanted status, and particularly degrees, it had to conform. And this was the easier because the means were already there. It was merely a question of overcoming resistance, not of creating previously unknown attitudes and organization.

At Liverpool little effort was required to produce conformity. With ample funds, agreed purpose, sympathetic non-academics and, no doubt, the example of Owens' success, it had travelled far along the road to academic power in the few years before it joined the Victoria University.

Constitutions and De Facto Powers

This study of governance has deliberately given little attention to the formal organs of government and the constitutions which defined their powers. Not only were practice, interpretation, and custom more important than statute, as is so often the case in England, but statute tended to recognize what had already become reality.

The formal organs of faculty representation and power evolved over thirty years at Owens, and in general they recognized accomplished facts. A proto-Senate, the College Meeting, arose from the already ingrained habits of faculty discussion (after all there were only a handful of professors) and of consultation of the faculty on matters of importance. The parlous state of enrolment's by the mid-50s led to a series of faculty reports to the Trustees. Included were at least two proposals for regular meetings of faculty and Principal, and the suggestion that they report regularly to the Trustees.[87] These suggestions were adopted and the recommendations of subsequent meetings concerning changes in entrance exams and fees were immediately accepted,[88] thus beginning, or rather transferring to a formal body, the tendency toward faculty control. By 1857 the decision of a majority of the professors in concurrence with the Principal was to be valid unless subsequently annulled by the

Trustees;[89] after that the day-to-day business of the College steadily disappeared from the Trustees' Minutes.

The Extension scheme made a new and more complete constitution necessary. This was provided by the Owens College Extension Act and subsequent Bye-Laws, which defined the powerful position of the Faculty, now embodied in a Senate. The 1869 draft of the Act, and the faculty's comments, solicited by the Trustees, are most revealing.[90] The Senate was given broad powers over "Education and Discipline", particularly in matters of curriculum and examination, scholarships and prizes, admissions, and even the employment of junior faculty. Their right to advise on all matters was also recognized. In reply the Faculty requested powers of expulsion and various alterations of detail, but "recognize most entirely the considerable share of power and independent action which the draft proposes to give them."[91] In fact, as the preceding pages have indicated, what they saw was formal recognition of powers they already exercised and would extend further.

The authorship of the constitution which was embodied in the Owens College Extension Act is a further testimonial to the faculty's position. In 1869 the Extension Committee entrusted the drafting of the new constitution to a faculty member whose skill was likely to make the faculty's position legally impregnable, and the constitution the model for many future ones. The Act of 1870 may be considered one of the first of James Bryce's influential writings.[92]

It certainly influenced the founders of University College, Liverpool. Their Charter not only gave the same powers to the same officers and bodies as at Owens; it also did so in nearly identical language. Owens College's steadily growing size, wealth, efficiency, and repute made it an almost irresistible model. Leeds resisted somewhat longer. A formally constituted Senate only appeared in 1884, and its powers, and those of the Principal, were less than at Manchester. But membership of the Victoria University, achieved in 1887, meant increasing assimilation to the Manchester model, since the federal university itself was immensely influenced by its first and most important constituent.

By 1900, when the Victoria University dissolved into its constituent parts, both the formal constitution and the actual practices first developed by Owens College had been tested and found satisfactory. The new University of Birmingham had adopted a very similar system; Manchester, Liverpool, and Leeds did not significantly alter their internal arrangements when they parted company;

and newer colleges followed the trend. They have continued to do so. The 20th Century universities of Britain, the Empire, and the Commonwealth have followed what by now seems this traditional course.

7

The Colleges and Their Environment

In order to succeed the civic colleges had to make places for themselves in Victorian society. Developing good relations with a wide range of people and organizations was a necessity. The colleges became part of a spreading network of intellectual, educational, and cultural institutions via interlocking directorates, shared facilities and personnel, and mutual support of various kinds. If they were to fulfill the founders' and faculties' intentions they needed to attract students to a new sort of higher education, at first accepting such students as were available, but working to create a potential student body interested in and prepared to receive this innovative instruction. This involved attention to such varied subjects as scholarships, the quality of secondary schools, and the development of public examinations.

Growth, prestige, and public support all required a broad base, and the colleges steadily expanded their range of services and persons served. Evening classes at low prices extended higher education beyond the comfortable middle class. The incorporation of medical schools linked the colleges to a powerful profession and to an important service function in society. The colleges also incorporated both the cultural roles and the clienteles of the museums and intellectual societies which they absorbed from time to time.

In search of prestige and efficiency the colleges collaborated among themselves and with the older institutions of higher education. At the same time they sought to control their own destinies and to attract students by acquiring university status with its power to grant degrees. This involved the consent, if not the active participation, of government. The Owens, Yorkshire, and University colleges linked themselves in a federal university in order to establish their position, offer a full range of services and certifications, and strive for parity with the older institutions.

Links were established with an extraordinary number of societies and institutions. The offer by a college of the use of a room, hall, or lab was a common encouragement to good will and familiarity. Space was provided for dozens of associations including: the Ladies Education Association, the Liverpool Teachers' Guild, the Technical Education Association, the Church Schools Association, the Biblical Archaeological Association, the Iron and Steel Institute, the Women's Literary Society, the Society of Chemical Industry, the St. Johns Ambulance Brigade, the Priestley Club of Leeds, and the Manchester German Gymnasts.[1] In the 80s wider renown was encouraged when the colleges played hosts to the great meetings of societies like the British Medical Association and the British Association for the Advancement of Science.

Closer relationships were also common. Members of the Leeds Geological Society and Naturalists' Field Club went on Professor Green's "weekly excursions" for a small fee. At Liverpool the College and its professors were instrumental in founding and supporting the Marine Biology Committee which created an important centre of research. Owens was well represented when the Society of Arts, in London, discussed industrial and scientific education.[2] The colleges provided services to associations and communities, examining students and pupil teachers, awarding prizes, and lecturing to a wide range of societies and classes at home and in neighbouring towns.[3] By 1881 Owens found it convenient to establish standardized procedures for the loan of apparatus. The service relationships might also work the other way: Liverpool borrowed lithographs from the Arundel Society; Leeds regularly thanked industrial firms for loans of equipment and tours of works.

Links with local government were obviously necessary. Support in the form of municipal resolutions and public meetings was always available. More tangible support ranged from the willingness of Manchester and Chorlton-on-Medlock to macadamize roads to reduce noise to Liverpool's provision of a site for University College.

The Owens and Yorkshire Colleges' close relations with the press, especially with Scott's *Guardian* and Baines' *Mercury*, have been discussed. The newspapers supported the colleges' efforts, the editors were intimate with the faculties and governors, and the papers' correspondence columns were effectively used by Principals and professors. University College also benefitted from friendly publicity and support.[4] The foundation of the college was reported *in extenso*, as elsewhere. The *Daily Post* and the *Daily Mercury* were particularly interested in and sympathetic to the College: they reported its affairs and supported its efforts throughout the 80s. The College's beneficial effect on the community was a constant theme, and one whose elaboration involved specific support for business classes, chemistry, etc., as well as general statements about raising the intellectual tone of the city and providing a capstone for the local system of education. Support ranged across such varied fields as the value of higher education for women, always available at University College, the need for new buildings to alleviate overcrowding (a mark of success) and favourable reviews of the college's new literary magazine. All in all, the press served effectively to define, publicize, and perhaps enlarge and improve the colleges' positions in their surrounding communities.

All these relationships were encouraged, even made possible, by the close-knit nature of each city's intellectual and political elite. Important examples of interlocking memberships and directorates can be found in Chapter 5; the list could be vastly extended. Colleges encouraged the process by electing political and other officials to their governing bodies. By 1890 Leeds' list of "Representative Governors" included men from ten schools, the Corporation and the School Board of Leeds, six intellectual societies, and the Worshipful Company of Cutlers of Sheffield.[5]

Schools

Perhaps most important were the ties with local networks of educational institutions. The colleges' general purposes in developing these connections were summed up by the Victoria University when it offered a scheme for affiliating local institutions: "... by the establishment of such a connection the efficiency of the institutions in question may be increased, a waste of power prevented, and a greater degree of unity and solidity given to many educational efforts in this part of the country."[6] Assistance to school boards and local forms of adult and popular education was always provided.[7] Mechanics institutes and other institutions which might prepare working men for the colleges' evening classes were viewed with especial favour; their students received fee reductions, and scholarships were created. Other local efforts to provide science teaching, evening classes, etc. were supported by the colleges' faculty and governors.[8]

The education of teachers naturally received attention. While early efforts to affiliate the colleges with government training school schemes foundered on the rocks of professorial independence and a reluctance to do elementary teaching, by the late 80s an assortment of evening and Saturday schoolmasters courses and scholarships were being consolidated into regular forms of affiliation with government and private training colleges for teachers. Secondary education received special attention. From the very first the colleges recognized that the deficiencies of local secondary education were the greatest obstacle in the path of offering higher education, and they hoped that through example, entrance examinations, exhortation, and assistance they could raise the level of secondary schools.[9] The process was necessarily slow, and at one point Owens seriously considered establishing its own school to prepare potential students.[10]

Another means of setting and raising standards in secondary education was the developing system of Oxford and Cambridge Local Examinations, often significantly called "Middle Class Examinations". The colleges provided halls for these exams, and for the London Matriculation which also became a mark of high attainments in secondary education, and further encouraged the system by offering scholarships to high-scoring candidates.

The colleges made advice and equipment available to secondary schools and provided courses suitable for their staff. In some cases professors even gave courses of lectures at secondary institutions. As the Charity Commissioners overhauled more and more grammar schools and other educational foundations the colleges found themselves electing members of the governing bodies of dozens of grammar schools and other educational trusts. As Principals and professors were usually chosen, this gave the colleges a close and powerful oversight over much of the local supply of secondary education.

The local grammar schools were most important sources of well-prepared students, and the colleges sought good relations. Unfortunately schools like Leeds Grammar and the Royal Institute School at Liverpool sometimes saw the colleges as *competition* for the best students, especially those preparing for Oxbridge.[11] The colleges eventually solved the problem by elevating their levels of work and entrance requirements; in the meantime University College encouraged students to remain at school.[12]   Scholarships formed important links between colleges and grammar schools; Liverpool Institute students won a scholarship a year in the 80s, while Owens advertised the exhibitions available to students of Manchester Grammar, and had induced a steady and growing flow from that source by the 80s.

Scholarships and prizes added to the general attractiveness of the colleges and also served more specific purposes in attracting particular types of students or encouraging particular studies. Scholarships were offered for women, for artisans, and for students from a wide variety of schools.[13] Evening class scholarships and exhibitions encouraged the working class.   In 1880 Owens was offering scholarships and prizes to reward proficiency and encourage further study in classics, English, mathematics, Greek Testament, political economy, history, engineering, physiology, natural history, and law.   As they matured, the colleges were increasingly able to offer substantial fellowships, like the Langton and Bishop Berkeley at Manchester and the Sheridan Muspratt Chemical Scholarship at Liverpool, to encourage advanced study and research. The number of scholarships at each college at least kept pace with its growth.

Students

The colleges were determined to serve, and if necessary, to shape, a particular type of student. They were intended primarily for the middle classes, and their course offerings and fees were designed with this in mind. A survey of students' parentage undertaken at Owens in 1867 reveals the success of this design: 73 of 113 day students were sons of merchants, manufacturers, professionals, and persons of independent means, while another 20 were of "the trading classes".[14]

The next concern was the students' age: the colleges regretted the practical necessity of admitting students of 14 and 15, and made every effort to encourage longer school attendance, using entrance examinations and regulations for this purpose. The major hindrance apart from the want of secondary facilities was that late admission deferred entrance into business or other remunerative employment. By the later 70s the attractions of the colleges, the improvement of secondary education, and the increased social and economic value of advanced education were apparently overcoming these problems. Owens College first reduced the percentage of students under 18 below 50% in 1870-71, and entrants under 16 were a rarity by 1872.[15]. This satisfied not only the faculty but also those critics who had tended to describe the colleges as glorified schools. The maturity of students was also an important argument in justifying claims to university status.

Greater maturity meant better preparation, particularly as the colleges' efforts to improve secondary education bore fruit. The colleges steadily divested themselves of their more elementary studies. By 1895 at Owens when 36% of the new students came from a grammar or public school and another 10% had received some higher education,[16] a recognizably university-type clientele had clearly been created.

The colleges also worked, with less immediate success, to encourage the taking of a regular, full-length course leading to a degree. The increasing demand for this form of certification worked in their favour, but throughout the first decade of the Victoria University the vast majority of students in the three constituent colleges sought only some lesser qualification or some more specific information or instruction, in spite of incentives to prolonged and regular study which included prizes and reduced fees.[17] As graduation, and the customarily resulting alumni records, remained relatively rare and scarce, the exact purposes of students and results of their studies can only be inferred from the information on demand provided in Chapter 4.

Throughout the 19th Century the vast majority of students were apparently local, a natural result of the colleges' newness, nonresidential character, and deliberate efforts to serve their own cities and region. Leeds was pleased to report that it attracted students from throughout Yorkshire. By the late 70s Owens' size and reputation had at least begun the slow process of enlarging its catchment area. The records of the Friends Hall, established near Owens and approved by the college, reveal the beginnings of cosmopolitanism. Quakers and others came to reside from an extraordinary variety of places. A majority of the 16-18 students in residence at any time were from distant parts of England and Ireland, while students from Calcutta and New Zealand gave an imperial flavour to the list.[18]

The colleges found the creation of a disciplined student body surprisingly easy. There were never any major disturbances comparable to Oxbridge "rags" or Continental riots. Perhaps the generally disciplined character of the Victorian middle and upper working classes had something to do with this, as certainly did the fact that a majority of students lived at or near home and were under familial constraint and discipline. There were of course some exceptions to Greenwood's usual description of student conduct at Owens as "unexceptionable". These infrequent outbursts usually involved drink, rarely theft or women, a proportion which no doubt still obtains today. The rising age and maturity of students produced a corresponding change in disciplinary style. Where Owens' detailed regulations in the 50s demonstrated the college's position in loco parentis, by the time University College was founded a simple code similar to today's was found sufficient.[19]

Though working with some new materials, the colleges were trying to create a fairly traditional form of student, recognizable at Oxbridge then and at British universities today. The student whose age, preparation, or intentions were peculiar might be accepted, but he was then encouraged to conform to the norm, not make a unique contribution. Some diversity was of course tolerated, though less as the colleges became more popular and respected, and hence able to dictate to their potential clientele. The preferences of the new civic colleges became the predominant practice of the mature civic universities. In the interim, however, the colleges made good use of the flexibility which went with newness and a lack of fixed tradition.

Evening Studies

The colleges knew that the numbers of regular, middle class students age 16 to 20 would remain quite small for some years. Evening classes offered a chance to broaden the scope of the colleges' clientele and services, as well as increasing total enrolments. The idea was by no means new: educational and philanthropic efforts had been providing increasing amounts of adult and technical education since the 30s, ranging from elementary literacy to the moderately advanced classes of some mechanics institutes and new technical schools.[20] The colleges hoped to cap this rather haphazard edifice with increasingly advanced courses which might even lead to a university degree.[21] In providing these services the colleges could expect support from the accustomed and established advocates of "continuing" education.[22]

Their intentions were not solely altruistic. Every effort was made to propagate the middle class science of political economy, including the endowment of prizes and the provision of free admission to lectures. The results were limited, which is not surprising in light of the doctrines professed: Jevons' attacks on strikes provoked a spirited exchange in the local newspapers, and were hardly likely to encourage working class interest in the subject as then taught. More general, and perhaps more attractive intentions were summarized in a statement of the purposes of the Working Men's College, which was soon to be absorbed into the Owens evening classes. It spoke of the removal of class distinctions through freer social intercourse, and went on: "The number of cultivated working men being increased, a necessary modification will result in our social condition, and the relations of the country as a whole will be affected by it." Presently less appealing, but perhaps more soothing to the employing classes, was a later statement of intent: "We do not propose to take working men from their own proper sphere of duty ... they wil learn the true worth and dignity of their calling, and will fear to debase it ...."[23]

The Yorkshire College defined the desired clientele and purpose of the evening classes: "... the diffusion of knowledge and the awakening of new interests in classes of whom the traditional academic learning of England has generally taken too little account."[24] This covered a very wide range given the very narrow definition of traditional academic education in the Victorian era. Obvious barriers were poverty, social standing, religion, and previous education. Equally significant, especially in the great Northern cities, was the tendency to enter business or commerce at a very early age; this portion of the middle class, particularly the lower levels of white collar workers, was as effectively barred from the traditional higher education as artisans and labourers. The classes at Owens were intended to offer "thorough and patient study, after strict academical methods ... to young men of all ranks whose occupations prevent their attendance in our ordinary classes."[25]

The hours and subjects of the classes would be adjusted in response to demands; but "strict academical methods" would be maintained. The colleges' faculties intended to offer *higher* education only, even at the expense of popularity.[26] This, after all, was in keeping with their professional dignity, the original plans of the colleges, and their intention to provide a capstone, not a competing part, of continuing education. It also made the evening classes a useful step on the way to full time study.[27] Scholarships to the day classes were offered to exceptional evening students; exhibitions to the evening classes were offered in conjunction with a variety of firms, schools, mechanics institutes, etc. In this way a student might, and occasionally did, rise from an elementary school background to a university degree. Such successes were acclaimed at public meetings and in the college calendars.

Mere numbers made the evening classes important to the Colleges. They gave an appearance of usefulness and success in the early years when other enrolments were small, and this appearance encouraged both support and new enrolments. Evening classes also provided faculty members with an often small but no doubt useful supplement to their salaries, as well as a sense of contribution to education and the community. Many courses were taught at the faculty's request even when small numbers made the remuneration derisory. Owens began to offer evening classes "designed to lay a foundation of accuracy and method for reading and inquiry ..."[28] in the session 1853-54. Natural history and history were added to the "Schoolmasters' Classes" in classics and mathematics begun the year before at "the request of a large number of persons, actually engaged in teaching ...."[29] Numbers rose, English, jurisprudence, and chemistry were soon offered, and by 1859 "the range of evening instruction was made co-extensive with that of the Ordinary Classes."[30]

In 1861 Owens more than doubled the size of its evening classes[31] by absorbing the Working Men's College which had been founded in 1858, largely by Owens professors and others who supported both institutions. The WMC had offered intermediate and higher education at very cheap rates, after the fashion of Frederick Maurice's foundation in London.[32] Its very complete records[33] and the ease with which it was assimilated by Owens make it a good example of the early years of an evening program.[34] (It may have been more exclusively working class-oriented than the colleges' programs: Owens agreed to a considerable reduction of evening fees when the amalgamation took place.) A first burst of enthusiasm (231 enrolments) was quickly followed by a decline, with less than a hundred students after three years. This may well have represented a potentially steady state, as classes per student, which had quickly dropped from 2.24 to a low of 1.38, had then climbed steadily to 1.58, a ratio which remained typical of Owens evening classes for the next ten years. Teachers, librarians, and shopkeepers formed a small proportion of students, "operatives" provided from 25 to 30%, a proportion considered too low by the founders and faculty, while the lowest branches of the black-coated middle class, "clerks, bookkeepers, warehousemen, etc.", provided 46 to 66%. English, Latin, Chemistry, History, and Maths were the most consistently popular subjects, roughly in that order. Continuity of enrolment was insufficient to satisfy the founders, but nearly a third of the third year students had been continuously enrolled, and a few seemed headed toward eventual degrees or other qualifications.

This would seem to be a typical picture of the evening students. The majority sought some portion of a liberal education or instruction in a science. Most took one or two courses for a year or two. This might be both a practical and a rewarding endeavour: enhancing status, employability, or self-respect; increasing the skills of a teacher, foreman, artisan, or clerk.[35] Smaller numbers sought university degrees, a more complete education, or admission to the day classes, possibly through the exhibitions offered to successful evening students or by preparing for such major schemes as the Whitworth scholarships. By the mid-60s Owens, aware of student demands and preparation, had created a successful formula through deliberate trial, experimentation, and amalgamation. While constantly encouraging prolonged and thorough study, they accepted the lesser role as well. In fact the formula was so successful that evening numbers were double those of day students for the succeeding decade.

Throughout the 70s Owens continued to note the problems of short-term attendance and limited interests among evening students, but the college was increasingly pleased with the successes of those students who did take examinations and acquire degrees.[36] The move into new buildings in 1873 produced a tremendous increase in student numbers as well as a rise from one-and-a-half to around one-and-three-quarter classes per student. Modern subjects increased their share of enrolments, and had outstripped classics by 1875. Numbers fell off slightly at the end of the 70s but this appears to have reflected the maturity of both the college and the community. Improvements in secondary education and the increased differentiation and specialization of education allowed the college to shed those courses and students which were incompatible with its image and intentions. The continued popularity of classics coupled with the steadily increasing demand for modern languages and physical sciences suggests that the college was meeting a substantial demand for cultivation and useful knowledge at an advanced level.[37]

Medical Schools and Museums

The colleges enlarged their scope by absorbing entire institutions with their members, clientele, and functions. The most important incorporations were of medical schools. The details of acquisition varied but the benefits sought and the eventual results were the same everywhere.[38] In their day, in the first half of the 19th Century, the proprietary medical schools had represented a successful effort of the medical profession to unite its members and increase their status and competence, but by the 70s and 80s limited resources and part-time staffs were unable to meet the need for new subjects and new facilities, and the growing demand for degrees. Amalgamation with Owens in the 70s gave the Manchester medical school access to excellent labs, arts teaching, and the permanent and professional character and discipline of collegiate education. Joining Yorkshire and University Colleges in the 80s offered the additional benefit of their likely admission to the Victoria University with its degrees.

The colleges also benefitted. They acquired the property and assets of the schools, though these were usually little beyond collections of specimens and teaching appliances. More important was the influx of regular students attending science classes as well as preparing for their preliminary examinations in the liberal arts. At Liverpool the small numbers of the first four years were doubled by the first influx of medical students, while even the well-established enrolment of Manchester had been increased by 40%. Connections with both the general public and the medical profession were encouraged and likely to grow steadily. The medical schools' relations with the growing networks of hospitals, clinics, and other medical services in the cities linked the colleges to the public and its services. The support of the members of an important and powerful profession was also desirable. At Owens, where the local medical society offered to deposit its valuable library, "second only to Edinburgh...," on condition of continued access and some monetary support, the college noted that: "The close friendly relations which the arrangement can scarcely fail to maintain between the College and so cultivated and influential a section of the community as the Members of the Medical Profession cannot help proving most valuable to the College."[39] Training the members of a much-needed profession must also have increased the colleges' prestige.

The incorporation of local intellectual and scientific societies was usually of minor importance, involving some new supporters and small libraries and collections. One case, that of Owens College's absorption of the Natural History and Geological Societies of Manchester was of considerable importance, however. Their collections were extensive, they possessed some endowments, and the college agreed to create a museum open to the public and was able to attract support for this undertaking.[40] Once established as part of the new range of buildings erected during the 70s, the museum quickly became an important public service. The curator gave demonstrations, public lectures were offered, and by 1877 the College was receiving " ... frequent applications from Mechanics Institutions, Working Men's Natural History Societies, and the like to be allowed to visit the Museum."[41] Old photographs reveal that by the 80s the museum had become one of the recreations of middle class society as well.

Other Universities

The colleges' connections with the rest of British higher education were various. With Oxford and Cambridge they were entirely informal but in many ways pervasive. While characterized in some ways by a reaction against the matter and manner of Oxbridge, the colleges always seem to have had the ancient institutions in mind. Founders defined the purposes of colleges in terms of the traditional universities, and critics and supporters invariably compared the standards and curricula of the civic colleges to those of Oxbridge, whether in praise or derogation of the new. As the major producers of scholars, in the liberal arts and mathematics at least, Oxbridge also trained the vast majority of the new colleges' faculty in those areas. This background, added to the interest in Oxbridge-dominated exams for scholarships, the Civil Service, etc., produced a strong influence upon governance, curriculum, and the less measurable but important matter of style. Owens, Yorkshire, and University Colleges all realized the necessary limits of this influence, however. They never allowed a reverence for academic traditions to override their primary concern with the needs and wants of a middle class and predominantly nonconformist clientele. And they discouraged suggestions and refused tentative offers of formal affiliation and/or subordination to Oxbridge, explaining that their institutions were essentially unique and must ultimately be independent.

Scotland and Ireland provided useful models for imitation and comparison, as well as most of the faculty not trained at Oxbridge. The lecture system of the Scottish universities was recognized as an economical teaching technique. The idea of a professoriate partially remunerated through fees, and thus subject to the checks and sanctions of an academic marketplace, was perhaps congenial to some, and certainly an answer to critics. Equally important, the Scottish and Irish institutions were encouragingly successful models of regional universities appealing to a middle class clientele and, particularly in the Scottish cases, to the aristocracy of labor as well. In addition, the fact that they received recognition and even money from the state provided the newer colleges with an argument for university status and eventual subvention.

Connections with London were the most important. The University of London provided well thought of degrees; even its matriculation examination became a valued qualification. Throughout the second half of the 19th Century the University's prime purpose was to serve as an examining board before whom any candidate might appear. The civic colleges could attract advanced and ambitious students with the promise of preparing them for these degrees. Their students' successes in turn reflected luster on the colleges, testifying to the efficiency and standards of their instruction. Whatever else it may have demanded, and there were endless accusations of requiring "cram" and the acquisition of an undigested smattering of knowledge, London degrees encouraged students and the schools which prepared them to develop a broad range of liberal and scientific studies. Each college in its infancy appreciated the advantages of its relationship with London; each, as it reached maturity, found the relationship increasingly irksome, a hindrance to the independence of faculties and institutions.[42]

The Victoria University

The civic colleges, and especially Owens, had always had great things in mind; John Owens had directed that a university curriculum be offered. By the time Owens' growth and success had produced the Extension movement the idea had become public property: in February of 1867 the *Guardian* printed a letter from Kay-Shuttleworth advocating Owens' expansion into a university in the interests of a higher education for the middle classes which would not divorce them from their origins. This was followed by a leading article supporting Extension to make the College a "provincial university". The *Courier* concurred.[43] Further expansion led the Owens' faculty to assert, in 1874, that: "If account be taken of the kind as well as of the comprehensive range of the teaching given, Owens College may fairly claim to take the same position in relation to its district as the University of Glasgow, for instance, holds in the West of Scotland..." and that degree granting status would perhaps follow.[44]

A year later the Senate had concluded that the College both needed and deserved university status. They and the Council proceeded to issue pamphlets, solicit and analyze expert opinion, combat criticisms, and generally define the position, purpose, and prospects of a civic university[45] with such success that a Royal Charter was obtained in 1880. The variety of supporters revealed both an interest in the expansion of higher education and the developing repute of Owens College in academic circles.[46] Indeed the only serious objections arose in Liverpool and Leeds, where present or potential colleges were threatened with a hopelessly overshadowing competitor. A constitution permitting their federation within the new Victoria University assuaged their fears and assured them of equal advantages. As their size, wealth, and level and range of teaching became adequate they were admitted, Liverpool in 1884 and Leeds in 1887.[47]

Four major arguments were offered in favour of the university plan. They were thoroughly summarized by a committee of Council and Faculty members in 1877.[48] First, the district was capable of supporting a university in point of wealth and numbers. That it was willing was shown by Owens' steady growth in enrolments and endowments, as well as the increasing refinement and expansion of culture in the district. Given the moribundity of Durham, the fact that Oxbridge was more or less antithetical to certain middle class values, and the limited and non-collegiate nature of London University provision, only a local university could provide for an area at least as large and populous as those served by Scottish and Irish universities already chartered and supported by the state. The high tone in which the suitability of Lancashire was often asserted was intended to counter the common assertion that the Northern districts were crude, Philistine, and even vicious; unsuitable realms for a university.

Second: "Owens College is fairly adequate to the assumption of the more dignified position, whether regard be had to its past history and development, to the range and character of its teaching, to its constitution, academic and extra-academic, or (account being taken of its age) to the number of its teachers and its students, and to the amount of its endowments." Ample statistical support of this assertion appeared in the petition to the Privy Council.[49]

The last two arguments were more complex. The college claimed that elevation of rank would improve its efficiency in many ways and also "... greatly extend and strengthen its influence as an independent source of intellectual culture and activity in the district in which it is placed."[50] This meant several things. Encouragement and a higher tone would be imparted to the teaching and research of faculty, and to the efforts of students. The new university would be supported as evidence of the cultural and intellectual maturity of the industrial North. In particular, it would stimulate the local agencies of secondary education by encouraging students to prepare themselves for admission to a convenient university, and providing advanced training and certification for teachers. In a letter supporting Owens' bid the Secretary to the Charity Commissioners said that a university would upgrade the grammar schools of the North which, with the exception of Manchester Grammar, sent few students to any university. A new institution would provide an alternative to Oxbridge or business at age 17. University status would thus further one of Owens College's first and constant intentions.

The most important advantage of a university charter in increasing popularity, prestige, and influence would be the privilege of granting degrees. It would provide both positive advantages and relief from the burdensome restrictions involved in preparing students for London external degrees. This burden loomed so large that it formed the fourth major argument for university status, and produced more faculty comment than any of the others. Existing relations were said to prevent "that rapport between teaching and examining which is necessary to a thoroughly efficient system of instruction." The examinations themselves were said to cover too wide a range of subjects in an eccentric fashion, encourage cram, and represent a test which was simultaneously too difficult yet an insufficient test of thorough education. Furthermore, the external degree did not constitute certification of the receipt of a supervised collegiate education. As the constitution of London made no provision for the representation of provincial institutions there was little likelihood that this situation would improve.[51] While testifying to the good effect of the London influence on a fledgling institution, Manchester was sure that maturity required freedom.

The positive advantages of a charter and degree-granting status were several. The growing demand for degrees and their increasing value on the job market were discussed in Chapter 4. This demand was especially important for the recently amalgamated medical school; a degree meant elite status within the medical profession, and the flood of candidates to Scottish universities[52] revealed the competitive advantages of university status over medical schools which could only prepare for qualifying examinations. One of the first actions of Owens' professors when seeking university status was to prepare a detailed statement rehearsing the needs of the medical profession and the College's capacity to supply these.[53] A charter would also give the faculty the power to create and implement an attractive and complete course of higher education as they and their middle class Northern clientele understood it. Furthermore, the very difficulty involved in acquiring a charter and the rarity of university status would testify to the soundness and distinction of institution, faculty, and studies.

Supporters of the university were unanimously agreed that these benefits could not be obtained through the awarding of a lesser or different certificate. Given the antiquity and repute of the bachelors degree, a new institution of limited repute could not hope to convey similar cachet to any newly created certificate. British experience has since shown the correctness of their estimates both of the attractions and values of bachelors degrees and the inferiority of any other certificates. An alphabet soup of degree substitutes, and the institutions that award them, have spent the 20th Century unsuccessfully attempting to establish their parity with the traditional certificates and the schools which grant them, whether new or old.

Owens accepted a federal constitution as the price of silencing the objections of Liverpool and Leeds to any grant of a charter. The conditions for incorporating a college were "(1) that it has established a reasonably complete curriculum in Arts and Sciences at least; (2) that its means and appliances for teaching are established on a sound basis; and (3) that it is under the independent control of its own governing body."[54] Affiliation was sought to acquire the benefits of university status, particularly degrees. It was urgently sought by Liverpool and Leeds because competition with a degree granting institution would become increasingly difficult, especially in attracting the best students, while achieving entire independence as universities would require much more time and wealth and meet with many objections to the multiplication of institutions. Medical schools had affiliated with the colleges in the hope of offering degrees, and their needs increased the urgency. At Liverpool the process was simple.[55] The college was in many ways modelled on Owens, it had quickly acquired a substantial endowment, and when informal negotiations revealed the need for some expansion of teaching £30,000 was immediately raised to satisfy these demands. Poorer, technically oriented, and lacking unanimity among its own governors and supporters, Leeds found affiliation more difficult. Where Liverpool had ascertained its inadequacies through informal conversations, Leeds made formal application and then learned of its failings. It was eventually admitted in 1887, but, in the words of a modern commentator, it remained "a rather vulnerable poor relation."[56]

The federal university had various effects on its junior partners. They were able to use the possibility of admission to stimulate local support.[57] The tendency to imitate Owens, already strong because of its relative age, success, and prosperity, was increased by the recognition of Owens by both the academic world and the government as deserving of high status. Furthermore, the Owens' faculty and governing bodies naturally formed an influential majority of the officers and members of the new university, and their definition of curricula, degree requirements, etc. were inevitably influenced by the practices of their college.

In spite of differences of degree or specifics, Owens, Yorkshire, and University Colleges all sought essentially similar benefits from University status. The new charter enhanced the colleges' attractions, capacities, and position within their cities and region, Victorian society, and the evolving system of British higher education. Being part of the Victoria University reinforced already pronounced tendencies among the colleges, allowing them to play few new but many enlarged roles. It is time to review the colleges' position in their environment and their importance and influence in the historical development of British higher education.

The Colleges and the Community

As civic colleges Owens, Yorkshire, and University met the needs of the surrounding communities and their members. The growing population of Lancashire and the West Riding was increasingly interested in education, and the growth of facilities and maturity in primary and secondary education culminated logically in locally provided higher education. The sense that education was necessary in the interests of both individuals and society produced elementary education for the poor, middle class secondary schools, technical instruction, and higher education for a growing and newly defined professional, social, and intellectual elite.

The demands of a variety of individuals were studied and catered for by the new colleges. Supports for status and preparation for social mobility were in great demand, and education provided these in several ways. Liberal education was itself a mark of status, as well as adding social cachet to professions. Professional education offered both the chance of social mobility and social defenses for the sons of the bourgeoisie. Technical courses and education for teachers provided routes into the middle classes for the ambitious and intelligent.

College attendance provided economic as well as social returns; indeed the two were growing less distinguishable as class was increasingly defined in economic terms. In addition to the high salaries of professionals and the competitively selected members of the Civil Service, such specific studies as a foreign language, mathematics, or a technical course could lead to promotion for clerks, foremen, and other workers.

The colleges also met the demand for high culture born simply of intellectual curiosity. Fascination with both science and the more traditional learned studies had long marked the middle and upper classes of Northern urban society. Local intellectual societies provided the birth places of many of the colleges themselves. For those seeking the rarefied heights of the intellect, of academia, or even of the Establishment, the colleges could assist a brilliant or persistent student toward Oxbridge. And, by the 80s, they could offer increasing opportunities for research, advanced study, and intellectual employment within their own walls.

The colleges also provided suitable and satisfying outlets for a common form of philanthropic interest, and for commemorative urges. Gifts to the general funds would aid the community at large, while scholarships and the endowing of chairs might support some particular group or study. The amount of energy thus channeled can be seen in the devoted service of many persons to the colleges. Individual needs and demands were often those of the community as well. An educated populace and elite were increasingly seen as necessary to the continued growth of the economy, the success of the increasingly complex and democratic state, and the happiness of society and its members in general. The need for expert professionals was constantly increasing, and in the case of such professions as medicine the connection with the welfare of the community was unmistakable. Though the colleges limited their range of technical subjects, the technical and scientific education which they offered was increasingly appreciated in communities which were beginning to feel the pressure of foreign competition, and to suspect that technological and scientific backwardness were causes of the relative decline in Britain's position.

The colleges were also both a method of expressing local pride and of elevating the tone of local society. The necessity of combatting the coarsening influences of commercial life was a constant theme of influential promoters of colleges, liberal education, and culture generally. The civic college was an important part of the attempt both to create and to publicize the creation of a well-rounded culture in the new industrial and commercial centres of England. It also represented an aspect of this culture which united otherwise disparate groups. Religion and local politics, the two most important public concerns, were divisive in the extreme, but bishops and non-conformists, liberals, incipient laborites, and all but the most obscurantist Tories in the area supported the colleges.

The key to the colleges' success in meeting local needs was their adaptability. Though determined to establish high standards they accepted the necessity of tailoring their lower level teaching to the capacities of available students while making determined and effective efforts to increase those capacities by helping to upgrade secondary education and offering the encouragement of exhibitions, prizes, and scholarships. The curriculum was also adjusted to suit local needs. Textile technology undoubtedly made Leeds a viable institution, while chemistry first established the national and international reputation of Owens not only because it was well taught but because it was well supported and much in demand.

The Colleges and English Higher Education

In addition to their local importance the civic colleges made major contributions to the evolution of the system and the style of English higher education. Here too their adaptability was one essential component. By first accepting a variety of new subjects into their curricula and then being themselves admitted within the pale of university status they substantially broadened the scope of higher education in England. Seeking areas in which to excel outside Oxbridge's dominance in classics and mathematics they placed a strong emphasis on the development of new disciplines, particularly those like chemistry, and later engineering, for which there was a growing demand. In addition to these popular subjects other newly developing areas of academic interest such as English literature, language, and history "got in on the ground floor" at the civic colleges. Their small size made the single professor of a new subject an important figure, thus giving the subject a reasonable chance of growing with the college and becoming eventually an important department of a university. The introduction of new subjects at the ancient universities was usually, contrariwise, hindered by the almost permanent insignificance of scale of any new subject when compared to the old.

Even after the civic universities had reached substantial size the form they had taken in their early years made curricular innovations easier than at Oxbridge. Essentially unified institutions divided into academic departments could subdivide these or add new ones with far less effort than that necessary to establish the position of a new discipline within the intricate and sometimes conflicting bureaucracies of Oxbridge and their colleges.

The exemplary force of the revised curriculum, and the general prestige of the colleges, was reinforced by their intellectual repute. By the end of World War I the civic universities were arguably at the intellectual summit of British higher education, drawing their students from a larger pool of talent than that available to Oxbridge, and excelling in the study and teaching of many subjects. Owens had led in chemistry, as early as the 70s. By the 90s civic colleges were leading the nation in many experimental and technical sciences. The 20th Century saw the addition of supremacy in such fields as history and social sciences.

While the civic colleges increased the adaptability of English higher education and its receptiveness to change, the colleges' limits of adaptability also became those of the system from the 1880s to the 1950s. Their increasing size and growing number absorbed the energy and funds devoted to the expansion of advanced education, and so the formula developed by Owens and the later colleges became the accepted norm for most of higher education. In curricular terms this obviously represented a vast broadening of the old basis of classics and mathematics; the colleges nonetheless imposed limits. A subject must have a well-developed theoretical basis and it must require a rigorous and lengthy period of instruction and study. This made it possible to envision the study as fulfilling the more general purposes of higher education, particularly training the mind and disciplining the individual. Borderline subjects such as technology were acceptable only insofar as they could be made to meet these criteria by emphasizing their theoretical content; Roscoe had insisted that technological chemistry could only be taught upon a foundation of pure chemistry, while the engineering taught in English universities has been called over-theoretical and impractical ever since its inception. The relegation of subjects which did not meet these criteria either to a peripheral place in the universities or outside them became a prominent characteristic of English higher education, particularly when compared with the almost anarchic openness of American colleges and universities to any new study, or to the deliberate and successful attempts of Continental states to create and support high-status institutions offering those subjects relegated to inferiority in England.

The civic college style broadened the range of students as well as studies, but placed limits on this expansion as well. The middle classes, particularly the professional, managerial, and entrepreneurial classes were to be deliberately recruited rather than merely tolerated as in the past. And the ambitious among the labouring classes were to be welcomed and encouraged as well. Yet in many ways the definition of a suitable student did not alter significantly from that of Oxbridge; it was merely that a broader range of candidates could now learn to approximate themselves to it. The preferred student was a late adolescent who had completed an academic secondary education. He should attend full time for the purpose of taking a degree, and at least cloak his more crassly economic interests in a semblance of scholarship. While the evening student remained important to the college and the few mature students were welcomed, all were encouraged to resemble the regular student; fees were reduced for regular as opposed to occasional students, and the best evening students were encouraged to enter the day classes by means of scholarships and no doubt through less formal means. The English system, relying on the efficiency of its universities and their traditions, which in this case were reinforced rather than radically altered by the civic universities, has remained peculiarly resistant to the influx of other categories of students into higher education.

Thus the civic colleges essentially defined the limits of both students and studies in the most prestigious forms of English higher education. They were just sufficiently adaptable to prevent the rise of any really successful rivals. With the traditional clientele still satisfied by Oxbridge and the newly strong classes served by the civic universities, all other forms of higher education were relegated to inferiority of status and support, a position which remained essentially unaltered at least until after World War II. Whether this has done more to protect the standards or to inhibit the development and extension of English higher education is a matter beyond the scope of this study.

The manner in which the civic colleges were created and organized also created or reinforced models and traditions in English higher education. The way in which the colleges were financed is almost unique in the history of education. Only in the United States were larger or similar amounts contributed to universities by private, non-governmental benefactors. In every other European state the 19th Century saw the reorganization or creation of a state-funded, state-sponsored, and state-controlled system of higher education. The civic colleges, and of course Oxbridge, remained predominantly independently funded until well into the 20th Century. Apart from the greater independence inherent in the government's inability to starve a university into submission, the independent character of both the creation and financing of civic universities also made the government less desirous of exercising detailed control. At its simplest this meant that the government did not need to seek detailed accounts of the expenditure of large sums of public money. More complex matters of tradition, precedent, and habit were also involved, however.

No doubt much of the unique character of the relationship between government and higher education in England in the 19th and the first half of the 20th Century is simply due to the general tendency of the British to govern and administer far less than Continental governments. A country whose police forces, sanitary services, hospitals, and schools were all the results of private enterprise, local effort, and philanthropy naturally applied the same techniques and motives to the provision and operation of new universities. But the manner in which the civic colleges were created reinforced as well as reflected the prevailing form of relationship between such institutions and the government. By seeking only recognition for already created institutions they did nothing to encourage or require the creation of a body of administrative or statute regulations of higher education or the bureaucracy necessary to administer them. By the time this recognition came to include charters and the right to grant degrees the colleges were able to seek only the privileges which well-reformed and widely respected ancient institutions already possessed. The government was asked only to grant, never to define or regulate.

The contrast with the circumstances and consequences elsewhere is most instructive. American institutions at this time found no reason or precedent to seek any governmental warrant for their activities. This certainly led to a chaos of dubious credentials but it also permitted practically unlimited innovation. The worth of an institution and its certificates came to be judged entirely on the basis of past and present performance, without concern for precedents or the opinions of established institutions. Continental institutions, on the other hand, found themselves subject to minute regulation particularly in the matter of credentialling, where the degrees awarded were defined, and the necessary examinations prescribed, by the state. As these were generally intended to be identical throughout a country, innovation could only come from the central bureaucracy, not from individual institutions. The creation of the civic universities defined the modern English compromise between these two extremes. In seeking their charters and in expanding their scope thereafter the colleges would use their own judgment. The only formal constraint was that of consideration of their petition for a charter. Thereafter self-imposed constraints similar to the formal ones set the limits of innovation. Standards must be commensurate with those at other institutions, and curricula should not be expanded beyond those subjects widely accepted as academically respectable. To insure this degree of uniformity, the Victoria University was one of the first to mandate the use of external as well as internal examiners, a system which has since done much to maintain the standards and also the standardization of British higher education. Within established institutions the English thus had much more freedom than their Continental peers. But only in the United States could a new institution hope to make its own way to first class status without preliminary recognition from either the state or its peers.

The way in which government financial support eventually came to the colleges did little to hinder their freedom, and in fact established the precedent and system by which government subvention of education was operated and controlled until the 1970s. The small size of government contributions militated against the creation of elaborate mechanisms for their regulation and distribution. The colleges were given a few thousand pounds, and the distribution of this largesse, which was based on the individual college's importance, seems to have been agreed upon in consultation with the colleges. Once received, the colleges were entirely responsible for the distribution and expenditure of the funds. Using the expertise of concerned professional educators was obviously a far more economical way of taking decisions than creating a new government bureaucracy to administer what remained, until the 1920s at least, very small grants. And the efficiency of the system was undoubted. As a characteristically English result, the increasingly formal deliberations of the leaders of the civic universities were not replaced by a government department, but were themselves erected into a unique agency, the University Grants Committee, which continued until recently to administer the government subvention of British universities in a way envied by academics throughout the world.

The civic colleges quickly established themselves as suitable models for the expansion and modernization of British higher education. They also contributed, by the very nature of their creation and development, to the peculiar relationship which long subsisted between British universities and the British government, in which the government maintained legislative and judicial powers but failed, or chose not, to develop an administrative, bureaucratic system of supervision. The civic college model even extended its influence beyond Britain to the Empire. Oxbridge could never be exported, but the civic colleges were adaptable, modern, and simple enough to be adopted throughout the Empire. Their excellences in terms of standards usually went with them; their limitations became more obvious and serious in environments requiring greater flexibility than they possessed. They have nonetheless remained influential and admired institutions throughout the 20th Century.

Notes

Note on Abbreviations

Three abbreviations are used throughout the notes to designate materials from the archives of the three colleges:

O.C. for Owens College, Manchester
Y.C. for Yorkshire College, Leeds
U.C. for University College, Liverpool

followed by some such more specific designation as "Council Minutes", "Document Books", etc. These sources are discussed and itemized in the Bibliographical Note.

Introduction

1.   The term "civic colleges" is not generally found in the literature of British higher education. It is used here as a convenient means of referring to institutions without university status, as in the case of all the proto-civic universities before 1880 (London is not usually designated a civic university), and the constituent colleges as distinct from the whole of the Victoria University thereafter.

Chapter One: Background

1.   Burn, *The Age of Equipoise.*
2.   Tholfson, "The Intellectual Origins of mid-Victorian Stability", *Political Science Quarterly.*
3.   See especially Anderson, *Family Structure in Nineteenth Century Lancashire.*
4.   While the customary indices of middle class status, occupation and income (and income tax), are too variable to provide reliable figures, it is certain that the middle class was growing rapidly in proportion to the total

population during the Victorian era. Most debate over the growth rate has centered on the question of which levels within the middle class grew fastest. The argument is relatively unimportant for our purposes, as anyone paying income tax or employed in a middle class occupation could plausibly consider educating himself or his children at a civic college.

Best's *Mid-Victorian Britain* contains a useful summary of the economic and employment circumstances of the middle class (pp.81-91).

5. Young, *Victorian England: Portrait of an Age.*

6. By about 2 million per decade in the 30s, 40s and 50s, 2-1/2 million in the 60s, and 3 million in the 70s and 80s. The population of England and Wales was 13,897,000 in 1831 and 29,003,000 in 1891. These and the following figures on contributions are most readily available in Mitchell and Dean, *Abstract of British Historical Statistics.*

7. Summarized in Best, *Mid-Victorian Britain*, p.85.

8. See, particularly, Briggs, *Victorian Cities* and Thornhill, *The Growth and Reform of English Local Government.*

The Free Trade Hall, dedicated, as A.J.P. Taylor and Asa Briggs have both pointed out, to a mighty proposition, is perhaps the precedent of these evidences of the creative capacity of the great provincial cities of Victorian England. See Taylor's *Essays in English History* and Briggs'*Victorian Cities.*

9. See Roberts, *Victorian Origins of the British Welfare State.*

10. See, for example, Thompson, *The Owens College. Its Foundation and Growth*, Chapter III, for biographies of the original trustees.

11. Yates, *Thoughts on the Advancement of Academical Education in England*, pp.25-28.

12. Armytage, *The American Influence on English Education*, p.6.

13. The founders' views of religious education are succinctly and lucidly put in Macaulay's essay on London University, *Edinburgh Review*, vol. 43, p.315. Also available in numerous editions of Macaulay.

14. Quoted in Charlton, *Portrait of a University 1851-1951*, p.26, and elsewhere.

15. This explanation of Durham's foundation is elaborated in Armytage, *Civic Universities*, pp. 175-76. An uncritical narrative of Durham history is Whiting's *The University of Durham 1832-1932.*

16. See Stone on "The Size and Composition of the Oxford Student Body", in *The University in Society* and Rothblatt, *Revolution of the Dons*, charts pp.280-284 for the continued gentry and professional character of Oxbridge students. The likely exceptions to Northern non-attendance would be physicians and clerics.

17. These in general run to a type well-summarized by Mortimer Proctor:

> The freshman, armed with parental advice from either a father who is a country vicar or a widowed mother who plans to live in penury to educate her son, arrives at the university aboard a coach driven by a cigar-smoking, horn-tootling undergraduate (though later, of course, he comes by train from London). The formalities of matriculation performed, he meets his uncongenial tutor to determine a course of study; this, however, is at once neglected in favor

of more diverting pastimes when he learns that college life is a highly social affair. Vigorous wine parties, a bonfire in the quad, tricks played upon unpopular students, midnight excursions to screw shut the doors of offending tutors, days in the field with hounds and horses and on the river in punt and shell, all take up too much time to permit him much study. Even if he is a quiet creature, he is drawn by the more sprightly into some form of undergraduate foolishness; if he is a wild one, he lives a very full life indeed.

From this point on affairs may take a tragic turn, or more often the hero may recover his senses and graduate with honor, but in either case there is little here to attract a good middle class parent. Proctor, *The English University Novel*, p.1. This paragraph and the next are based on his study.

18. Simon, *Studies in the History of Education, 1770-1870*, p.91.

19. The growing power of the fourth estate, while not in itself an educational pressure, served as a transmitting and amplifying agent for such pressures. The periodical press in Britain, particularly the influential critical reviews such as the *Edinburgh, Westminster*, and *Quarterly* helped to create public opinion and also served as barometers of it. When a review maintains a reasonably consistent editorial policy and a large and faithful readership, as did the three mentioned above, it may reasonably be assumed that the editorial positions both represent and encourage the opinions of a significant segment of the literate, articulate public. The introductory chapter of Ellegard's *Darwin and the Common Reader*, contains a thorough discussion of the legitimacy and use of this sort of evidence.

The education criticism in the *Westminster* and *Edinburgh Reviews* represented a broad spectrum of intellectual reform opinion. These reviews were considered at the time to be the house organs of the radicals (particularly Benthamites and utilitarians, but not Chartists or Socialists) and Whig liberals respectively. Should the opposing views of Tory opinion be wanted, the *Quarterly Review* may always be consulted for defenses of the Established Church, the rights of collegiate foundations, and the dangers of an educated proletariat.

How many people were swayed by the reviews remains a moot point, even after such studies as Clive's *Scotch Reviewers: The Edinburgh Review 1802-1815*. However, the intellectuals who founded London University and some of the businessmen who were to administer Owens College were probably readers of and in some cases writers for the *Westminster* and *Edinburgh*.

20. Rothblatt, *The Revolution of the Dons*.

21. Stone, *The University in Society*, vol. 1, pp.78-80, 102.

22. *Edinburgh Review*, vol. 35, p. 302 (1821).

23. *Westminster Review*, vol. 24, p.102.

24. *Victoria History of Middlesex*, "University College," p.357.

25. *Victoria History of Middlesex*, "Kings College," p.349.

26. *Edinburgh Review*, vol. 48, p.235.

27. *Edinburgh Review*, vol. 42, p.346.

28. See Ch. 4.

29. Dent, *1870-1970 : A Century of Growth in English Education*, p.37.

30. A large percentage of the original faculty had attended Edinburgh University. Bellot, *University College*, p.47. Two standard sources on London are Bellot's *University College* and Hearnshaw's *Centenary History of Kings College*. An excellent shorter account is contained in the *Victoria County History of Middlesex*, "The University of London" , pp. 315-360.

31. Cottle and Sherborne's *The Life of a University* provides a brief history. There is no major study.

32. Balliol and New College made substantial financial contributions and helped to recruit a faculty.

33. The standard account is Chapman, *The Story of a Modern University*.

34. See Hughes, *The University of Birmingham*.

35. An enormous and interesting descriptive catalogue of possible predecessors is found in Armytage's *Civic Universities*. It is not, however, an analytic work, and the possible relationships between most of these institutions and the civic colleges are not considered.

36. See Parker's *Dissenting Academies in England* for a general account which confirms this view.

37. The various reasons were well discussed at the time in Hole's *Essay ... on Mechanics Institutions*.

38. The standard history is Tylecote, *The Mechanics Institutes*.

39. Reader use expanded almost a hundred-fold between 1799 and 1835. Parliamentary funding grew steadily; enlarged grants from 1845 marked the beginning of the building of a great modern national library by Panizzi and others.

Arundell's *The British Museum Library* is a useful general history. On Panizzi's intentions and achievements see Miller, *Prince of Librarians*.

40. Minto, *A History of the Public Library Movement*.

41. *Westminster Review*, vol. 98, p.343, statistical chart.

42. The intentions, philosophy, and purpose of library foundations are discussed in Munford, *Penny Rate*.

43. See Ch. 5.

44. See Ashton, *Economic and Social Investigations in Manchester* and Cullen, *The Statistical Movement*.

Chapter Two: Preconditions

1. O.C. Trustee Minutes, report "On the Experience of the Session 1851-2 at Owens."

2. They were encouraged by the realization of the talent revealed by universal elementary schooling and by the possibility of funds from the Science and Art Department. See, e.g., Lawson and Silver, *A Social History of Education*, Ch. IX.

The opinion of the Bryce Commission (1895) is noteworthy. A very high level was occasionally reached. "There are cases in which a higher grade elementary school carries on the education of some of its best pupils for some time after the age of 15, preparing them for a scholarship competition, or for matriculation at the local university college ...," G.B., *Royal Commission on Secondary Education*, 1895, p.53.

3. Notably by Kelly, *A History of Adult Education in Great Britain* and by Harrison, *Learning and Living*, 1870-1960.

4. Figures taken from the Education Census, 1851 and quoted in Stephens, *Regional Variations in Education*.

5. A convenient summary of the development of "ladders" up to 1900 is Lawson and Silver, *A Social History of Education*, pp.337-40.

6. G.B., *2nd Report of the Royal Commission on Technical Instruction*, 1884, pp. 29, 425.

7. Growing numbers of pupil teachers were receiving an essentially secondary education by the 70s, a process begun considerably earlier. Simon, *Education and the Labour Movement*, p.180.

8. G.B., Education Department, *Special Reports on Educational Subjects 1896-7*, vol. I.

9 Emphasis in original.

10. Arnold, *Schools and Universities on the Continent*, pp.276-77.

11. See Mack, *Public Schools*.

12. One of the 9 schools investigated by the Clarendon Commission, or possibly one of a few others. Honey's *Tom Brown's Universe* is the most elaborate study of the rank order of the various public schools.

13. Naturally there were exceptions, particularly those interested in science or medicine. London or the Continent would however remain more likely choices than the provinces until the 20th Century. See Bamford, *The Rise of the Public Schools*, pp. 264-65 for the further education of Winchester and Harrow men.

14. Canon Woodard made the class basis of these assumptions clearest in his plans to cover England with a system of Church of England secondary schools. Their subject matter, duration, fees, and student recruitment would all separate them into three social class categories, and these were clearly and specifically described as such. Heeney's *Mission to the Middle Classes* describes the proposed system. It is interesting to note that the actual schools which Woodard founded suffered from a sort of early academic drift and steadily attempted to recruit higher class students, keep them to a later age, and give them a classical preparation for university entrance.

15. See G.B., *Royal Commission on Secondary Education, 1895*, pp. 230-31, which summarizes the testimony of the principals of the constituent colleges of the Victoria University on the subject.

16. Bamford, *Rise of the Public Schools*, pp. 270-72.

17. At the Manchester Grammar School, for example, enrolments more than doubled between the 60s and 90s. G.B., *Royal Commission on Secondary Education, 1895*, p.43.

18. The working men's movement for shorter hours was linked to the notion of further education and cultivation. The T.U.C. began to tackle the interlocking questions of the 8 hour day and education from the 80s, though the WEA and the 8 hour day were both to be 20th Century phenomena. See Simon, *Education and the Labour Movement, 1870-1920*. The rise and fall of such institutions as mechanics institutes and working men's colleges

indicates the growing determination to provide higher education, as well as demonstrating the inherent difficulties.

19. See Chapters 2, 4, Tables III and IV. The later decline is usually and reasonably attributed to the general expansion and diversification of adult and evening education.

20. Musgrove and Taylor, *Society and the Teacher's Role*, p.3.

21. Musgrove and Taylor, *Society*, Appendix, p.90.

22. Lowndes, *The Silent Social Revolution*.

23. Adapted from a table in G.B., *Royal Commission on Secondary Education, 1895*, vol. 9, pp. 426-29.

24. See Jordan, *Philanthropy in England*, Ch. 2, and below, Ch. 5.

25. Lawson and Silver, *A Social History of Education*, Ch. VII.

26. *Edinburgh*, vol. 48, "London University and King's College."

27. *Edinburgh*, vol. 48, "Library of Useful Knowledge."

28. *Edinburgh*, vol. 99.

29. "... the most important interests of the public have been sacrificed to private advantage ...", (*Edinburgh*, vol. 54, "English Universities -- Oxford.") By the mid 30s universities are described as betraying their commitments and the "National Trust"; the commitments had been defined in 1834 as: "... the University so called, i.e. the necessary national establishment for General Education ...", (*Edinburgh*, vol. 60, "The Universities and the Dissenters," and "Admission of Dissenters to the Universities.")

30. For a thorough survey of 19th Century contributions to higher education see Owen, *English Philanthropy*, pp. 356-67.

31. Cardwell, *The Organization of Science in England*, p.126.

32. Local rates had been part of the Poor Law at least since the time of Elizabeth, but the system was more an anomaly than a precedent, and was extensively reworked with doubtful success throughout the 19th Century.

33. The expansion of public and government interest may be seen from two different but complementary points of view in Maclure, *Educational Documents, England and Wales, 1816-1963* and Simmonds and Nicholls, *Law of Education*, Ch.1. On the general trend toward "collectivist" activities, and on the more specific and useful idea of the shift from statutory toward administrative control of society and its affairs, the classic work is Dicey, *Law and Public Opinion in England*.

34. Berdahl, *British Universities and the State*, provides a good historical survey of the state's concern for higher education.

35. Hobhouse's *The Dead Hand* is perhaps the best description of, and certainly one of the strongest attacks upon the continued strength of, the traditional regulations governing charitable trusts.

36. Hamilton, "Building and Civil Engineering Construction", in Singer et al., *A History of Technology*, vol. 4.

37. In the 1820s by the *Edinburgh* and *Westminster*.

38. Russian competition seems to have produced a precursor to the threat of Continental competition in the 70s. Armytage notes that the pressure of Russian expansion on the North of India, led by engineers and others trained in Imperial schools, led to the creation of the East India Company colleges at Haileybury and Addiscombe in 1813 to train administrators and engineers. (*The Russian Influence on English Education*, p.24). The cur-

riculum of studies at the new schools was considered of greater usefulness than that offered at other institutions, at least by the *Edinburgh Review* in 1816 (vol. 27, p. 511).

39. *Edinburgh Review*, vol. 129, "The Competitive Industry of Nations", reviewed the Paris Exposition, remarked on the greatness of Prussian firms, and descried a need for highly educated managers as well as technically trained workmen in British industry.

40. "Our foremen, chosen from the lower industrial ranks, have no sufficient opportunities of correcting the deficiencies of their early education. Our managers are too apt in every case of novelty to proceed by trial and error, without scientific principles to guide them; and the sons of our great manufacturers too often despise the pursuits of their fathers as mere handicrafts ...", *Edinburgh Review*, vol. 127, "Technical and Scientific Education," p.442.

41. Cardwell, *The Organization of Science*, pp. 125-26.

42. The *Westminster* analyzed German universities in 1836, vol. 24, p.102.

43. *Westminster Review*, vol. 99, "The National Importance of Scientific Research."

44. See for example Rothblatt's table on the occupation of Cambridge's engineering graduates in 1910, *Revolution of the Dons*, p. 285.

45. Arnold, *Schools and Universities on the Continent*.

46. Habakkuk, *American and British Technology in the 19th Century*.

47. "The first phase of industrialization -- up to World War I -- shows three different occupational groups in industry, more or less corresponding to the phases of technical development -- unskilled manual workers, skilled workers, and commercial and clerical personnel." H. Schelsky, "Technical Change and Educational Consequences", in Halsey, Flood et al., *Education, Economy and Society*. These categories of men are largely trained and/or educated by traditional methods.

48. See Charlton, *Portrait of a University*, Ch. II, "The Preparation".

49. Thackray, "Natural Knowledge in Cultural Context", *AHR* no. 79 (1974), pp. 672-709.

50. Thompson, *The Owens College*, Chapter III.

51. See Chapter 3.

52. Briggs has chosen three of them as the classic Victorian cities and his subtitles express their character: "Manchester, Symbol of a New Age; Leeds, a Study in Civic Pride; Birmingham: The Making of a Civic Gospel." *Victorian Cities*.

53. Owen, *English Philanthropy*, pp. 469-70.

54. See Hall, *The Organization of American Culture, 1700-1900*.

55. E.g., the Owens Extension Committee decided not to canvass generally in Manchester during the bad year 1869. O.C., "Extension and Amalgamation" volume. Liverpool's founders made a similar decision a decade later.

56. "... gas encouraged evening classes in the Mechanics' Institutes, and aided the new literacy and education. That people could congregate after their working hours in well-lit halls encouraged the processes of popular government. The social, industrial, and communal life of the nineteenth

century could not have developed as it did without gas-light." Elton, "Gas for Light and Heat," Ch. 9, p. 274, in Singer et al., *A History of Technology*, IV.

57. Professor Roscoe reported to the Council in February 1874 on his testing and alteration of the new gas lighting. O.C. Council Minutes.

Chapter Three: Colleges and Cities

1. Freeman, "The Manchester Conurbation", Ch. 3 in the British Association's excellent survey, *Manchester and its Region*.
2. Redford and Russel, *History of Local Government*, p. 208.
3. Redford and Russel, *History of Local Government*, Ch. 21.
4. Love, *Manchester As It Is*, Chs. 6 and 7.
5. Briggs, *Victorian Cities*, pp. 91, 125.
6. Liverpool had created a cultural base earlier, but Liverpool was a pre-industrial mercantile city, whereas Manchester's character, while mercantile, was based on industry.
7. Shils, "The Intellectuals", *Encounter*, April, 1955.
8. See Thompson, *The Owens College*, pp. 19-31.
9. "Substance of Report of a Committee of the Trustees, 1850", by Messrs. Kay, Neild, Fletcher, Foster and Heywood, in O.C. Archives.
10. Passages from Owens' will, quoted in various sources including Clapp's *John Owens* and Fiddes' *Chapters in the History of Owens College*.
11. O.C. Trustees Minutes, report from the faculty, 28 June 1852.
12. Useful charts of student numbers, college income, etc., can be found in Fiddes, *Chapters*.
13. Bryce, James, Viscount Bryce. A distinguished jurist, historian, author, and political figure. His early career was much concerned with education and when he came to Owens as Lecturer, later Professor of Law, he had already acquired an intimate familiarity with Lancashire education as an assistant commissioner of the *Schools Inquiry Commission*. He had then recommended improvements including co-ordination of secondary and higher education.

Jevons, William Stanley. An economist, statistician, and logician, he achieved an international reputation in economics and a professional one in logic before his early death, age 47.

Reynolds, Osborne. Engineer and physicist, he taught engineering at Owens for 37 years. An effective teacher, he was best known for original researches which had practical consequences. His work was recognized by the Royal Society's gold medal in 1888.

Roscoe, Sir Henry Enfield. After training at London and Heidelberg under Bunsen, Roscoe rose with the Owens College, becoming a well known chemist and teacher, and the acknowledged leader of a great school. His importance was recognized by appointment to Royal Commissions, knighthood, and eventual election to Parliament.

Ward, Sir Adolphus William. An historian of England and its literature, and of foreign affairs, he edited the Cambridge *Histories of English Literature* and of *British Foreign Policy*. He established his reputation while at Owens, and became Vice Chancellor of the Victoria University. His local repute gained him the "freedom of the city" of Manchester in 1897.

14. Unfortunately there is no study of Leeds like Redford and Russel's of Manchester. An impressionistic study centering on the construction of the Town Hall can be found in Briggs, *Victorian Cities*, which also contains a useful bibliography.

15. A good, analytical history of the Yorkshire College and the University of Leeds is Gosden and Taylor (eds.), *Studies in the History of a University*.

16. "Yorkshire College of Science: Report of the Committee ...", Leeds, 1872, in Y.C. Archives. The report went on to define the intended clientele as "... persons who will afterwards be engaged ... as foremen, managers, or employers ... [or] teachers of technical science."

17. Weaving instruction began in 1875, Engineering in 1876, Coal Mining in 1877, and Dyeing in 1879.

18. The historical background and the establishment of the College are treated in Supplements to the *Liverpool Daily Post* of 24 and 25 May 1978, in honor of the College Centenary.

19. White's *History of the Corporation of Liverpool* discusses voluntary efforts as well as the activities and inadequacies of the Corporation.

20. See Sadler, *Report on Secondary Education in Liverpool*.

21. Liverpool Daily Post, 23 May 1878. This article touches on all the points mentioned by other papers and foreshadows the Daily Post's position as the Liverpool paper most consistently and deeply interested in the College.

22. The outline of the following account can be found in Campbell Brown, *The First Page*, supplemented by Henry Ormerod's unfinished history of University College. These have been superseded by Kelly's *For Advancement of Learning*.

23. The close linking of these two groups was particularly appropriate in Liverpool, where important schools had grown out of the associations.

24. *Liverpool Daily Post*, 25 May 1878.

25. Many of its students, especially evening students, would be continuing an interrupted education rather than proceeding direct from secondary schools. Many would be seeking specialized training or education and would have little interest in computing academic years toward a degree they did not expect or desire.

26. The Roger Lyon Jones Chair.

27. The original parsimony had been wise, and was perhaps a result of the founders' familiarity with previous Liverpool educational endeavours. The Royal Institution had crippled itself for years by the expense of its original building, though some no doubt felt that the college had gone too far in the other direction by opening in a reconditioned lunatic asylum.

Chapter Four: Demand and Supply

1.   The culture-seeking manufacturers in Mrs. Gaskell's novels were undoubtedly drawn from the life by one in a position to observe them. Elizabeth Gaskell's husband was a classically educated clergyman and one of the strongest supporters of education projects in Manchester.

2.   "Substance of Report of a Committee of Trustees", 1850 (Kay, Neild, Fletcher, Foster, and Heywood).

3.   Inaugural Address, 6 October 1851.

4.   Their attention also extended to those lesser certifications achieved in a variety of other examinations; the colleges were willing and eager to administer the Oxford and Cambridge Local Exams and those of various other groups which certified education of a more or less secondary character.

5.   See, for example, Greenwood's comments on the growing number of regular students concerned with London degrees, and his expectation that the new science degree will attract additional students interested in those subjects, O.C. Minutes of Trustees: "Report to Trustees", 27 October 1859. Also O.C. Annual Report, 1859-60.

6.   The civic college might prepare them to win a scholarship as well. College Calendars regularly announced the successes of past students at Oxbridge scholarship and degree exams.

7.   The various subjects and possible marks receivable in them were published in the following places.

ICS: 1858 in Heywood, *Academic Reform*, p. 11; 1885 in U.C. Calendar 1885-86.

Woolwich: 1857 in Heywood, *Academic Reform*, p.11; 1885 in U.C. Calendar 1885-86.

Direct Commissions in the Army in O.C. Calendar, 1862-63.

8.   A small alteration was made in the early 60s, giving increased weight to maths, Arabic, and Sanscrit.

9.   By the 80s the maximum allowable age of candidates had been lowered, and Sanscrit and Arabic removed from the exam. Successful candidates were expected to spend two years in preparation after the exam.

10.   Reader, *Professional Men*, pp. 100-104.

11.   Cohen, *The Growth of the British Civil Services*.

12.   E.g., O.C. Calendar, "The Principal's Report for 1874-75" announced that a student had been placed 15th in the ICS competition for 37 appointments and another had placed first in the competition for draughtsmen for the Hydrographical Department of the Admiralty.

An interesting juxtaposition and succession of announcements in the Liverpool Calendar and records is even more revealing of the college's attention to this demand. The Calendar for 1885-86 published a description of the Home and Indian Civil Service exams and also an advertisement for a cramming establishment, a "Civil Service Academy" which offered preparation for all the various Civil Service clerkship exams. The next year's Senate minutes reveal the appointment of a professor as counsellor to students preparing for the exams. U.C. Minutes of Senate, 9 March 1887.

13.   O.C. Minutes of Trustees, June 1860.

14. *Manchester Guardian,* 6 October 1870.
15. O.C. Minutes of Trustees, December 1870.
16. O.C. Minutes of Council, 21 April 1876. The Principal drew attention to an exchange in the Commons which clarified the new regulations of the ICS regarding the further training of candidates. The rules, calling for residence at a University exercising "moral control" would be "liberally construed"; that is, they were not intended to exclude Scottish universities and the affiliated colleges of London, such as University, Kings, and Owens. The new regulations required some time to effect and the College asked the India Office to allow selected ICS candidates to spend their probationary time at Owens, residing in an affiliated hall or with a professor. O.C. Minutes of Council: "Principal's Report", 20 February 1880.
17. Millerson, *The Qualifying Associations,* Ch. 5.
18. Each of the following organizations represented both new students and new subjects for higher education.

1800	Royal College of Surgeons of London
1818	Institution of Civil Engineers
1825	Law Society
1834	Royal Institute of British Architects
1841	Pharmaceutical Society of Great Britain
1844	Royal College of Veterinary Surgeons
1847	Institution of Mechanical Engineers
1848	Institute of Actuaries
1860	Royal Institution of Naval Architects
1866	Royal Aeronautical Society
1868	Royal Institution of Chartered Surveyors
1871	Institution of Electrical Engineers
1873	Institution of Municipal Engineers
1877	Royal Institute of Chemistry
1877	Library Association
1879	Institute of Bankers
1880	Institute of Chartered Accountants in England and Wales
1882	Chartered Institute of Patent Agents
1885	Institute of Municipal Treasurers and Accountants
1886	Chartered Auctioneers and Estate Agents Institute
1886	Institute of Brewing
1889	Institute of Marine Engineers
1889	Institution of Mining Engineers
1891	Chartered Institute of Secretaries
1894	Chartered Society of Physiotherapy
1897	Chartered Insurance Institute

This list is a conflation of those in Millerson, *The Qualifying Associations,* Ch. 5.

19. In 1858, with the College at low water, the new Principal elaborated on this problem, discussing Owens' uniqueness "In not standing in a distinctively recognized relation with any of the Branches of Professional Life ...." Attempts to join with the medical school had been unsuccessful

and further connections with teacher education were being considered on the basis of a proposal by J.D. Morell. O.C. Minutes of Trustees: Principal's Report, 25 March 1858.

20. O.C. Calendar, 1862-63.

21. "Meanwhile, ..., it repeatedly happens that aspirants to the several professions, or those who for other reasons wish to supplement their school training by a year or two of collegiate study, seek to enter some classes in a college like this for which they are indeed well fitted, while they are seriously deficient in respect of other, perhaps only less necessary, branches of knowledge. To apply an unbending standard, and to exclude all such applicants from this or other like institutions, would be scarcely possible, and certainly in true interests of education inexpedient." O.C. Calendar 1869-70: "Principal's Report".

22. See Chapter 5.

23. The Yorkshire College of Science, Report of the Committee Chairman, Lord F.C. Cavendish (Leeds, 1872).

24. Pamphlet, U.C. archives, marked: "A dozen copies of this pamphlet were distributed to each member of the Committee 26 March 1879."

Awareness was not confined to the committee: the Council of the School of Medicine offered to endow the chair of experimental physics almost before a College Council was there to accept it. U.C. Council Minutes, 23 April 1881. A request by law students for a course of lectures was also quickly approved. U.C. Council Minutes, 25 June 1881.

25. Reader, *Professional Men*.

26. Carr-Saunders and Wilson, *The Professions*, p.365.

27. The exempting exams were a Matriculation at London or Dublin, Mods at Oxford, and the Previous at Cambridge. All were listed in the O.C. Calendar of 1862-63, but London Matric, which was actually administered, as well as prepared for, at Owens, was emphasized with italics. Any one exempted the holder from one year of articles. A B.A. reduced the requirements by two years.

28. Peterson, *The Medical Profession in Mid-Victorian London*. See also Reader, *Professional Men*, Ch. 1, and Newman, *The Evolution of Medical Education in the 19th Century*.

29. At Liverpool, the need for instruction in chemistry, physics, and botany turned the members of the Medical School into one of the earliest and strongest groups advocating the foundation of a college. Campbell-Brown was particularly well informed on this subject, as he was in fact the chemistry lecturer at the Medical School.

30. St. Mary's Hospital Medical School sought affiliation with Owens as early as 1858, though all it received was an agreement by the college to remit the general admission fee for its students. O.C. Minutes of Trustees, July 1858.

At Leeds, the Medical School arranged for chemistry teaching at the college in 1875, and by 1878 was making a permanent arrangement for courses in botany and comparative anatomy which were evidently already under way. Y.C. Council Minutes, 25 February 1875; 27 September 1878.

31. In 1859 Greenwood advised the Owens trustees to consult the medical schools about the new education requirements of the General

Council of Medical Education and Registration prior to their coming into effect. O.C. Minutes of Trustees, 24 November 1859. The next public report pointed out the college's suitability as a place of preparation. O.C. Annual Report, 1859-60.

32. O.C. Minutes of Trustees, November 1868.

33. O.C. Minutes of Trustees, May 1869.

34. "It is hardly possible to mention any topic, or any subject upon which, sooner or later, a solicitor in large practice may not find himself deeply engaged. It is quite impossible to define within a narrow compass the nature of a solicitor's business -- it extends to anything; it extends to everything: the fact is, we are, as professional men, entrusted to a very great extent with the confidence of gentlemen; we are entrusted to a very great extent with the most sacred matters connected with gentlemen. It often happens that the protection of their honour and their character, and of course of their property, is left to our zeal and integrity, and when we are brought into this confidential and habitual intercourse with men of every class in society, the highest as well as the lowest, I think that it is most important that the profession should be so educated as to be qualified for carrying on that intercourse as gentlemen themselves; but I apprehend that that qualification can't be attained except by educating them as gentlemen with much greater attention to their general endowments and information than is at present the case." Sir George Stephen before the Select Committee on Legal Education (1846), quoted in Christian, *A Short History of Solicitors*, p. 183.

35. Birks, *Gentlemen of the Law*, pp.238-39.

36. A Select Committee of Commons in 1846, a Royal Commission on the Inns of Court and Chancery in 1854.

37. Birks, *Gentlemen of the Law*, p. 237.

38. See footnote 28 above.

39. Carr-Saunders, *The Professions*, pp. 49-50.

40. Emphasis in original.

41. O.C. Minutes of Council: "Principal's Report", 16 November 1871.

42. O.C. Extension: "Copy of letter from Prof. Bryce to The Trustees of Owens College ... read 18 May 1871." He added that, "Now it would be a serious hardship for Manchester Law Students to be obliged to go for Law teaching to London, or to Oxford or Cambridge, and a still more serious one to be required to pass the examination on the strength of their own reading only without having had the benefit of any oral instruction. There is likely therefore to be a real demand for such instruction, and Owens College is just the institution which may fairly be asked to provide it. I believe I am right in saying that a large proportion of the professional men in Manchester and the neighbouring towns, while welcoming the scheme of the Legal Education Association, will be especially eager to support it if they see that it is likely to be the means of causing better provision for the education of young Lawyers to be made in Manchester, which may for so many purposes be regarded as a local Metropolis. There is therefore good reason to hope that they will be glad to promote and encourage by their sympathy and by

practical suggestions any scheme of legal education which you may think fit
to establish in Owens College, and that they will induce a very considerable
number of their Clerks to attend such Law Lectures as may there be deliv-
ered." Though the particular exam he envisioned was not established,
exams continued to gain importance in the profession.

43.   Total fees for the course would be 2/2/0 plus a 7/- annual entrance
fee, the course would last one or two years, and hours would be "fixed to
meet the convenience of Articled Clerks, say at 4 or 4.30 p.m." O.C. Extension "Copy Letter from Mr. R.D. Darbishire, to the President of the
Manchester Incorporated Law Association" May, 1871. Flexibility on the
part of the members of the Association was also needed, as the letter pointed
out: "... probably Clerks would be more willing to avail themselves of the
advantages of the courses of Lectures if the Solicitors to whom they may be
articled would allow the time occupied in attendance at the College to count
as part of the Clerk's service. This plan would not cause much inconvenience, if, as is proposed, the Lectures were arranged near, but before the
end of the usual Office hours. It is a plan which has already been put in
practice after negotiation between the Trustees and the employers of pupils
in engineering establishments, and, in another case, with members of the
Parmaceutical Society, and in both of these cases with advantageous results."

44.   O.C. Minutes of Governors: Report of Council, 28 March 1872.

45.   O.C. Document Book, no. 90, 1872. While further exams were not
mandated, the Law Society itself extended and increasingly thoroughly controlled the exams begun under the Act of 1860.

46.   The Law Society and the college collaborated in funding the department. In 1875 they invited those concerned to a meeting to raise funds.
O.C. Document Book, no. 52, 22 April 1875. The fund raising was evidently accomplished by September. O.C. Minutes of Council: "Report of
the Law Department Committee", 22 September 1875. By 1878 the college
established its own preliminary and advanced exams the passing of which
gave exemption from the preliminary exam before being articled and from
the first year of articles, respectively. O.C. Minutes of Council: "Principal's
Report", 15 March 1878.

47.   There is evidence of legal or preparatory studies at Leeds. The Incorporated Leeds Law Society did propose some collaboration in 1879.
Y.C. Council Minutes: "Letter to the Council", 1 December 1879.

48.   U.C. Council Minutes, 7 February 1882. Co-operation among these
institutions seems to have been thorough: the college offered a 50% reduction in its fees for F.W. Maitland's lectures on The Courts of Law and Eq-
uity to all articled clerks and law students, the Law Students' Association
offered prizes and conferred with the college about the lectures, and in 1886
the Law Society and the College Senate formed a Board of Legal Studies to
which the College contributed £40 per annum. U.C. Calendar, 1884-85;
U.C. Council, 7 November 1882; U.C. Council Minutes, 12 January and 23
March 1886.

49.   Y.C. Council Minutes, 14 January 1880.

50.   The early "Principal's Reports" at Owens frequently remarked the
diligence and maturity of the students from the Lancashire Independent
College.

51. Y.C., 9th Annual Report, 1882-83.

52. O.C., "Notices, etc.", 16 June 1854: 9/71 ordinary students in 1853-54 were from L.I.C. O.C. Minutes of Trustees, Appendix "Extract from a report ... Oct. 15, 1855": 11/58 from L.I.C. in 1854-55.

53. *Manchester Guardian*, 8 October 1873, on the opening of the new buildings.

54. O.C., Minutes of Trustees: "Principal's Report to Trustees", 31 October 1861.

55. O.C., Principal's Annual Report, 1873-74.

56. Bond, *The Victorian Army and the Staff College*. Bond discusses inter alia, the development of all facets of educational interest in the Army.

57. For these exams see above footnotes 7, 8, and 9.

58. E.G., O.C. Calendar, 1862-63, contains: (1) "Abstract of Regulations in regard to the examination of gentlemen preparatory to their receiving commissions in the army"; (2) "Abstract of Regulations for the admission of gentlemen cadets" (Woolwich); (3) ditto (Sandhurst).

59. Reader, *Professional Men*, p.97.

60. Tropp, *The School Teachers*. He doubts the reality of this perceived flood, but it was the perception which would stimulate men to defend or better their position.

62. Quoted in Tropp, *The School Teachers*.

63 Carr-Saunders, *The Professions*, pp. 252-53.

64. Archer, *Secondary Education*, Ch. XII.

65. Edmonds, *The School Inspector*.

66. O.C., Minutes of Trustees, 1853.

67. O.C. Prospectus, 1854-55.

68. O.C., Principal's Annual Report, 1852-53: "In the history of the session now concluded, nothing calls for warmer congratulation than the opening of the Schoolmasters' Class. The request of a large number of persons, actually engaged in teaching, to be furnished with the means of higher instruction for themselves, was in itself a good omen for popular education in and around Manchester .... How it [the courses] may be yet more beneficially conducted, we trust to learn by experience ...." O.C., Principal's Annual Report, 1854-55: "In the Schoolmasters' Classes, it is very gratifying to state that there is no diminution of numbers or of zeal."

69. O.C. Principal's Annual Report, 1854-55.

70. O.C. Document Book, no.90, 28 February 1877.

71. Leeds and Liverpool began by offering classes at suitable hours and low rates. Both colleges evidently found the arrangement satisfactory and steadily expanded their offerings; they also began to associate themselves with such organizations as the Leeds and District Teachers' Association and the Liverpool Teachers' Guild.

Y.C., Calendar 1875-76; Principal's Annual Report, 1878-79, 82-83. U.C., Senate Minute, 10 December 1884. The Senate is already considering offering classes for teachers. U.C., Calendar, 1886-87.

Co-operative arrangements were made with the new school boards, and Liverpool in 1890 was preparing to associate itself with the Liverpool Day Training College.

Y.C., Annual Report, 1881-82: The increase in part-time students "... is largely due to the efforts made this session by the College Staff in conjunction with the Rev. Dr. Barnes, Chairman of the Education Committee of the Leeds School Board, and other members of the Board, to interest Certificated Teachers in the work of the College ...." By 1884 a more detailed scheme had been developed, the object being "... the provision of systematic instruction for teachers who become candidates for certificates without attendance at a Training College. Such persons have hitherto in general acquired their knowledge either through unaided private study or through attendance at 'private adventure classes.' The need of more systematic instruction has been felt for some time past, both by the Department and by those interested in elementary education in our large towns ..." Courses were to be offered in mathematics, history, English composition, grammar, and literature, history, geography, Latin, and French. Small rearrangements of the College teaching were all that were necessary to meet these demands. Y.C., "Scheme for the Training of Elementary Assistant Teachers"; memorandum prepared apropos the Council resolution of 31 October 1884 by Bodington as Principal. U.C., Council Minutes, 1888; "Consultations are being held with the school board and College faculty to examine pupil teachers."

U.C.: Report of a Committee of Senate upon the Liverpool Day Training College Scheme, November 1890. Thirty students a year were expected as a result of the scheme of collaboration. Yorkshire College also established Day Training in 1891.

The Liverpool scheme may well have been encouraged by the college's awareness that its numbers had for some years been swelled by students from the Edgehill Training College for Teachers.

U.C., Annual Report, 1884-85.

72. See Chapter 7.

73. See Engel, *From Clergyman to Don*, and Rothblatt, *Revolution of the Dons* for discussions of professionalization in Oxford and Cambridge respectively.

74. Adapted from figures on p.2 of Anderson, *Victorian Clerks*.

75. Lockwood, *The Blackcoated Worker*, p.21.

76. Houlstons Industrial Library No. 7, *The Clerk: a sketch in outline of his duties and discipline* (London, 1878), p.13. Quoted in Lockwood, *The Blackcoated Worker*, p.20.

77. Calendars and Prospectuses of evening classes refer to their suitability for persons engaged in business pursuits. The connection was signalized in Manchester by the establishment in 1865 of an evening class exhibition to be awarded to a student at the Manchester Commercial School. By 1867 arithmetic and the principles of bookkeeping were being taught by "an experienced accountant ... once of the University of Heidelberg. "Minutes of Trustees: Principal's Report", 26 September 1867. At Leeds a business course curriculum even included such practical subjects as shorthand. Y.C., Council Minutes, 1887.

78. On the pressures upon the clerks, see Anderson, *Victorian Clerks*, Chs. 4, 5, and 6.

79. At Leeds, the Annual Report for 1886-87 points out that languages were offered with specific attention to business needs, and were well attended. The applicability of language courses was seriously considered. Y.C. Minutes of Council, 22 September 1886. By 1887 the Council was expanding the French classes and raising the instructor's salary as University and business oriented study of the subject had both increased. Y.C. Council Minutes, 14 December 1887.

80. Pollard, *The Genesis of Modern Management*.

81. The Institute of Secretaries was established in 1891.

82. Pollard, *The Genesis of Modern Management*.

83. The use of insurance companies implied the development of a small and highly specialized profession, the actuaries. They required a high degree of mathematical training, which might certainly have been acquired at a civic college, but their total numbers were so few as to make any demand from this source problematical.

84. Parker, *Dissenting Academies*. Priestley had defined such a course in 1765 in his "Essay on a Course of Liberal Education for Civil and Active Life."

85. "Owens College, Manchester. Courses of Instruction." No date, but c. 1855-56. The recommended course was as follows:

1st year - Latin. Mathematics Modern History. History Language and Literature French History

3rd year - Mental and Moral Philosophy English Constitutional Chemistry, or Natural History Political Economy Law French, or German

2nd year - Latin. Mathematics English Language and Literature. Modern History Jurisprudence Chemistry, or Natural History, French or German

86. O.C. Minutes of Trustees, 1854.

87. In a few specific cases, the college worked to meet special demands. It collaborated with the Institute of Bankers to provide evening instruction for candidates for the Institute's examinations, but this appears to have consisted mostly of advertising the college's regularly scheduled courses in mathematics, political economy and law. O.C. Senate Minutes: "At a meeting of the (Bankers') Committee held Monday, 7 March 1881."

88. Pollard, *The Genesis of Modern Management*, pp. 120-21.

89. Gosden and Taylor, *Studies in the History of a University, 1874-1974*, p.43, citing the evidence of the Y.C. Annual Reports.

90. See Caton, et al., *The Making of the University*.

91. Carr-Saunders, *The Professions*, p. 297.

92. Beard's *Manual of Hydrology* (1852), Glynn's *Rudimentary Treatise on the Power of Water* (1853), Fairbairn's *Mills and Millwork* (1862), and perhaps most notably Rankine's *Steam Engines and Prime Movers* (1859).

See Armytage, A *Social History of Engineering*, p. 152, and Singer et al., *A History of Technology*, vol.4, p. 445.

93. He also notes that the link was much delayed by the engineers' justified suspicions that many of the mid-century scientists whom they consulted were hopelessly inept in dealing with practical problems, and even inaccurate in the data they provided to engineers. See Rolt, *Victorian Engineering*, Ch.6, for the egregious errors of such scientists, particularly the Astronomer Royal, whose comments and inadequacies cannot have endeared Oxbridge and its science to the engineers.

94. The first major branch of engineering to depend on new scientific discoveries was electrical engineering, which only became important in the last decades of the century.

95. Rothblatt, *Revolution of the Dons*, p. 285.

96. O.C. Trustees Minutes, "Report by Prof. Clifton", 18 April 1863.

97. A memorandum by Osborne Reynolds, written for the information of the "Mechanical Workshops Engineering Syndicate" at Cambridge (c. 1890) and quoted in Hilken, *Engineering at Cambridge*, p. 103.

98. O.C. Trustees Minutes, "Report of the Committee on the Engineering Department", 31 October 1867 speaks of "... the danger of discouraging this branch of instruction, comparatively so new in this district, by publishing too strict, or too comprehensive a scheme in the first instance ...."

99. O.C. Trustees Minutes, Appendix, "Report on the Condition of the Engineering Department", 21 July 1870.

100. O.C. Trustees Minutes, June 1868; O.C. Calendar, 1868-69; O.C. Trustees Minutes, 1870.

101. O.C. Senate Minutes, "Report of the Engineering Committee to the Senate", June 1876; O.C. Council Minutes, 7 April 1876.

102. Y.C. Annual Report, 1877-88.

103. Y.C. Annual Report, 1880-81. Lectures would be offered in the winter, permitting field work in the summer. "This arrangement will, it is hoped, make it possible for many young men engaged in engineering works to obtain the best form of education for their profession, by devoting alternate periods of six months to theory in the college and to practice in the workshop."

104. Y.C. "Appointment of a Professor of Civil and Mechanical Engineering; Information for Candidates", 17 April 1884.

105. U.C. Annual Reports, 1884-85 and 1885-86.

106. U.C. Annual Reports, 1887-88.

107. By 1890 the Council had concluded that the emphasis on Engineering and practical mechanics had met expectations of efficiency, had made and received contributions to and from engineering, attracted students, and brought the college into touch with the national movement for technical education. U.C. Annual Report, 1889-90.

108. That is: it might not be the right thing to teach, it might not be possible to teach, and it might expose trade secrets.

109. See Cotgrove, *Technical Education*, for a thorough discussion of this peculiar arrangement.

110. Sanderson, *The Universities and British Industry*, especially Ch. 1 and pp. 16-18 in particular.

111. Habakkuk, *American and British Technology in the 19th Century*.

112. "The first phase of industrialization -- up to World War I -- shows three different occupational groups in industry, more or less corresponding to the phases of technical development -- unskilled manual workers, skilled workers, and commercial and clerical personnel." Schelsky, "Technical Change and Educational Consequences", in Halsey, Flood et al., *Education, Economy and Society*. These categories of men are largely trained and/or educated by traditional methods.

113. Distinguishing between the growth of new techniques and that of technology may help to clarify the English situation. Techniques are empirically derived and defined, and skill and efficiency are the products of practice and experience; hence the reluctance to alter techniques. Technology is a body of more or less theoretical data and constructs, whose rules are then applied to actual situations; both the generalized character of the rules and the possibility of formulating and testing hypotheses by scientific method encourage innovation. The two employ radically different forms of education, with apprenticeship the most effective in the first case, and prolonged theoretical training necessary in the other. Britain, however, had achieved industrial supremacy largely by means of a compromise between these two systems. Innovation arose out of increasingly systematic studies of techniques, but without a previous theoretical basis.

The most famous incidence is the development of the steam engine prior to thermodynamic theory. A more revealing one may be Wedgewood's improvements in the production of pottery. While these are frequently spoken of as scientific, they were in fact a highly systematized series of trials which tested variations in the previously accepted techniques, but were not based upon hypotheses which the then state of chemistry could not in any case have provided. (See Burton, *Josiah Wedgewood*, for a simple account of Wedgewood's investigations.)

Such remained the investigative and operational methodologies well beyond 1850. Landes, in a thorough discussion of the gradual entrance of science into technique, that is, into the development of technology as we know it, finds that there is general scholarly agreement that the process had hardly begun at mid-century, and many plausible arguments for placing its achievement of supremacy well within the 20th Century. Landes, *The Unbound Prometheus*, especially pp.104-14 and 323-26.

114. Sanderson's study of *The Universities and British Industry* may at first appear to support the idea of the primacy of industrial demand as an influence on the new colleges. In fact, however, it helps to establish the late and rather uncertain arrival of industry as a demand factor in higher education. The great industries which Sanderson links to the colleges only began their expansion in the 60s and 70s and reached a size capable of making significant demands only in the 90s.

115. See below, Chapter 5.

116. In coal mining (the largest branch of the profession) mechanical and technical developments were applied sporadically from the 70s onward, and the development of marginal coal fields and the rise in wages and shorten

ing of working hours as the century drew to its close all acted as stimuli. Allen, *British Industries and Their Organization*.

117. In this field the term manager has generally been applied to a technical expert, particularly concerned with those safety devices and regulations mandated by government, and with the mechanics of mining, rather than with the business side of the mining industry. See Carr-Saunders, *The Professions*, pp. 151-53.

118. O.C. Extension, 1867. The faculty proposed a chair of geology, to be connected with mining.

O.C. Council Minutes, 1875. An extensive "Report of the Geology and Mining Department Committee" emphasized the needs of the potential students in the area and the ability of the college to offer an appropriate course, but apparently little came of this. Perhaps the relatively low productivity of the Lancashire mines was a factor. While falling returns may theoretically call for technological change, they are practically likely to encourage conservatism and retrenchment, and it was the schools at Leeds and Newcastle, serving the expanding fields of the North, which prospered.

119. Letter from Arnold Lupton to the Coal Mining Committee of the Yorkshire College 18 April 1894. Lupton was requesting a raise in salary, pointing out that he gave 67 lectures, conducted 6 examinations, and 3 mining excursions, etc., per annum.

120. Y.C. Council Minutes: Letter "To the Board of Examination for the Mining District of Yorkshire and Lincolnshire", 17 June 1881.

121. Lupton to Coal Mining Committee, 18 April 1894.

122. The essential problems involved in mechanization were solved between the 30s and 70s with worsted production fully mechanized by the 50s. Murphy, *A History of the British Economy*, pp. 578-79. Whether these technical achievements would stimulate an interest in technology or rather encourage the faith in informal methods of invention and development is an open question.

123. See, e.g., Baines, *Account of the Woolen Manufacture of England*, pp. 112-13, and evidence to the Samuelson Committee quoted in Singer, et al., *A History of Technology*, vol.5, pp. 789-90.

124. Gosden and Taylor, *Studies in the History of a University*, p. 248, contains a useful summary. The role of the Livery Companies is described in Chapter 5.

125. The situations included the appointment of J. Clapman, a student for 3 years, as Instructor in the Technical School of Stroud. Y.C. Annual Report, 1877-78. The appointment is suggestive of the beginning of what became a fairly substantial form of employment for the best products of the new colleges.

126. Y.C. Annual Report, 1882-83.

127. Y.C. Annual Report, 1883-84. It was, however, strongly emphasized that a student could also benefit from a less exhaustive course involving only chemistry and dyeing.

128. Carr-Saunders, *The Professions*, pp. 175-76.

129. See, for example, T.H. Huxley's lectures on this subject between 1854 and 1857, available in *Essays*, vol. 3, "Science and Education".

130. For a good summary see Pilcher and Butler-Jones, *What Industry Owes to Chemical Science*.

131. The very foundation of the Institute marks the growth and professionalization of the field. Concern for professional qualifications had arisen in the 60s and with it the realization that the Chemical Society, with its amateur tradition and limited aims, was no longer entirely satisfactory. Pilcher, *History of the Institute of Chemistry*, from which the requirements for membership are quoted.

132. The mention of published research is both symptomatic of professional interests and an indication of a new demand upon civic colleges. The growing numbers of students doing advanced research in Roscoe's labs at Owens undoubtedly had varied motives, but one certain outcome would be fulfilling the Institute's membership qualifications.

133. Haber, *The Chemical Industry*, pp. 190-91.

134. The provision of chemistry teaching is detailed in Pilcher, *History of the Institute*, pp.12-22.

135. The links between academic scientists and industrial requirements in Manchester are articulated by Kargon, *Science in Victorian Manchester*.

136. The Society brought together industrialists and chemists. Roscoe was also instrumental in making it a national rather than merely local organization. See Thorpe, *Roscoe*, Ch. IX, "Roscoe and the Organization of Scientific Societies".

137. Roscoe, *Record of Work*.

138. Roscoe, *Record of Work*.

139. Y.C. Annual Report, 1883-84. The course in chemical technology was abandoned a few years later, as the students were insufficiently prepared and the divorce of the course from practice hampered both students and staff. However, much of the material was reabsorbed into the other classes, and the success of the Dyeing Department prevented any total divorce from technological chemistry. Y.C. Annual Report, 1887-88.

140. U.C. Council Minutes, 9 June 1885.

141. See Dyer and Mitchell, *The Society of Public Analysts*.

142. Stieb, *Drug Adulteration*. See especially p.78: "It seems clear that a turning point was reached in food and drug analysis around 1875 ...." Dyer and Mitchell, *The Society of Public Analysts*.

143. Dyer and Mitchell, *The Society of Public Analysts*.

144. Y.C. Annual Report, 1883-84.

Chapter Five: Founders and Benefactors

1.   Charlton, *Portrait of a University*, 1851-1951, Appendix III, pp. 148-49.

2.   Gosden and Taylor, *Studies in the History of a University 1874-1974*, p.93.

3.   Evaluating the success or failure of new colleges in another laissez-faire society, Curti and Nash summarized the American experience: "The successful colleges found a single wealthy benefactor, obtained money abroad, collected a large subscription, or were taken under the patronage of

state or city. This windfall pushed the struggling institution out of purgatory into permanence." Curti and Nash, *Philanthropy in the Shaping of American Higher Education*, p. 45.

4. Outside of the Victoria University, U.C. Bristol was particularly successful in getting official civic support.

5. Jordan, *Philanthropy in England*.

6. In fact, the colleges rapidly realized that unspecific gifts for general purposes were most desirable. Joseph Thompson, student of Owens, member of Council from 1870, and treasurer and historian of the college, repeatedly remarks on the special desirability of this form of gift in *The Owens College, Its Foundation and Growth*.

7. Jordan, *The Charities of London*, pp.48-49.

8. Jordan, *The Charities of London*, pp. 67-68.

9. London's other great group of educational philanthropists were the professionals. Their benefactions were concentrated upon the universities which had nurtured them. In Victorian England such support might continue, but might also extend to civic colleges offering professional or pre-professional training, particularly in medicine and to a lesser extent in law.

10. "The close connection between the city and the college was emphasized by the use of the same bell to call merchants to the Exchange, and to summon students to a lecture." Armytage, *Civic Universities*, pp. 78-79. While never a great success as a formally pedagogic institution, it supported some great scholars and led to the founding of the Royal Society.

11. Owen, *English Philanthropy*, 1660-1960, p. 103.

12. Owen, *English Philanthropy*, p. 165.

13. Carnegie, "Wealth" and "The Best Fields of Philanthropy", in the *North American Review*, CXLVIII, CXLIX, 1889.

14. See the brief biography in Owen, *English Philanthropy*, pp. 395-401.

15. Quoted in *Fortunes Made in Business*.

16. Eddison and Thompson, *A Sketch of the ... Yorkshire Ladies Council*

17. Quoted in the Annual Report for 1881-82.

18. Smaller subscriptions also came from special interest groups. The Annual Report for 1882-83 records the guaranteeing of £70 per annum for 3 years for a German Instructor by the German residents of Liverpool.

19. Data taken from a donation list published in conjunction with an appeal by the New Laboratories Building Committee, 29 November 1883. Copy in the U.C. Archives.

20. There were doubts about whether a broad appeal to Yorkshire might lessen civic support, and whether such independent communities as Bradford could be induced to contribute. Nevertheless, the broad appeal was made from the first. The public meeting of 30 April 1874 reported the raising of £25,000, and it was said that the West Riding was surely capable of providing the necessary additional sums. Lord F. Cavendish observed that with some assistance from the older Universities, "Leeds should be in a position to offer to the people of Yorkshire what Owens College gave to the people of Lancashire ...."

Every year's Annual Report appealed to Yorkshiremen and 1885 saw a new twist to the appeal:

"It is greatly to be desired that the amount invested should be so increased as to enable future current expenditure to be borne by the yearly income, especially just now, when there is reason to believe that the College would obtain admission to the Victoria University if its funds were placed on an adequate footing.

Attention may be called to the fact that University College, Liverpool, has been enabled by the more liberal contributions of its endowment funds, to become a part of the Victoria University. The Yorkshire College, on the other hand, although of earlier foundation, and the only College mentioned in connection with Owens College in the Charter of the University, and although it will also most favourably compare with any college of equal age, in respect of number of students and of good and useful work, still remains outside, waiting for Yorkshiremen to give it the means of claiming admission to the University as a right."

21. Y.C. Annual Report, 1886-87.

22. A convenient summary of the growth and general acceptance of this attitude will be found in Musgrave, *Sociology, History, and Education*, Ch. 5, "The Definition of Technical Education, 1860-1910".

23. Sanderson, *The Universities*, pp. 86-87.

24. Bankers, M.P.s, and Oxbridge trained men who supported reform and expansion of higher education, contributing time and money in Manchester and expertise in Parliament.

25. Owen, *English Philanthropy*, p. 165.

26. Owens announced its pleasure at receiving contributions from a distance to its extension fund. The examples of £500 donors were not merely distant, however; they were the late Lord Derby, Lord Egerton of Tatton, Lord Overstone, and Mr. Lewis Lloyd.

27. Other institutions followed suit. When Sheffield became a University College in 1897 the Duke of Norfolk became President.

28. Thompson, *The Owens College*, Ch. XXIII.

29. Class pride, particularly in the great new Northern cities, would be closely allied with civic pride since civic status was usually the result of middle class efforts. See Ch. 2, Preconditions.

30. O.C. Minutes of Trustees, 31 January 1861.

31. See below.

32. *Manchester Guardian*, 22 August 1865.

33. Ayerst, *Guardian, Biography of a Newspaper*, pp. 188-89.

34. *Manchester Guardian*, August 1874. *The Courier* was equally helpful.

35. O.C. "Report of the First Session", 1852.

36. At the first public meeting in May, 1878, the Mayor had remarked that "... such had been the care exercised by his predecessors in calling such meetings that towns' meetings in Liverpool were always considered by the inhabitants as important gatherings which were only justified by important events". *Liverpool Daily Post*, 25 May 1878.

37. U.C. Archives: pamphlet marked "A dozen copies of this pamphlet were distributed to each member of the Committee, 28 March, 1879". Subscriptions could be given in at variety of banks and at public news rooms.

38. "The importance of this phenomenon of habit, of the tradition of social responsibility, cannot be too strongly stated. We have observed in many hundreds of parishes that one substantial foundation of say an almshouse would very quickly draw many other gifts either for the support of that institution or some other equally ambitious undertaking for still another need in the community. A grammar school founded in one parish would inevitably tend to inspire a similar foundation in a nearby community." Jordan, *Philanthropy*, pp. 153-54.

39. O.C. Annual Report, 1852-53.

40. E.G. The Langton Fellowships and History Scholarships were founded in 1877 by "friends of Mr. William Langton, for many years a resident in Manchester." Council Minutes, 5 October 1877.

41. In Fairbairn's case the memorial committee first erected a statue and then endowed a scholarship with £1,150. Council Reports, 1881. A classical scholarship, endowed with £1,000, was the result of a public subscription in testimony of respect for the Bishop. "Principal's Annual Report, 1880-81".

42. The advice of lawyers and bankers was of considerable importance in many American benefactions. Curti and Nash, *Philanthropy*, p. 165.

43. As with much of the information on benefactions, this was calculated from Appendix III of Thompson, *The Owens College*. It does not include testamentary bequests which were posthumously named for the donor by the college, though it is of course conceivable that this sort of memorial might well have been envisioned by the donor. Donations bearing a family name, but not testamentary, were generally made in honor of some non-participating member of that family, usually deceased. These gifts ranged in size from the £5,500 for the Fielden Lectureship in Mathematics to the £250 given by S. D. Bles to endow a prize in Hebrew in memory of his father. Some were as obviously motivated as Mrs. J.F.C. Crace-Calvert's endowment of a chemistry scholarship in memory of her husband, who was a most distinguished chemist, while others remain more or less enigmatic.

44. The rather ironic commentary on the teaching of the principles of laissez-faire appeared in the Annual Report for 1864-65, where Shuttleworth was described as "... one of the earliest and most zealous friends of this college, and one of the most enlightened and energetic promoters of education of whom Manchester can boast."

Mrs. Shuttleworth's letter to the trustees offers a rare insight into a donor's motivation: "It was my late husband's wish to found in connection with Owens College a Scholarship such as while it had the effect of leading competent students to devote themselves more thoroughly than many do to the study of the science of Political Economy should also be of sufficient intrinsic importance to afford to a young man material assistance on his entrance into life -- Mr. Shuttleworth had himself throughout the course of a long life, spent in more or less anxious self education for the better discharge of the duties which he always acknowledged and as constantly conscientiously laboured to fulfil as a citizen of his own town, and of his country, became so persuaded of the value of adequate theoretical cultivation at the beginning of life and of the great advantage to a young man of some resources of his own beyond the ordinary fruits of early industry, that it was his frequent pleasure to plan some such endowment as I have mentioned." O.C. Minutes of Trustees, January 1865.

45. Any remaining funds were to be used to provide prizes in the evening classes in political economy. O.C. Minutes of Trustees, 1866.

46. The Council in accepting the gifts, explained its motivation: "the donors being of opinion that a general knowledge of that Science is one of the best securities for perpetuating perfect free trade in food products, which was the object of the League". O.C. Council Minutes, 15 October 1875.

47. Thompson, *The Owens College*, Ch. 1.

48. Derived from lists in Maltby, *Manchester and the Movement for National Elementary Education*, Appendix XIII.

49. Manchester MPs were automatically Trustees of the College under Owens' will until the reorganization of 1870.

50. Ashton, *Economic and Social Investigations in Manchester*.

51. Thompson, *The Owens College*, Ch. 1.

52. Its then President, John Marshall of the famous family of industrialists, had described a plan as early as 1826.

53. Shimmin, *Leeds*, Ch.1.

54. The Society had continued to hear about education after Marshall's proposal of 1826. Papers on Oxford were read in the 50s and 60s, 1869 saw two lectures on technical education, and during the 70s papers on various educational questions were presented.

55. Information in this paragraph from Kitson Clark, *Leeds Philosophical and Literary Society*.

56. Life Governors were those who had contributed at least £250 to the College; Perpetual Life Governors, those whose contributions had reached £1,000 (their number, 23, is included in the total of 225) had a membership rate in the Phil. and Lit. of 52%, including Sir Edward Baines, the Duke of Devonshire, Sir Andrew Fairbairn, and at least 5 MPs, clearly a distinguished group.

57. Thorpe, "Personal Reminiscences", in Kitson Clark, *Leeds Phil. and Lit.*

58. As of 1890 37% of the College's past and present faculty were or had been members of the Society, including Bodington, Marshall, Lupton, and other distinguished names. By the mid-80s Rucker was an Honorary Secretary, Professor A.H. Green was the Honorary Geology Curator, and Professor Miall had been doubling as curator of the museum.

59. Ashton, *Economic and Social Investigations in Manchester*.

60. See Grindon, *Manchester Banks and Bankers*.

61. A useful biographical sketch will be found in the "Supplement to the *Liverpool Daily Post*", 24 May 1978.

62. U.C. Annual Report, 1886-87.

63. Data has come from the accurate list of benefactions in Thompson, *The Owens College*, and from various city directories and collective biographies.

64. Important discussions of Extension can be found in Thompson, *The Owens College,* and Chaloner, *The Movement for the Extension of Owens College.*

65. O.C. Minutes of Trustees, 20 December 1866.

66. See, for example, the histories of the College by Thompson and Hartog, and Roscoe's *Life and Experiences.* Ashton evidently believed in setting an example for those who might contribute to any part of the Extension Fund. Besides £4,000 to the general fund he gave £1,000 each to the Geology and Mining and the Endowments and Scholarships Funds, and £500 to the Medical School Fund.

67. Potter, no doubt like other members of the committee, was not new to the work. He had been involved with earlier schemes for a college in Manchester as mentioned above.

68. Apart from the histories of the movement by Thompson and Chaloner, information is contained in three "Reports of the Executive Committee", several printed broadsides and appeals (of which the first is a proof copy dated 1 June 1866, revealing the long and careful gestation which preceded the public appeal) and memorials to the Lords of the Treasury all contained in a volume marked "Owens College Extension and Amalgamation 1870-1" in the university archives.

69. Printed sheets issued by the Executive Committee, 1 March 1867.

70. Broadside of the Executive Committee dated: "Royal Institution, Manchester. 28 August, 1868".

71. O.C. Cuttings Books, in Archives.

72. *Guardian,* 27 February 1868.

73. As reported *in extenso* in all Manchester newspapers.

74. O.C. Archives.

75. The Second Report of December, 1869, remarked on the bad times, and the consequent decision not to canvass generally, but noted that funds had reached £89,405. The Third Report in July, 1870, found times still bad but the fund at £102,030. In 1872 a further appeal was made; funds had reached £130,000, but student numbers were growing even faster, and the amalgamation with the medical school and the wants of the museum required more money. (O.C. "Extension and Amalgamation" vol. 133, headed "Proof-Private; the Owens College.")

76. These figures, in great detail, will be found in Thompson, *The Owens College,* Appendix III.

77. An appeal was made to the Association of Coal Owners of South Lancashire and Cheshire, asking them to provide for something like the schools of Freiberg and Saxony. The examples of engineers and chemical manufacturers were cited. O.C. Document Books, Vol. I, no.13, 7 December 1870. Also, O.C. Minutes of Council, "Report of the Geology and Mining Department Comm. to the Council".

78. O.C. "Extension and Amalgamation" vol. 142, headed "Observation ... To Foster the Fine Arts".

79. The Annual Report for 1882-83 found the Building Fund £10,000 short of the amount necessary to complete buildings already under way!

80. The amount lost from capital in 1882-83 was £1,364. Y.C. Annual Report 1882-83.

81. In a report to the College Council made in 1883 the necessity for providing Arts teaching was proved by the example of other institutions including Liverpool, Nottingham, Sheffield, Bristol, and Birmingham. In the last case the original absence of Arts and the almost immediate decision to add them was cited. The clincher was the certainty that the Victoria University would not admit a college which lacked an adequate Literature Department. Even after these overwhelming arguments were marshalled it took considerable time to effect the change from incidental to regular status.

82. Y.C. "A", 4 March 1877. The University Extension Committee, pleased with the College's proposal for two chairs offered £350 per annum for 3 years, on condition of being represented on a College Committee. They received three representatives on the Education Committee.

83. The circumstances are summarized in Gosden and Taylor, *Studies*, "Curriculum".

84. By 1881 the £100 subscriber had died, and a total annual subscription of £355/9/6 was derived from 13 subscriptions of between £10 and £50, and 42 smaller subscriptions. Members of the Baines, Lupton, Marshall, and Tetley families were providing nearly a third of the total. "List of Subscriptions", Y.C. Archives.

85. The noted philanthropist and creator of Saltaire, a model town for factory workers.

86. William Rathbone's unpublished "Sketch of Family History" quoted in Kelly, *For Advancement of Learning*, and elsewhere.

87. U.C. Council Minutes, 1 May 1883 and 5 February 1884.

88. U.C. Council Minutes, 7 May 1881.

89. "A sum of over £100,000 has been collected within the last two years, and the Special Committee to which was entrusted the task of framing a Constitution, and upon which both the Committee appointed at the Town's Meeting and the donors were equally represented, has completed the draft of a Charter which will shortly, it is hoped, obtain the Royal sanction. University College, Liverpool, will then have commenced its corporate existence, and will, thenceforth, be entitled to rank as one of the public institutions of this City. It has met with large and generous support from all classes without distinction of creed or politics, and whether we regard the amount of the endowments which it has received, or the importance of the objects for which it has been founded and the great advantages to the City and neighborhood which must follow upon its success, its present position is such as to justify those who have striven to give effect to the wishes of the inhabitants expressed at the two Town Meetings, in seeking the aid of the City Council to bring those endeavours to a successful issue ....

"If the Council of the College may, without presumption, submit a definite proposal through your Worship to the City Council, it would be that the Corporation should become the purchasers of the buildings and area above mentioned, [an asylum on Brownlow Hill] and should let them to the College on a lease of 75 years, at a nominal rent.

"Such support is not without precedent. What the comparatively small town of Nottingham has done ... might surely be done by the large and wealthy City of Liverpool, in aid of an institution to which her Citizens have contributed ten times that amount.

"I trust that this appeal may meet with a favourable consideration and in conclusion will only add, that, by the terms of our Constitution, the Mayor for the time being and five representatives selected by the City Council will be members of the Supreme Governing Body of the College."

Printed copy in U.C. Archives. The Corporation of the City of Liverpool did indeed buy the College its site, worth about £30,000.

90. "In order to prevent this quite irreparable misfortune, Messrs. Rathbone, Holt, Tate, Sinclair, and others have promised the sum of nearly £20,000 provided the remainder necessary to fulfill all requirements for entering as a coequal member of Victoria University be raised. The required sum is about £30,000, towards which nearly £10,000 has been promised, and a vigorous effort is now on foot to raise the remainder, in the hope that the handsome, but strictly conditional, offer of the above-named gentlemen may not be forfeited, and an all-important department of University College be allowed to collapse." Printed copy of a letter headed "Liverpool University College" and signed by Malcolm Guthrie; copy in U.C. Archives.

Chapter Six: Governance

1. The terms "lay" and "layman" refer to those who are not engaged in academic activity for their livelihood. Such persons may, of course, be highly educated and engage in scholarly pursuits.

2. The organizational arrangements of civic universities have been frequently described. The most thorough analysis of the acquisition and exercise of power in British universities is contained in Moodie and Eustace, *Power and Authority*, and in various papers by these authors, notably Eustace's "The Origins of Self Government of University Staffs", presented to the 1970 Annual Conference of the British Sociological Association, and Moodie's "Academics and University Government: Some Reflections on British Experience", presented to the Seminario "Politicas y Estructuras Universitarias: Antecedentes y Experiencias Internacionales", Vina del Mar, Chile, November, 1979. See also Van de Graaf, et al., *Academic Power*.

The present author is indebted to this body of work for many ideas on the subject of this chapter, though the application and perhaps distortion of them to the specific circumstances of the 19th Century is his own responsibility.

3. Lord Ashby has published versions of this explanation in several places, most completely in "A Postscript on Self-Government in Civic Universities", in Ashby, *Technology and the Academics*.

4. Eustace, "The Origins", p.16. See footnote 2 above.

5. Representatives and organizations of students only acquired significant powers after the period under study, though social organization had already begun. Ashby and Anderson, *The Rise of the Student Estate*, p.43.

Non-academic staff, other than senior administrators, have only very recently acquired a voice in university affairs.

6. And revealing them very publicly, via a series of parliamentary investigations and a body of polemical literature ranging from works like those of Arnold and Pattison to a vast assortment of diatribes.

7.   Notably the University of London, which was originally governed entirely by shareholders, without academic input. Moodie and Eustace, *Power and Authority*, p.27.

8.   The charitable Livery Companies of the City of London found it easy to understand a government so like their own when they decided to support the Yorkshire College, and their members were no doubt comfortable as Governors and Council members of the College in consequence.

9.   Thomas Ashton, explaining the proposed constitution of the Owens Extension College, spoke of a governing body small enough for an individual sense of responsibility but large enough to include the opinions of the community. *Manchester Examiner and Times,* report of the "Owens College Extension" meeting, 4 December 1869. The representative character was evidently enhanced at the expense of the sense of responsibility, as the Court was quite large, while even the Council had occasional trouble achieving a quorum.

10.   Donors of £1,000 or more became "Perpetual Life Governors", while gifts of at least £250 earned a "Life Governorship". The qualifications, and the names of those so qualified, were prominently displayed in the College Calendar.

11.   These links were quite deliberately fostered. The Duke of Devonshire inquired of the new University College, Liverpool, whom he might usefully nominate in his capacities as Chancellor of both Victoria and Cambridge universities. James Stewart of Trinity, Cantab., and H.E. Roscoe of Owens were suggested. U.C. Council Minutes, 22 December 1881.

12.   Moodie and Eustace, *Power and Authority*, Ch. V.

13.   See *DNB* entries under Heywood and Thompson, *The Owens College.*

14.   Thompson, *The Owens College,* especially Ch. III.

15.   See his comments on professors, particularly Theodores, in *The Owens College.*

16.   Y.C. Council Minutes, letter to Clothworkers, 5 June 1875.

17.   Y.C. Council Minutes, letter from J.J. Hummel to the Chairman of the Textile Industries and Dyeing Committee, 31 January 1885. Also see, more conveniently, Gosden and Taylor, *Studies,* "Government and Staff", p.198-200, 219-20. The title Instructor was ostensibly merely an indication that certain departments were externally maintained, but it is worth noting that Technology and its Instructors achieved the status of a faculty of the college only with great difficulty.

18.   Lupton's receipt of the Cross of the Order of St. John and an illuminated address from his colleagues and students was reported in the *Leeds Mercury,* 1883.

19.   Greenwood married the daughter of a prominent bank manager (Langton, whose retirement was commemorated by a large gift to the college), Roscoe the daughter of Edmund Potter, M.P.

20.   Edmund Muspratt, influential supporter of College and University, said that the professors' evening lectures and contact with influential residents soon earned respect. Muspratt, *My Life and Work,* pp.276-78. Rathbone's friendship with several professors, and particularly with Oliver

Lodge, is mentioned in Rathbone, *A Memoir*, Ch. IX, supported by an assortment of letters catalogued as IX. 6. 175-204, in the "Rathbone Papers" at the University of Liverpool.

21. E.g., Professor Green's FRS appears in the Y.C. Annual Report for 1885-86. The value of professors' public activities in enhancing the colleges' repute was appreciated, and this no doubt redounded to the professors' credit vis a vis Councils and others. When Roscoe was appointed to a government "Noxious Vapours Commission" Greenwood pointed out to the Council that "it was clearly in the interest of the College that he should act on the Commission". O.C. Council Minutes, October 1876.

22. Leeds' first three professors, Rucker, Green, and Thorpe, became respectively Secretary of the Royal Society and Principal of London University, Professor of Geology at Oxford, and Director of Government Laboratories. Gosden and Taylor, *Studies*, "Introduction".

23. Moodie, "Academics and University Governance", (Chile), pp.6-7.

24. Three quotes from O.C. Trustees Minutes, October 1868.

25. Information on the relationships among income, expenditure, and status will be found in Banks, *Prosperity and Parenthood*.

26. This may have been especially significant at Leeds, where the faculty were striving for a position similar to that at Owens. In the mid-80s Stroud, who had been a Gilchrist Scholar at Owens, became Cavendish Professor of Physics, and was soon followed by Smithells (chemistry), who had been a Dalton Scholar at Owens and had taught for two years under Roscoe.

27. O.C. "Substance of a Report ...", 1850.

28. Y.C. "Report of the Committee ...", 1872.

29. O.C. Council Minutes, 1853.

30. O.C. "Substance of a Report ...", 1850.

31. U.C. Council Minutes, 1881.

32. For example, in 1875 the Manchester Senate's recommendation that a new Lectureship in English Language be established (in keeping with the then current trend in scholarship) was immediately approved by the Council, apparently without debate. O.C. Council Minutes, March 1875.

33. Except by or to academics elsewhere. From Owens College's inception to its achievement of university status professors had complained of the way in which University of London exams had distorted Owens' curricula.

34. Presumably the faculties' expertise was what led donors to leave the details to them. In any case the Owens faculty were defining conditions of scholarships at least from 1857. See O.C. "Minutes of College Meetings", vol. 1, 1857-1869.

35. In addition to new clinical fields, physics, more botany, and a new form of anatomy were added to the medical curriculum in the late 19th Century.

36. The Council was to advertise professorships and to refer all applications and testimonials to the Senate for advice, though it was not to be bound by that advice.

37. For examples, see the appointments of assistants by Professors Frankland and Roscoe, and of an evening teacher by Greenwood, O.C. Trustees Minutes, October 1853, 1859, and 1865, respectively.

38. Uncontested and unsupervised faculty appointment of assistants appears as early as 1874 and was common by the late 70s. Y.C. Council Minutes, 1874, 1878-79.

39. O.C. Senate Minutes, 1873-74, and Council Minutes, 1875-76. The new regulations directed the Principal to present a form of advertisement to the Council. The Principal and the Registrar were to summarize all replies for members of Council and Senate; then the Senate was to examine, arrange, and report on the applications, after which the Council was to invite one or more candidates for interviews. Council Minutes, June, 1876.

40. The examples of Schorlemmer and Toller reveal the reality of faculty power. Each had been hired by the faculty as an assistant, and each later received a newly created chair on the faculty's recommendation without even the formality of an advertisement. O.C. Senate Minutes, 1874 for Schorlemmer's chair in organic chemistry, 1880 for Toller's Smith English chair.

41. By 1878 at Leeds the faculty was creating appointment short lists for the Council. Y.C. Council Minutes, 1878. As early as 1884 at Liverpool Senate recommendations for guest lecturers and two new professorial appointments were accepted by Council, apparently with little or no discussion. U.C. Council Minutes, May-July, 1884.

42. Leeds did dismiss technical faculty, and all the colleges at one time or another had troubles with the relatively large, transitory, and uncontrolled medical faculties.

43. In the last decade, for example, most British and American discussions of the state's powers over higher education have dealt with governments' financial activities.

44. O.C. Trustees Minutes, 1858-59; Minutes of College Meetings, 1858; Council Minutes, 1871.

45. The faculty had buttressed their opinion with outside professional opinions. Thompson, *The Owens College*, pp. 214-17.

46. See, for example, the O.C. Senate Minutes, June, 1875, and Council Minutes, April, 1881.

47. O.C. Trustees Minutes show regular acceptance of faculty claims for repayments and allotments for lab equipment, materials, etc.

48. U.C. Council Minutes, 25 June 1881, and November, 1881.

49. U.C. Council Minutes, 28 February 1882. Expenditures by professors were generally authorized in advance and seldom discussed or audited. E.g., Council Minutes, 22 May 1883; 2 October 1883; Senate Minutes, 1884.

50. This power had existed informally at least as early as 1868. O.C. Trustees Minutes, 1868, 1870.

51. The Langton Fellowship, created in 1878, and the Bishop Berkeley Fellowships, 1881, provided for research fellows at Owens. See Fiddes, *Chapters*, pp. 114-16.

52. U.C. Council and Senate Minutes, May-July, 1884.

53. In 1869 the Owens faculty were providing the Trustees with detailed reports on the costs of running new labs. O.C. Council Minutes, 1869. In 1871 the Council directed that: "Senate be requested to send to the treasurer for embodiment in his estimate a statement of all grants which they think it desirable to apply for during the session." O.C. Council Minutes, 1 November 1871.

54. The process can be traced in the Minutes of Liverpool's Council. In 1884 a small committee of Council and faculty was appointed to draw up forms, make estimates, present accounts, etc. Small annual grants were made thereafter, and financial affairs generally seem better arranged by 1886. By October of 1889 a Finance Committee was appointed to consider the "annual reports" of departments, and next January the committee recommended small annual grants to some departments. It was not yet a modern budget, but it was a far cry from the earliest years. U.C. Council Minutes, November, 1884, 1886, October 1889, January, 1890.

55. U.C. Council Minutes, 3 July 1888.

56 "Substance of a Report of a Committee of the Trustees", 1850, O.C. Archives. Advice was solicited from a wide range of individuals, universities, and other educational institutions.

57. O.C. Trustees Minutes, 1858. Greenwood's quick grasp of all College business was impressive but not really surprising. Since 1851 he had served practically as acting Principal during Scott's many illnesses, and in 1857 he gathered the reins into his own hands with quiet efficiency. O.C., Trustees Minutes, 1851-57.

58. The logic was obvious, for example, to the vast majority of American colleges which gave their chief academic/executive officer a place, or even the headship of, their governing bodies. See Schmidt, *The Old Time College President*, pp.48-49, 73-74. The typical American college president of the 19th and 20th Centuries of course had considerably greater powers than his English counterpart.

59. O.C. Trustees Minutes, 1859-61.

60. The new Principal was immediately authorized to arrange for demonstrators, etc., and then report. U.C. Council Minutes, 22 December 1881. For the growing range of his duties, see U.C. Council Minutes, 1890.

61. See, as a not unrepresentative example, Thompson's laudatory Chapter VI in *The Owens College*.

62 See below for statistical evidence of his diligence. His qualities were publicly recognized at the time. See a series of articles on "The Principal and Present Professors of Owens College" published in the Manchester *Free Lance*, 8 and 29 February 1868.

63. Indeed, they travelled together on the Continent, examining foreign educational institutions at the College's behest.

64. O.C. Senate Minutes, 18 October 1873, and Council Minutes, 1874. Note that it was the Senate which had acquired the power to elect a Vice-Principal. Further evidence of the general respect for the Principal's qualifications and activity can be found in the raising of his salary to £700 in 1873. O.C. Council Minutes, 4 April 1873.

65. See footnote 62 above.

66. Good examples include his quick response to complaints about a change in certification of evening class work. Correspondents in the public press had regretted a loss of previously available honors and convenience of transfer; Greenwood immediately assured them that the new arrangements would take care of this. *Manchester Guardian*, April, 1874.

His diplomatic skills were also equal to a complaint from the medical students, again in the public press, that they had been deprived of the right to address their own annual gathering. Greenwood replied with an apology and the scheduling of an extra address. O.C. Cutting Books, June, 1872.

67. All the colleges seem to have followed Owens' lead in this matter. Scott had been assigned the duty of examining candidates for admission to Owens in 1851.

68. Annual attendance records of Councils and committees of Council are available in the Liverpool and Manchester archives for the years mentioned in the text. They are frequently printed with the Annual Reports. By simply adding together Council and committee attendances I have created a crude, but, I believe, informative measure of interest in and influence on college business. Certainly the names of the most regular attenders at Owens from 1870-1872 are those of men prominent in all aspects of the College's life. Greenwood and Roscoe are joined by Thomas Ashton, R.C. Christie, R.D. Darbishire, Alfred Nield, and Joseph Thompson.

The choice of seven or eight most frequent attenders is not arbitrary; in most years frequency of attendance falls off greatly outside this inner circle. By 1874 at Owens a circular to Council members reminds them that regular attendance is necessary to avoid further problems in attaining a quorum. O.C. Council Minutes, 5 June 1874.

69. See Thompson, *The Owens College*, Ch. VIII.

70. Thompson, *The Owens College*, pp. 241-42.

71. The Trustees had requested faculty advice, and this was embodied in a series of reports, many of whose recommendations were accepted (see below, p.252). O.C. Trustees Minutes, "Copy Statements and Summary read at the Meeting of 20th May 1856."

72. O.C. Trustees Minutes, 1865-66.

73. See Thompson, *The Owens College*, pp. 313-15 for a description of their activities. See also, in addition to the Trustees Minutes, a volume titled "Owens College Extension and Amalgamation 1870-1" in the University archives.

74. Copy of letter to the Hon. Sec., Mr. Reynolds, dated June 25th, 1877, and signed by Green, Thorpe, Rucker, Miall, and Armstrong; in the Council Minutes.

75. Y.C. Council Minutes, September, 1877.

76. Gosden and Taylor, *Studies*, "Government and Staff," p.201. This chapter, by F.T. Mattison, provides a conveniently available summary of the development of governance at Leeds.

77. Y.C. Academic Board Minutes, 1878-79.

78. Y.C. Council Minutes, 1874. The committee was entrusted with "... the more strictly academical administration and discipline of the College

...", a definition of duties which surely seems to suggest faculty control under normal circumstances.

79. The difficulties surrounding the office and appointment of a Principal are well covered in Gosden and Taylor, *Studies*, "Government and Staff", pp.187-91.

80. See below

81. Here, as elsewhere, both faculty and laymen eventually agreed that the permanent Principal should be an arts professor, and preferably a classicist. Gosden and Taylor, *Studies*, "Government and Staff", p.190.

82. Y.C. Board of Governors Minutes, 14 April 1886.

83. Y.C. Board of Governors Minutes, 16 May 1888.

84. Even after 1878 the Principal was the sole, and non-voting representative of the faculty at Council meetings.

In 1878 the Academic Board was seeking assurance that its reports were being heard by the Council. In 1879 a communications failure held up the approval of regulations for the new Coal Mining Associateship. (In that year the Council also rejected a Board resolution concerning library fees, an action inconceivable at Owens or Liverpool.) Communications remained uncertain, causing difficulties with the engineering course in 1881, etc. Y.C. Academic Board Minutes, 1878-82.

85. Y.C. Academic Board Minutes, December, 1880.

86. A regular Senate was created only in 1884.

87. O.C. Trustees Minutes, "Copy of Statements and Summary read at the Meeting of 20th May 1856". Professor Frankland recommended "... a closer co-operation amongst the Professors, by periodical meetings with the Principal ...." Professor Christie went further: "4. That if possible there should be combined action of the Professors among themselves, and of the Professors with the Trustees and that with a view to this, monthly meetings should be held by the Principal and Professors and occasional reports presented to the Trustees."

88. Thompson, *The Owens College*, p.159.

89. O.C. Trustees Minutes, February, 1857, "As to the Principal and Professors", in which the rules and powers of "College Meetings" were defined.

90. O.C. Trustees Minutes, 1869, "Draft of Owens College Extension Act". "The Owens College Bye-Laws", Manchester, 1873.

91. O.C. Trustees Minutes, 1869, including a report by the Professors upon the new draft constitution, as requested by the Trustees.

92. Bryce's instructions from the Trustees explained that Owens had become a public service and should therefore become a public institution, not a private trust with private trustees. Governors were to represent the government, local dignitaries, men of University training and distinction, interested men of standing familiar with practical life, Faculty representatives, the Bishop, representatives of the alumni, etc. O.C. "Extension and Amalgamation 1870-1" volume, entry 37, "Instructions to Mr. Bryce ...."

Chapter Seven: The Colleges and Their Environment

1. These last rented Owens College's new gymnasium. These and numerous other similar arrangements will be found in the various Council and Trustees Minutes.
2. The Principal and a Trustee were actually invited to London by the Society. O.C. Trustees Minutes, December, 1867.
3. In 1875 Owens was offering very popular public lectures in groups of 3 or 4; subjects included Roscoe on "Earth, Air, Fire, Water" and Stewart on "The Energies of Nature".

   The Yorkshire College specialized in extra-mural lecture courses of 8 or 10 lectures. During the later 70s they offered them in such towns as Bradford, Darlington, Harrogate, Halifax, Hull, Rotherham, and Wakefield, in some years offering as many as 7 courses. Y.C. Calendar, 1879-80.
4. U.C. Archives, "Cutting Books".
5. The list was prominently displayed in the Yorkshire College Calendars.
6. O.C. Archives, "Victoria University: Affiliated Institutions, Draft Scheme ...", March, 1886.
7. Professors examined students, classrooms and meeting space were provided, and special schoolmasters' classes were offered.
8. Examples include the Executive Committee of the Association for the Promotion of Evening Science and Arts Classes in Leeds, which included a large proportion of the faculty and council of the Yorkshire College, and the Liverpool School of Science, linked through its directorate with University College.
9. O.C. Annual Report, 1852.
10. This expedient, adopted by many American colleges in similar positions, was thoroughly described in a report, "Recommendations to the Trustees on The Plan of a School". O.C. Trustees Minutes, 25 May 1857. No action was taken.
11. Price, *A History of the Leeds Grammar School*. Brown, *Some Account of the Royal Institution School*.
12. The college advertised the fact that especially well prepared students could proceed to a Victoria degree in two years.
13. At Owens, schools so favored included the Manchester Jews School, the Commercial Schools, and the Grammar School. Scholarships were offered to "Artisan Members" of any Mechanics Institute, and to employees of the London and North Western Railway Co.
14. O.C. Document Books, 2 February 1867. The other 20 students' parentage was unknown.
15. Percentages derived from the Principal's regular reports to the Trustees and Council.
16. O.C. Annual Report, 1896.
17. At Owens in 1863 a detailed study showed that a majority of recent students had attended only one session. Formally advertised regular courses and fee reductions presumably helped produce the longer attendance and greater courses per student ratios of the late 60s and 70s.

   O.C. Trustees Minutes, 26 March 1863.

18. The reports of the Hall's principal to the Owens College Council will be found in O.C. Council Minutes. The Friends Hall was one of several established in affiliation with the college, and the only one which, during the 70s and 80s, remained solvent for any length of time.

19. The growth of corporate student life, including sports teams, clubs and societies, and a union, no doubt began to absorb excess student energies. The origins of these activities are seldom recorded in detail, but all were apparently active in the 80s, by which time colleges were allotting meeting space and purchasing sports grounds and gymnasia.

20. Convenient histories of the movement include Harrison, *Learning and Living*, and Kelly, *A History of Adult Education*.

21. In 1862 Greenwood's summary history of the Owens' evening classes spoke of schoolmasters desirous of carrying their studies to a more advanced stage, and of artisans "obtaining a higher training than is generally to be found in institutions expressly designed for them". O.C., Annual Report, 1862.

All the colleges announced the successes of evening students in university and other exams, and encouraged transfer to the day classes and/or the taking of degrees.

22. In 1879 Owens noted that increased fees, and consequent falling numbers, would "curtail the activity and usefulness of the College in a direction in which some of its warmest friends see one of its most important claims to public support". O.C. Senate Minutes, 15 March 1879.

In this context "public support" may mean state support. If so, it further indicates the significance of meeting the demand for part-time higher education.

23. "Inaugural Address of the Working Men's College", 1858, by A.J. Scott.

24. Y.C. Annual Report, 1883.

25. O.C. Annual Report, 1861.

26. In 1860 Greenwood noted that "our demand of work, and not of passive attendance merely, interferes with their popularity". Then, as earlier and later, the solution was to be encouragement, but without any relaxation of standards.

27. By 1858 Owens was encouraging regularity and progression among its evening students by standarizing its course offerings and allowing fee reduction for logical and progressive courses of study. O.C. Annual Report, 1858.

28. O.C. Annual Report, 1854.

29. O.C. Annual Report, 1853.

30. O.C. Annual Report, 1859.

31. Enrolment leaped from 102 to 234.

32. See Sadler, *Continuation Schools in England* and Harrison, *The Working Men's College*.

33. The most detailed records were discovered in the Owens bursars' strongroom, wrapped in an incredibly filthy package which had evidently lain unopened since the 1880s. They, in addition to reports printed in the Working Men's College Magazine, provided the data for this paragraph.

34.   This detailed information is similar at all points to the less complete data on the evening divisions of the civic colleges. Their rough estimates of the social class of students agree with these exact ones, as do descriptions of attitudes, intentions, and reasons for short attendance.

35.   Gosden and Taylor, *Studies*, p. 43.

36.   In 1863 the Annual Report recorded appointments of one-time evening students to important posts. The classes could certainly be a road to the top. T.E. Thorpe, the distinguished chemist, began his career by gaining the exhibition to the Owens evening classes from the Manchester Commercial Schools.

By the late 70s the evening classes produced 7 or 8 London matriculation passes and one or two degrees per year.

37.   The Annual Report for 1870 is most illuminating:

A careful analysis has been recently made by the Registrar, at the suggestion of the Senate, of the statistics of the six years which have been passed in the new buildings under the present system, and of the six years next preceding passed in the old building and under the old system. Some of the results are interesting and significant. In the six Sessions from 1867 to 1873 the average number of students was 471, the average number of classes held was 37, and the average number of classes attended by each student was 1.6: in the six Sessions from 1873 to 1879 the average number of students has been 840, of classes held 56, and of classes attended by each student 1.75. These 56 classes have been classified into nine groups; viz., the group of classics, of English (including language, literature and history), of modern language, of the moral sciences (including logic and political economy), of pure mathematics, of engineering, of the physical sciences, of the biological sciences, and of the Fine Arts. There has been some fluctuation in the number of students entering in the several groups; but during each of the last six years the modern languages group has had the largest number of students, while the physical sciences group has stood second, and the classical group third, in this respect; and the fourth and fifth places have been divided between the groups of English, pure mathematics, and engineering.

Greater detail can be found in the O.C. Document Books, vol. 5, no.85.

38.   The details are available in the standard sources: Thompson, *The Owens College*, Gosden and Taylor, *Studies*, and Kelly, *For Advancement of Learning*.

39.   O.C. Council Minutes, 3 September 1874.

40.   O.C. Council Minutes, "Extract from an indenture ..." between the Natural History Society and Owens, dated 18 December 1872.

41.   O.C. Council Minutes, "Principal's Report", 2 November 1877.

42.   Owens sought this independence through the creation of the Victoria University. Liverpool sought it through the dissolution of the Victoria University after 1900; Leeds found it at the same time but still doubted its ability to stand alone.

43.   *Manchester Guardian*, 1 and 2 February 1867; *Manchester Courier*, 4 February 1867.

44. O.C. Council Minutes, August, 1874, "Memorandum of some considerations relied on by the Representatives of Owens College in their application to the Government for a Grant of Public Money." Emphasis in original. Nothing came of the application.

45. O.C. Archives, "Pamphlets Concerning University Status", 1876. These include the original faculty proposal, a report by a medical professor, published letters, a pamphlet analyzing the reaction of the press, memoranda, etc. Detailed information in the following paragraphs derives mainly from this source.

46. Supporters included Matthew Arnold, Edward Frankland, Mark Pattison and Lyon Playfair. O.C. Archives, "Pamphlets ...", 1876.

47. Concise accounts of the actual negotiations for a Charter can be found in Thompson, *The Owens College,* Chapter XXIII, and Gosden and Taylor, *Studies,* pp. 191-203.

48. O.C. Document Books, vol. 3, "Report to the Court of Governors ..." 22 March 1877. The Committee was impressively composed of Council members Neild, Ashton and Christie and Professors Greenwood, Roscoe, and Ward. Summaries of arguments 2, 3, and 4 are quoted from this source.

49. £326,000 of capital possessed by the College; £20,676 expended in 1876-77; 33 professors and lecturers in the Arts, Sciences, and Law, teaching 415 students; 15 regular Medical Faculty teaching 163 students; laboratories; a 25,000 volume library, £900 per annum in scholarships, etc. O.C. Document Books, vol. 3, "Memorial of the Owens College presented to the Lord President of the Privy Council", 20 July 1877.

50. O.C. Archives, "Pamphlets Concerning University Status". The Memorial to the Privy Council defined the recipients of these benefits as "those connected with the institution as graduates and past students ... schools and schoolmasters of the district ... professional men ... and its commercial and industrial classes."

51. Even University and Kings Colleges in London were complaining of the University's indifference to their concerns.

52. The price and inadequacies of Oxbridge and the rigors of the London course and exams restricted the flow to these sources and assured the success of a school convenient to the population of Northern England.

53. Manchester's excellence as a school, the size of its affiliated hospitals, and the wide range of clinical experience obtainable were all cited by Dr. J.E. Morgan of the medical school in this long, detailed memorandum, "Medical Education at the Universities". O.C. Archives, "Pamphlets Concerning University Status".

54. O.C. Annual Report, 1880.

55. It was described in *University College and the University of Liverpool.*

56. Gosden and Taylor, *Studies,* p. 203. Pp. 191-215 cover the relations of the Yorkshire College with the Victoria University.

57. Leeds, for example, described the establishment of Victoria and then said: "It must now be an object of honourable ambition of the Yorkshire College to secure the endowment and equipment which would warrant an application for admission ...." Y.C. Annual Report, 1880.

Bibliography

Bibliographical Note

The social, economic, political, and intellectual history of Victorian
England which forms the general background of this work is of
course treated in a practically limitless number of volumes. The
more specific studies which deal with local history, with the demand for higher education, and with the means of supplying it, deserve some more specific comment.

Major histories of Manchester and Liverpool are available. Redford and Russel, *History of Local Government*, and White, *History
of the Corporation of Liverpool*, go well beyond narrowly political
matters, and provide sound general histories of these cities. No
similar study of Leeds is available. Detailed studies of specific aspects of local and civic history abound; good recent examples from
Manchester include Williams, *The Making of Manchester Jewry*,
Ayerst, *Guardian: Biography of a Newspaper*, and Kargon, *Science
in Victorian Manchester*. All three are reminders that the history of
the growing cities of the North was very much the history of Britain
as well.

The demand for higher education was both social and economic.
Sources and commentaries on the socio-economic circumstances of
the Victorian middle classes are legion, but Banks, *Prosperity and
Parenthood*, remains perhaps the most convenient and informative.
Professionalization, which characterized much of the development
of the middle classes, is receiving increasing attention at present,
with new works utilizing the insights of history and the social sciences to produce such informative detailed studies as Peterson, *The*

Medical Profession in Mid-Victorian London. Though it does not encompass the most recent work, Reader, *Professional Men*, provides a useful survey of the growing professions and their members.

Specific studies of industrial and other non-professional employments are also available. There are histories of all major industries, while works like Tropp, *The School Teachers*, and Anderson, *Victorian Clerks*, treat of persons and employments most important to the civic colleges.

Studies of philanthropy are not nearly so numerous, but two major sources are available. Jordan, *Philanthropy in England*, treats of an earlier era but sets a standard of scholarship and offers generalizations of significance for more recent periods. Owen, *English Philanthropy*, has limited material on contributions to higher education but is an essential source of information on the general legal, social, psychological, and financial aspects of 19th Century charity.

There are many surveys of the history of English education; Lawson and Silver, *A Social History of Education in England*, is informative and up-to-date. Studies of various types of eduation, and of specific institutions, are very common and very variable in quality; Lawson and Silver's work provides a select bibliography. The history of education should not be narrowly construed: studies of other cultural institutions such as libraries, literary and philosophical societies, etc., are most informative, especially in the case of such thorough works as Tylecote, *The Mechanics Institutes of Lancashire and Yorkshire*, and the further studies stimulated by that volume.

Silver and Teague, *The History of British Universities, 1800-1969, A Bibliography*, excludes Oxbridge but provides an excellent guide to materials on the civic colleges and their successors. Armytage, *Civic Universities: Aspects of a British Tradition*, is the only general survey of the civic universities, but as it covers the era from the middle ages to the present and is also far broader in scope than its title suggests, it is neither detailed nor analytical. Recent works, notably Ringer's *Education and Society in Modern Europe* and Jarausch (ed) *The Transformation of Higher Learning, 1860-1930*, set the British experience in a broader international context.

Institutional histories of the colleges treated in this study are available. Of several dealing with Owens the first, Thompson, *The Owens College*, is a very thorough account of the early years. Leeds, on the other hand, is best studied in the most recent account,

Gosden and Taylor, *Studies in the History of a University*, which analyzes individually the various aspects of development including finance, governance, students, buildings, etc. Liverpool, after a century, has received its first major treatment by Kelly, *For Advancement of Learning*.

Unpublished Materials

The archival materials of the three colleges are similar in type, and of quantities proportional to their varying age and size. The materials at Liverpool and Leeds are well organized and conveniently available, while the more voluminous collections of Manchester are not presently consolidated in one accessible location.

The Trustees Minutes of the Owens College and the Council Minutes of all three colleges provide a great deal of information. In addition to recording the deliberations and decisions of the governing bodies they include copies of correspondence, reports made to the Councils, and other materials. The background and substance of decisions on almost every aspect of college affairs may be found here.

The Senate Minutes, and their predecessors the minutes of "college meetings", are more fragmentary and casually kept, revealing the faculties' opinions on some issues but otherwise paralleling the Council Minutes.

The Minutes of the Courts of Governors are brief, standardized, and of little or no value.

Each college also kept a wide assortment of miscellaneous materials, casually arranged in "Document Books" or stored haphazardly in some cases. Each college at some time maintained "Cutting Books" in which copies of local and sometimes national newspaper and periodical commentaries on the college were pasted. These provide a useful picture of the colleges' public face, and of public reaction and opinion.

Each college kept some records concerning students, but they are neither complete, uniform, nor particularly informative, which is unsurprising in view of the brief and irregular attendance of so many non-degree students throughout the 19th Century. Certainly no statistical analysis of them seems possible. Useful comments on students are to be found in the Council Minutes, however.

The most convenient running commentary on the progress of the colleges is their Annual Reports, which were presented publicly by the Principals. In addition to their place in the minute books these were regularly printed in the College Calendars, which provide a convenient source of statistics and reveal the colleges' pictures of themselves and the images which they wished to present to the public.

List of Published Material Consulted

Abramovitz, Moses and Vera F. Eliasberg. *The Growth of Public Employment in Britain.* Princeton: Princeton University Press, 1957.

Allen, G.C. *British Industries and Their Organization.* London: Longmans, Green, 1933.

Anderson, Gregory. *Victorian Clerks.* Manchester: Manchester University Press, 1976.

Anderson, Michael. *Family Structure in Nineteenth Century Lancashire.* Cambridge: Cambridge University Press, 1971.

Archer, R.L. *Secondary Education in the Nineteenth Century.* Cambridge: Cambridge University Press, 1921.

Argles, Michael. *South Kensington to Robbins: An Account of English Technical & Scientific Education since 1851.* London: Longmans, 1964.

Armytage, W.H.G. *The American Influence on English Education.* London: Routledge and Kegan Paul, 1967.

Armytage, W.H.G. *Civic Universities: Aspects of a British Tradition.* London: Benn, 1955.

Armytage, W.H.G. "James Heywood's Resolution: Prelude and Finale." *The Universities Review*, vol. 22, #3 (May 1950), pp. 139-153.

Armytage, W.H.G. *The Rise of the Technocrats: A Social History.* London: Routledge and Kegan Paul, 1965.

Armytage, W.H.G. *The Russian Influence on English Education.* London: Routledge and Kegan Paul, 1969

Armytage, W.H.G. *A Social History of Engineering.* Cambridge, Mass.: MIT Press, 1961.

Arnold, Matthew. *Schools and Universities on the Continent.* London: MacMillan, 1868.

Ashby, Eric. *Technology and the Academics.* London: MacMillan, 1959.

Ashby, Eric and Mary Anderson. *The Rise of the Student Estate in Britain.* Cambridge, Mass.: Harvard University Press, 1970.

Ashton, T.S. *Economic and Social Investigations in Manchester.* London: King & Son, 1934.

Axon, William E.A. (ed.). *The Annals of Manchester.* London: John Heywood, 1886.

Ayerst, David. *Guardian. Biography of a Newspaper.* London: Collins, 1971.

Baines, Edward. *Account of the Woollen Manufacture of England.* Reprinted from Thomas Baines, *Yorkshire Past and Present* (1875). Newton Abbott: David & Charles, 1970.

Bamford, T.W. *The Rise of the Public Schools.* London: Nelson, 1967.

Banks, J.A. and Olive Banks. *Feminism and Family Planning.* New York: Schocken, 1964.

Banks, J.A. *Prosperity and Parenthood.* London: Routledge and Kegan Paul, 1954.

Bibliography

Basalla, George, William Coleman, and Robert H. Kargon (eds.). *Victorian Science: A Self-Portrait from the Presidential Addresses of the British Association for the Advancement of Science.* Garden City, New York: Doubleday & Company, Inc., 1970.

Bell, S.P. (ed.). *Victorian Lancashire.* Newton Abbott: David & Charles, 1974.

Bellott, Hugh Hale. *University College, London.* London: University of London Press, 1929.

Berdahl, Robert O. *British Universities and the State.* Berkeley: University of California Press, 1959.

Best, Geoffrey. *Mid-Victorian Britain.* New York: Schocken, 1972.

Birks, Michael. *Gentlemen of the Law.* London: Stevens & Sons, 1960.

Bond, Brian. *The Victorian Army and the Staff College 1854-1914.* London: Eyre Methuen, 1972.

Briggs, Asa. *Victorian Cities.* New York: Harper & Row, 1970.

Briggs, Asa. *Victorian People.* New York: Harper & Row, 1963.

The British Association. *Manchester and Its Region. A Survey Prepared for the Meeting Held in Manchester August 29 to September 5, 1962.* Manchester: Manchester University Press, 1962.

Brockbank, Edward Mansfield. *The Foundation of Provincial Medical Education in England, esp. Manchester School.* Manchester: Manchester University Press, 1936.

Brown, E.J. *The Private Donor in the History of the University.* Leeds: University of Leeds Press, 1953.

Burn, W.L. *The Age of Equipoise.* London: George Allen & Unwin, 1964.

Burton, Anthony. *Josiah Wedgewood.* New York: Stein & Day, 1976.

Calvert, Monte A. *The Mechanical Engineer in America, 1830-1910: Professional Cultures in Conflict.* Baltimore: Johns Hopkins Press, 1967

Campbell Brown. *The First Page of the History of University College, Liverpool.* Liverpool: D. Marples & Co., 1892.

Cardwell, D.S.L. (ed.). *Artisan to Graduate.* Manchester: Manchester University Press, 1974.

Cardwell, D.S.L. *The Organization of Science in England.* London: Heinemann, 1972.

Carr-Saunders, A.M. and P.A. Wilson. *The Professions.* London: Oxford University Press, 1933.

Chaloner, W.H. *The Movement for the Extension of Owens College.* Manchester: Manchester University Press, 1973.

Chapman, Arthur W. *The Story of a Modern University: A History of the University of Sheffield.* London: Oxford University Press, 1955.

Charlton, H.B. *Portrait of a University, 1851-1951.* Manchester: Manchester University Press, 1951.

Christian, Edmund B.V. *A Short History of Solicitors.* London: Reeves & Turner, 1896.

City News-Notes and Queries. Manchester: Manchester City News, 1878.

Clapham, J.H. *An Economic History of Modern Britain.* Cambridge: Cambridge University Press, 1950.

Clapp, B.W. *John Owens, Manchester Merchant.* Manchester: Manchester University Press, 1965.

Clark, Burton R. *The Distinctive College: Antioch, Reed, Swarthmore.* Chicago: Aldine, 1970.

Clark, Burton R. and Ted I.K. Youn. *Academic Power in the United States.* Washington, D.C.: American Association for Higher Education, 1976.

Clarke, M.L. *Classical Education in Britain, 1500-1900.* OUP, 1959.

Clive, John. *Scotch Reviewers: The Edinburgh Review, 1802-1815.* Cambridge: Harvard University Press, 1957.

Cohen, Emmeline W. *The Growth of the British Civil Service.* Hamden, Conn.: Archon Books, 1965.

Cotgrove, Stephen F. *Technical Education and Social Change.* London: George Allen & Unwin, 1958.

Cottle, Basil and J.W. Sherborne. *The Life of a University.* Bristol: Arrowsmith, 1951.

Crowther, J.G. *Statesmen of Science.* London: The Cresset Press, 1965.

Cullen, M.J. *The Statistical Movement in Early Victorian Britain.* New York: Barnes and Noble, 1975.

Curti, Merle and Roderick Nash. *Philanthropy in the Shaping of American Higher Education.* New Brunswick: Rutgers University Press, 1965.

Curtis, S.J. *History of Education in Great Britain.* London: University Tutorial Press, 6th ed., 1965.

Davis, V.D. *A History of Manchester College.* London: George Allen & Unwin, 1932.

Dent, H.C. *1870-1970: Century of Growth in English Education.* London: Longmans, 1970.

Dicey, A.V. *Law and Public Opinion in England.* London: MacMillan, 1914.

Dore, Ronald. *The Diploma Disease: Education, Qualification, and Development.* Berkeley: University of California Press, 1976.

Dyer, Bernard and C. Ainsworth Mitchell. *The Society of Public Analysts.* Cambridge: W. Heffer, 1932.

Eddison and Thompson. *A Sketch of the Yorkshire Ladies Council.* Leeds: n.p., n.d.

Edinburgh Review. Assorted volumes.

Edmonds, E.L. *The School Inspector.* London: Routledge and Kegan Paul, 1962.

Ellegard, Alvar. *Darwin and the General Reader.* Goteborg, 1958.

Elliott, Philip. *The Sociology of the Professions.* New York: Herder & Herder, 1972.

Engel, Arthur Jason. *From Clergyman to Don: The Rise of the Academic Profession in Nineteenth Century Oxford.* London: O.U.P., 1983.

Esdaile, A.J.K. *The British Museum Library.* London: George Allen & Unwin, 1946.

Fiddes, Edward. *Chapters in the History of Owens College.* Manchester: Manchester University Press, 1937.

Foden, Frank. *Philip Magnus.* London: Valentine, Mitchell, 1970.

Fortunes Made In Business. London: Sampson Low, Marston, Searle, and Rivington, 1884.

The Free Lance, Manchester.

Galloway, Robert L. *A History of Coal Mining in Great Britain.* Newton Abbot, Devon: David & Charles, 1969 (1st ed., 1882).

Gathorne-Hardy, Jonathan. *The Old School Tie.* New York: Viking Press, 1977.

Ginsberg, Morris. *Law and Opinion in England in the 20th Century.* London: Stevens, 1959.

Girtin, Thomas Howard. *The Golden Ram: A Narrative History of the Clothworkers Company.* London: The Worshipful Company of Clothworkers, 1958.

Girtin, Thomas Howard. *The Triple Crowns: A Narrative History of the Drapers Company.* London: Hutchinson, 1964.

Gosden, P.H.J.H. and A.J. Taylor. *Studies in the History of a University 1874-1974.* Leeds: E.J. Arnold & Son Ltd, 1975.

Great Britain. *Commissioners Report on Scotch Universities 1831.*

Great Britain. *Report From the Select Committee on Scientific Instruction.* House of Commons, 15 July 1868.

Great Britain. *Report of the Committee on the Law and Practice Relating to Charitable Trusts.* London: HMSO, 1952.

Great Britain. *Report of Her Majesty's Commissioners Appointed to Inquire into the State ... of Oxford.* London, 1852.

Great Britain. *Reports of the Royal Commission on Technical Instruction.* 1884.

Great Britain. *Royal Commission on Secondary Education. Report of the Commissioners.* London: HMSO, 1895.

Great Britain. Education Department. *Special Reports on Educational Subjects, 1896-97.*

Great Britain. School Inquiry Commission. *Report of the Commissioners.* London: HMSO, 1868.

Grindon, Leo H. *Lancashire: Brief Historical and Descriptive Notes.* New York: Macmillan, 1892.

Grindon, Leo H. *Manchester Banks and Bankers.* Manchester: Palmer & Howe, 1878.

Habakkuk, H.J. *American and British Technology in the 19th Century.* Cambridge: Cambridge University Press, 1962.

Haber, Ludwig Fritz. *The Chemical Industry.* London: Oxford University Press, 1958.

Haines, George. *Essays Upon German Influence on English Education and Science, 1850-1919.* Hamden, Conn.: Archon, 1969.

Haines, George. *German Influence Upon English Education and Science, 1800-1866.* New London: Connecticut College, 1957.

Hall, Peter Dobkin. *The Organization of American Culture, 1700-1900: Private Institutions, Elites and the Origins of American Nationality.* New York: NYU Press, 1982.

Halsey, A.H., Flood, and Anderson (eds.). *Education, Economy and Society.* New York: The Free Press, 1961.

Harrison, J.F.C. *A History of the Working Men's College, 1854-1954.* London: Routledge & Kegan Paul, 1954.

Harrison, J.F.C. *Learning and Living, 1870-1960.* Toronto: University of Toronto Press, 1961.

Hartog, Philip Joseph (ed.). *The Owens College.* Manchester: J.E. Cornish, 1900.

Hearnshaw, F.J.C. *Centenary History of Kings College.* London: G.G. Harrap, 1929.

Heeney, Brian. *Mission to the Middle Classes: The Woodard Schools, 1848-1891.* London: SPCK, 1969.

Heywood, James. *Academic Reform and University Representation.* London: Whitfield, 1860.

Hilken, T.J.N. *Engineering at Cambridge.* Cambridge: Cambridge University Press, 1967.

Hobhouse, Sir Arthur. *The Dead Hand.* London: Chatto & Windus, 1880.

Hole, James. *An Essay on the History and Management of Literary, Scientific, and Mechanics Institutions.* London: Longman, Brown, Green & Longmans, 1853.

Hole, James. *"Light, More Light!" on the Present State of Education amongst the Working Classes of Leeds.* London: Woburn Press, 1969 (1st ed., 1860).

Honey, J.R. de S. *Tom Brown's Universe. The Development of the English Public School in the Nineteenth Century.* New York: The New York Times Book Co. (Quadrangle), 1977.

Houghton, Walter E. *The Victorian Frame of Mind, 1830-1870.* New Haven: Yale University Press, 1957.

Howarth, O.J.R. *The British Association for the Advancement of Science: A Retrospect 1831-1931.* London: The Association, 1922, 1931.

Huber, V.A., trans. and ed. F.W. Newman. *The English Universities.* London: W. Pickering, 1843.

Hudson, Derek and Kenneth W. Luckhurst. *The Royal Society of Arts, 1754-1954.* London: Murray, 1954.

Hughes, A.M.D. *The University of Birmingham: a short history.* Birmingham University, 1950.

Huxley, Thomas H. *Science and Education: Essays.* London: Macmillan, Ltd., 1910.

Inkster, Ian. "The Social Context of an Educational Movement: A Revisionist Approach to the English Mechanics Institutes, 1820-1850." *Oxford Review of Education,* vol.2, no.3 (1976), pp. 277-307.

Jenkins, Frank. *Architect and Patron. A survey of professional relations and practice in England from the sixteenth century to the present day.* London: Oxford University Press, 1961.

Jarausch, Konrad H. *The Transformation of Higher Learning, 1860-1980.* Chicago: U. of Chicago Press, 1983.

John, A.H. *A Liverpool Merchant House.* London: George Allen & Unwin, 1959.

Jordan, W.K. *The Charities of London.* London: George Allen & Unwin, 1960.

Jordan, W.K. *Philanthropy in England.* London: George Allen & Unwin, 1959.

Kargon, Robert H. *Science in Victorian Manchester.* Baltimore: Johns Hopkins University Press, 1977.

Kay, J.T. *The Owens College--A Descriptive Sketch.* Manchester: T. Sowler, 1891.

Keeton, George W. *The Modern Law of Charities.* London: Pitman, 1962.

Bibliography

Kelly, Thomas. *A History of Adult Education in Great Britain.* Liverpool: Liverpool University Press, 1962.

Kelly, Thomas. *For Advancement of Learning: The University of Liverpool, 1881-1981.* Liverpool: Liverpool U.P., 1981.

Kelsall, R.K., Anne Poole, and Annette Kuhn. *Graduates: The Sociology of an Elite.* London: Methuen, 1972.

Kitson, Clark E. *The History of the Leeds Philosophical and Literary Society.* Leeds: Jowett & Sowry, 1924.

Klingender, F.D. *The Condition of Clerical Labour in Great Britain.* New York: International Publishers, 1935.

Landes, David S. *The Unbound Prometheus.* Cambridge: Cambridge University Press, 1969.

Lawson, John and Harold Silver. *A Social History of Education in England.* London: Methuen, 1973.

Leclerc, Max. *L'Education des classes moyennes et dirigeantes en Angleterre.* Paris: Colin, 1894.

The Leeds Mercury, Leeds.

The Leeds Review, Leeds.

Lindblom, Charles E. "The Science of 'Muddling Through'," *Public Administration Review*, vol.19, no.2 (Spring, 1959).

Liverpool Daily Post.

Lockwood, David. *The Blackcoated Worker.* London: George Allen & Unwin, 1968.

Lodge, Sir Oliver. *Past Years.* London: Hodder & Stoughton, 1931.

Love, B. *Manchester As It Is.* Manchester: Love & Barton, 1839.

Lowndes, G.A.N. *The Silent Social Revolution.* London: Oxford University Press, 1969.

McCann, Phillip (ed.). *Popular Education and Socialization in the Nineteenth Century.* London: Methuen & Co. 1977.

Mack, Edward C. *Public Schools and British Opinion.* New York: Columbia University Press, 1939.

Mack, Edward C. *Public Schools and British Opinion Since 1860.* New York: Columbia University Press, 1941.

McLaren, Walter and John Beaumont. *Report ... on the Weaving and Other Technical Schools of the Continent.* London: Rivingtons, 1877.

Maclure, J.S. *Educational Documents, England & Wales, 1816-1963.* London: Chapman & Hall, 1965.

McPherson, Robert G. *Theory of Higher Education in 19th Century England.* Athens, Georgia: University of Georgia Press, 1959.

Maltby, S.E. *Manchester and the Movement for National Elementary Education. Manchester*: Manchester University Press, 1918.

The Manchester Courier, Manchester.

The Manchester Examiner and Times, Manchester.

Manchester Faces and Places.

The Manchester Guardian, Manchester.

Marsh, David C. *The Changing Social Structure of England and Wales 1871-1951.* London: Routledge and Kegan Paul, 1958.

Marshall, J.D. *Lancashire.* London: David & Charles, 1974.

Marshall, Leon Soutierre. *The Development of Public Opinion in Manchester.* Syracuse: Syracuse University Press, 1946.

Midwinter, Eric. *Old Liverpool*. Newton Abbot: David & Charles, 1971.

Miller, Edward. *Prince of Librarians*. Athens, Ohio: Ohio University Press, 1967.

Millerson, Geoffrey. *Qualifying Associations*. London: Routledge & Kegan Paul, 1964.

Minto, J. *A History of the Public Library Movement*. London: George Allen & Unwin, 1932.

Mitchell, B.R. and Phyllis Deane. *Abstract of British Historical Statistics*. Cambridge: Cambridge University Press, 1962.

Mitcheson, Richard Edmund. *Charitable Trusts*. London: Stevens & Sons and Maxwell & Son, 1887.

Montague, F.C. *Technical Education: A Summary of the Report of the Royal Commission*. London: Cassell & Co., c. 1884.

Montgomery, R.J. *Examinations: An Account of Their Evolution as Administrative Devices in England*. Pittsburgh: University of Pittsburgh Press, 1967.

Moodie, Graeme C. and Rowland Eustace. *Power and Authority in British Universities*. London: George Allen & Unwin, 1974.

Morris, R.J.B. *Parliament and the Public Libraries*. London: Mansell, 1977.

Mountford, Sir James. *British Universities*. London: Oxford University Press, 1966.

Munford, W.A. *Penny Rate*. London: Library Association, 1951.

Murphy, Brian. *A History of the British Economy 1086-1970*. London: Longman, 1973.

Murphy, James. *Church, State, and Schools in Britain 1800-1970*. London: Routledge and Kegan Paul, 1971.

Musgrave, P.W. *Society and Education in England Since 1800*. London: Methuen, 1968.

Musgrave, P.W. (ed.). *Sociology, History, and Education*. London: Methuen, 1970.

Musgrove, Frank and Philip H. Taylor. *Society and the Teachers Role*. London: Routledge and Kegan Paul, 1969.

Muspratt, Edmund Knowles. *My Life and Work*. London: John Lane The Bodley Head, 1917.

Newman, Charles. *The Evolution of Medical Education in the Nineteenth Century*. London: Oxford University Press, 1957.

North American Review.

Ogilvie, Vivian. *The English Public School*. New York: Macmillan, 1957.

Oliver, R.A.C. "University entrance requirements: whence & whither?" *Universities Quarterly*, June, 1966.

Ormerod, Henry A. *The Liverpool Royal Institution*. Liverpool: Tinling & Co., 1953.

Owen, David. *English Philanthropy, 1660-1960*. Cambridge: Harvard University Press, 1964.

Parker, Irene. *Dissenting Academies in England*. Cambridge: Cambridge University Press, 1914.

Perkin, Harold J. *Key Profession: The History of the Association of University Teachers*. London: Routledge & Kegan Paul, 1969.

Perkin, Harold J. *The Origins of Modern English Society 1780-1880*. London: Routledge & Kegan Paul, 1969.

Peterson, M. Jeanne. *The Medical Profession in Mid-Victorian London*. Berkeley: University of California Press, 1978.

Pickering, Sir George. *The Challenge to Education*. London: Watts, 1967.

Pilcher, R.B. *History of the Institute of Chemistry*. London : Bradbury, Agnew & Co., 1914.

Pilcher, R.B. and Butler-Jones. *What Industry Owes to Chemical Science*. New York: Van Nostrand, 1918.

Pollard, Sidney. *The Genesis of Modern Management*. Cambridge: Harvard University Press, 1965.

Proctor, Mortimer R. *The English University Novel*. Berkeley: University of California Press, 1954.

The Quarterly Review.

Rathbone, Eleanor F. *William Rathbone: A Memoir*. London: Macmillan, 1908.

Reader, W.J. *Life in Victorian England*. New York: Putnam, 1964.

Reader, W.J. *Professional Men: The Rise of the Professional Classes in 19th Century England*. New York: Basic Books, 1966.

Redford, Arthur and I.S. Russel. *The History of Local Government in Manchester*. London: Longmans, Green, 1940.

Regan, D.E. *Local Government and Education*. London: George Allen & Unwin, 1977.

Revue Scientifique, March, 1875.

Ringer, Fritz, K. *Education and Society in Modern Europe*. Bloomington: Indiana U.P., 1979.

Roach, John. *Public Examinations in England 1850-1950*. Cambridge: Cambridge University Press, 1971.

Roberts, David. *Victorian Origins of the British Welfare State*. New Haven: Yale University Press, 1971.

Roderick, Gordon W., and Michael D. Stephens. *Scientific and Technical Education in Nineteenth-Century England*. New York: Barnes & Noble Books, 1973.

Rolt, L.T.C. *Victorian Engineering*. Harmondsworth: Penguin, 1970.

Roscoe, Sir Henry E. *John Dalton and the Rise of Modern Chemistry*. New York: Macmillan, 1895.

Roscoe, Sir Henry E. *Life and Experiences.*

Roscoe, Sir Henry E. *Record of Work Done in the Chemical Department of the Owens College 1857-87*. London: Macmillan, 1887.

Rothblatt, Sheldon. *The Revolution of the Dons*. London: Faber & Faber, 1968.

Rothblatt, Sheldon. *Tradition and Change in English Liberal Education*. London: Faber & Faber, 1976.

Ryder, Judith and Harold Silver. *Modern English Society*. London: Methuen, 1970.

Sadler, M.E. (ed.). *Continuation Schools in England and Elsewhere*. Manchester: Manchester University Press, 1907.

Sadler, M.E. (ed.). *Essays on Examinations*. London: Macmillan, 1936.

Sadler, M.E. (ed.). *Report on Secondary Education in Liverpool*. London: Eyre & Spottiswoode, 1904.

223

Sanderson, Michael. *The Universities and British Industry*. London: Routledge & Kegan Paul, 1972.

Saul, S.B. *The Myth of the Great Depression, 1873-1896*. London: Macmillan, 1969.

Saunders, J.W. *The Profession of English Letters*. London: Routledge & Kegan Paul, 1964.

Saunders, W.L. (ed.). *University and Research Library Studies*. London: Pergamon Press, 1968.

Schmidt, George P. *The Old Time College President*. New York: Columbia University Press, 1930.

Scotland, James. *The History of Scottish Education*. London: University of London Press, 1969.

Shils, Edward. "The Intellectuals." *Encounter*, April, 1955.

Shimmin, A.N. *The University of Leeds. The First Half-Century*. Cambridge: Cambridge University Press, 1954.

A Short History of the City and Guilds of London Institute. London, 1896.

Silver, Harold and S. John Teague. *The History of British Universities 1800-1969: A Bibliography*. London: Society for Research into Higher Education, June 1970.

Simey, Margaret B. *Charitable Effort in Liverpool in the 19th Century*. Liverpool: Liverpool University Press, 1951.

Simmonds, H.J. and A.W. Nicholls. *Law of Education*. London: Pitman, 1933.

Simon, Brian. *Education and the Labour Movement*. London: Lawrence & Wishart, 1969.

Simon, Brian (ed.). *Education in Leicestershire 1540-1940. A Regional Study*. Leicester: Leicester University Press, 1968.

Simon, Brian. *Studies in the History of Education, 1780-1870*. London: Lawrence & Wishart, 1960.

Singer, Holmyard, Hall and Williams. *A History of Technology*. Vol. 4, *The Industrial Revolution*. London: Oxford University Press, 1958.

Smelser, Neil J. *Social Change in the Industrial Revolution*. Chicago: University of Chicago Press, 1959.

Smith, H. Bompas (ed.). *Education at Work. Studies in Contemporary Education*. Manchester: University of Manchester Press, 1927.

Stephens, W.B. *Regional Variations in Education*. Leeds: University of Leeds, 1973.

Streb, Ernest W. *Drug Adulteration*. Madison: University of Wisconsin Press, 1966.

Stone, Lawrence (ed.). *The University in Society*. 2 vols. Princeton: Princeton University Press, 1974.

Supple, Barry (ed.). *Essays in British Business History*. London: Oxford University Press, 1977.

Taylor, A.J.P. *Essays in English History*. Harmondsworth: Penguin, 1976.

Thackray, Arnold. "Natural Knowledge in Cultural Context", *American Historical Review* 79 (1974), pp.672-709.

Tholfsen, Trygve R. "The Intellectual Origins of Mid-Victorian Stability", *Political Science Quarterly* LXXXVI, pp. 57-91.

Thompson, Joseph. *The Owens College, Its Foundation and Growth*. Manchester: J.E. Cornish, 1886.

Thornhill, W. (ed.). *The Growth and Reform of English Local Government*. London: Weidenfeld and Nicolson, 1971.

Thorpe, T.E. *Essays in Historical Chemistry*. London: Macmillan, 1902.

Thorpe, T.E. *Roscoe*. London: Longmans, Green & Co., 1916.

Tropp, Asher. *The School Teachers: The Growth of the Teaching Profession in England and Wales from 1800 to the Present Day*. London: Heinemann, 1957.

Turner, D.M. *History of Science Teaching in England*. London: Chapman and Hall, 1927.

Tylecote, Mabel. *The Mechanics Institutes of Lancashire and Yorkshire Before 1851*. Manchester: Manchester University Press, 1957.

University College and the University of Liverpool 1882-1907. Liverpool, Liverpool University Press, 1907.

The University of Liverpool 1903-1928. Liverpool: Liverpool University Press, 1928.

Van de Graaff, J.H. et al. *Academic Power*. New York: Praeger, 1978.

Vaughan, J.E. and Michael Argles. *British Government Publications Concerning Education*. Liverpool: University of Liverpool Press, 1969.

The Victoria History of the Counties of England. *A History of the County of Middlesex*. London: Oxford University Press, 1969.

Vincent, Eric W. and Percival Hinton. *The University of Birmingham*. Birmingham: Cornish Brothers, 1947.

Wardle, David. *English Popular Education, 1780-1970*. Cambridge University Press, 1970.

Webb, R.K. *The British Working Class Reader*. London: George Allen & Unwin, 1955.

Westminister Review.

White, Brian D. *A History of the Corporation of Liverpool 1835-1914*. Liverpool: Liverpool University Press, 1951.

Whiting, C.E. *The University of Durham: 1832-1932*. London: The Sheldon Press, 1932.

Wiese, L. *German Letters on English Education*. London: Collins, 1877.

Williams, Bill. *The Making of Manchester Jewry 1740-1875*. Manchester: Manchester University Press, 1976.

Williams, James. *Education: A Manual of Practical Law*. London: Adam and Charles Black, 1892.

Williams, Tevor Illtyd. *The Chemical Industry*. 1953; republished E.P. Publishing Ltd., 1972.

Wood, Sir Henry Trueman. *A History of the Royal Society of Arts*. London: Murray, 1913.

Yates, James. *Thoughts on the Advancement of Academical Education in England*. London: Baldwin, Cradock & Joy, 1826.

The Year Book of Education, 1950. London: Evans, 1950.

Young, G.M. *Victorian England: Portrait of an Age*. London: Oxford University Press, 1953.

Index